PRACTICE FOR AIR FORCE PLACEMENT TESTS

PRACTICE FOR AIR FORCE PLACEMENT TESTS

SOLOMON WIENER
COLONEL, AUS-Ret.

E.P. STEINBERG

The views expressed in this book are those of the author and do not
reflect the official position of the Army or the U.S. Government.

ARCO

New York

Seventh Edition

Copyright © 1989, 1986, 1982 by Arco Publishing, a division
of Simon & Schuster, Inc.

 ARCO

Simon & Schuster, Inc.
Gulf+Western Building
One Gulf+Western Plaza
New York, NY 10023

DISTRIBUTED BY PRENTICE HALL TRADE SALES

Manufactured in the United States of America

2 3 4 5 6 7 8 9 10

Library of Congress Cataloging in Publication Data

Wiener, Solomon, 1915–
  Practice for Air Force placement tests / Solomon, Wiener,
E.P. Steinberg.
    p. cm.
  ISBN 0-13-689423-2
  1. United States. Air Force—Examinations. 2. Armed
Forces Vocational Aptitude Battery.   I. Steinberg, E. P.
II. Title.
UG638.W54 1989   88-34890
  358.4′0076—dc19   CIP

CONTENTS

OPPORTUNITIES IN THE AIR FORCE*

Over 600,000 highly trained officers and airmen make up today's Air Force. Some pilot aircraft—everything from helicopters to the Space Shuttle. Many others do the jobs that support the Air Force's flying mission; they may work as firefighters, aircraft mechanics, security police, or air traffic controllers or in many other Air Force career fields. The Air Force currently recruits about 60,000 men and women each year to fill openings in hundreds of challenging career fields.

THE ENLISTMENT PROCESS

Enlisting in the Air Force involves three steps:

1. Visit a Recruiting Office
   The first thing to do if you are considering a career in the Air Force is to visit the Recruiting Office nearest you. There a recruiter will answer your questions about the Air Force and evaluate your basic physical and moral qualifications.

   Applicants for enlistment in the Air Force must be
   —at least 17 years of age
   —a citizen of the United States or an immigrant alien legally admitted to the U.S. for permanent residence and possessing immigration and naturalization documents
   —in good health
   —of good moral character
2. Take the Armed Services Vocational Aptitude Battery. The Air Force, like the other brances of the armed forces, uses the Armed Services Vocational Aptitude Battery (ASVAB) to measure your ability to learn in four career areas: mechanical,

Adapted from *Aim High Straight Talk About Your Future in the Air Force.*

administrative, general, and electronic. You may have taken the ASVAB in school. If not, your recruiter will schedule an appointment for you to take this three-hour examination. Your ASVAB scores will help show specific skill and career areas for which you qualify. The higher your scores, the greater your job choices.

If your ASVAB scores qualify you for the Air Force, your recruiter will ask you to fill out an application. The application includes questions about where you have lived and the city, county and state of birth of you and your parents. You may need to take the application home with you to gather the information requested.

3. Go to the Military Entrance Processing Station. When the application is complete, your recruiter will arrange for you to go to a Military Entrance Processing Station (MEPS) for a physical examination, job counseling, and a job interview.

Your day at the MEPS will go something like this:

6:30 – 8:00 a.m.	Arrival and check in
8:00 – 11:30 a.m.	Orientation, physical exams and any special tests
11:30 – 12:30 p.m.	Lunch break
12:30 – 2:30 p.m.	Air Force Liaison NCO interviews
2:30 – 3:00 p.m.	Final enlistment processing
3:00 – 3:30 p.m.	Enlistment ceremony

The medical examination will be thorough. You will do a series of exercises to demonstrate strength and limb and joint movement. Your blood, urine, heart, hearing and vision will be tested. Your chest will be x-rayed and your general physical condition evaluated. At this point, the doctor will determine if you are physically qualified for the Air Force and note any restrictions.

The job interview is the most important activity of the day. The Air Force offers jobs in a wide variety of skill areas including:

Administrative Specialist
Aerospace Ground Equipment Mechanic
Aerospace Physiology Specialist
Airlift Aircraft Maintenance Specialist
Cryptologic Linguist Specialist
Explosive Ordnance Disposal Specialist
Engineering Assistant Specialist
Fire Protection Specialist
Food Service Specialist
Fuels Specialist
Inventory Management Specialist
Jet Engine Mechanic
Law Enforcement Specialist
Material Facilities Specialist
Morse Systems Operator
Munitions Systems Specialist
Personnel Specialist
Printer Systems Operator
Security Specialist
Tactical Aircraft Maintenance Specialist
Vehicle Operator/Dispatcher

To help you decide about your Air Force career, the Air Force Liaison Sergeant will enter your physical qualifications into a computer, add the skills you want, your ASVAB scores and the date you will be available. The computer matches this information with the Air Force's expected vacancies and then displays a list of available skills or career areas for which you are best suited. The Air Force will guarantee your skill or career area in writing as part of your enlistment agreement.

ENLISTMENT OPTIONS

The Air Force offers a choice of two basic enlistments:

1. The Guaranteed Training Enlistment Program guarantees training and initial assignment in a specific skill. In most of these specialties you may enlist for four or six years.
2. The Aptitude Area Enlistment Program guarantees classification into one of four aptitude areas (mechanical, administrative, general or electronic). Under this option, skill selection is determined during basic training. The program carries a four or six year enlistment.

After choosing one of these programs, you may also select the Delayed Enlistment Program which allows you to qualify for enlistment and training in a skill area but delays your entry into active duty for up to twelve months.

THE ENLISTMENT AGREEMENT

Once you have been accepted by the Air Force and have decided that the Air Force is for you, you will sign an agreement and take the oath of enlistment. The enlistment agreement is a complex and carefully worded legal document. If you are not sure about the wording or content, ask questions. Once you have chosen the skill or aptitude area you want guaranteed, it will be entered on the agreement and you will be asked to sign. Make sure that everything you expect is in the agreement before you sign because once you sign, the agreement is binding.

You will be sworn into the Regular Air Force (Reserve Air Force if you have delayed your reporting time) during a special enlistment ceremony. You probably won't leave for basic military training the same day you enlist, but you will be given a date on which to report for active duty.

When you return to the MEPS on the date scheduled, your physical status and enlistment documents will be reviewed. Any changes will be discussed and documented and your training will begin.

BASIC TRAINING

All Air Force Basic Military Training (BMT) is conducted at Lackland Air Force Base in San Antonio, Texas. The Air Force will arrange and pay for your trip to Lackland.

Upon arrival, you and about 45 other new airmen will be assigned to a group called a training flight.

Basic Military Training teaches enlistees how to adjust to military life both physically and mentally, and it promotes pride in being a member of the Air Force. It lasts six weeks and consists of academic instruction, confidence courses, physical conditioning and marksmanship training. Trainees who enlist without an aptitude area guarantee receive orientation and individual counseling to help choose a job specialty compatible with Air Force needs and with their aptitudes, education, civilian experience, and desires.

A typical day during basic training will be something like this:

5:00 – 6:15 a.m.	Reveille, physical conditioning, showers
6:15 – 7:30 a.m.	Breakfast
7:30 – 8:30 a.m.	Dorm preparation for inspection
8:30 – 11:30 a.m.	Academic classes or processing
11:30 – 12:30 p.m.	Lunch
12:30 – 4:30 p.m.	Academic classes Drill practice Inspection (personal) Retreat
4:30 – 5:30 p.m.	Dinner
5:30 – 6:30 p.m.	Mail call, briefings
6:30 – 9:00 p.m.	Dorm preparation, study time, personal hygiene
9:00 p.m.	Lights out

After graduation from Basic Training, recruits receive job training in their chosen specialty.

JOB TRAINING

Most enlistees go directly from Basic Military Training to one of the Air Force Technical Training Centers for formal, in-residence training. The Air Force's Technical Training Centers are Chanute Air Force Base, Rantoul, Illinois; Keesler AFB, Biloxi, Mississippi; Lackland AFB, San Antonio, Texas; Lowry AFB, Denver, Colorado; Sheppard AFB, Wichita Falls, Texas and Goodfellow AFB, San Angelo, Texas.

The training at Air Force Technical Training Centers is similar to that of high level vocational or college training. The length of technical school training varies from several weeks to a year, depending on the specialty.

Some airmen proceed directly from basic training to their initial duty station and receive instruction in their skill through on-the-job-training.

MANAGEMENT TRAINING

In addition to becoming skilled in their specialties, Air Force noncommissioned officers (NCOs) are also leaders and supervisors. Schools in the Noncommissioned Officer

Professional Military Education System teach NCOs to be more effective leaders and managers. They help NCOs to develop management abilities that are valuable in any chosen career, military or civilian.

ADVANCEMENT

Airman Basic (pay grade E-1) is the initial enlisted grade. However, if you have completed a Civil Air Patrol program or Junior Reserve Officer Training Corps (JROTC) for any service or have attained certain levels of college credit, you may qualify for enlistment in a higher grade.

Every job in the Air Force has a defined career path leading to supervisory positions. Airman Basic enlistees are normally promoted to Airman (E-2) upon completion of six months of service and to Airman First Class (E-3) after 16 months of service. Promotion to Senior Airman (E-4) usually occurs at the three-year point of service. Senior Airmen train for about 12 months before receiving the title of Sergeant. However, some airmen qualify for accelerated promotion. Local Air Force recruiters have all the details on qualifications for accelerated promotions and advanced enlistment grades.

Promotions to the higher enlisted grades of Staff Sergeant (E-5), Technical Sergeant (E-6), Master Sergeant (E-7), and Senior and Chief Master Sergeant (E-8 and E-9) are competitive. Eligible airmen compete with others worldwide in the same grade and skill, based on test scores, performance ratings, decorations, and time in service and grade. All airmen receive a promotion score that shows how they stand in relation to others in their specialty and where improvement may be needed. Additionally, E-8 and E-9 candidates are reviewed by a selection board.

OPPORTUNITIES FOR OFFICERSHIP

Normally, enlisted airmen and commissioned officers advance along separate career fields. However, the Air Force offers two programs through which airmen can receive commissions:

1. The Air Force ROTC Scholarship Commissioning Program allows airmen to complete their college degrees and earn officer commissions through two- or four-year Air Force ROTC Scholarships. Airmen selected for this program, transfer from active duty into the Air Force Reserve and enroll in the Air Force Reserve Officer Training Corps program at the college where they will get their degree. The ROTC Scholarship pays tuition, some fees and $100 during each school month. The ROTC scholarship commissioning program is highly competitive. To enter, you must qualify for pilot, navigator or missile training, or pursue a specified scientific, mathematical, technical, or engineering degree. Airmen are eligible to apply for this program after one year of active duty in the Air Force.

2. The Airman Education and Commissioning Program (AECP) is open to airmen who have been on active duty for at least one year and have 45 hours of college credit. AECP is limited to scientific and technical disciplines. Airmen who are selected attend college full time and draw the pay and allowance of a staff sergeant. Tuition, books and fees are paid by the Air Force. Once they have completed their degree requirements, these airmen are eligible to compete for entrance to Officer Training School. They are commissioned upon graduation.

EDUCATIONAL OPPORTUNITIES IN THE AIR FORCE

The Air Force has many special education programs to help men and women pursue their educational goals while serving in the Air Force.

1. The new G.I. Bill offers $10,800 in educational benefits. Your investment is $1200 which is deducted from your pay at the rate of $100 per month. To this the Air Force adds $9600. After two years of service you can start using your benefits. However, you must serve at least three years to get the entire $10,800 in benefits.
2. The Tuition Assistance Program will pay 75 to 90% of the tuition for off-duty courses taken at accredited colleges or universities.
3. The College-Level Examination Program allows airmen to receive credit for college courses by examination. This program is free to all airmen. Base education service centers maintain lists of tests available.
4. Extension Course Institute (ECI) is the Air Force's correspondence school. It offers nearly 400 courses which are free and open to all airmen and officers.
5. Community College of the Air Force allows your technical training to be converted into college credits. The CCAF keeps a computerized record of your educational progress. By combining your technical education, professional military education, and civilian college-level courses, you may earn an associate degree from CCAF in career areas such as:

- Aircraft and Missile Maintenance
- Electronics and Telecommunications
- Law Enforcement
- Public and Support Service

IS THE AIR FORCE FOR YOU?

In addition to the education and training opportunities previously discussed, the Air Force also offers

- Excellent starting salary, with regular pay raises
- Promotion opportunities
- Reenlistment bonuses
- Tax-free clothing allowance
- 30 days of vacation with pay each year
- Tax-free housing and food allowances
- A $50,000 life insurance policy for about $4 a month
- Complete medical and dental care
- Legal assistance
- Generous retirement system
- On-base shopping at reduced prices
- Complete medical care for dependents
- Variety of recreational facilities

Local Air Force recruiters have the latest information on enlistment programs and career opportunities. High school guidance counselors can provide information about Air Force ROTC programs and the United States Air Force Academy.

ALL ABOUT THE ASVAB

The ASVAB, a multiple aptitude battery designed for use with students in their junior or senior year in high school or in a postsecondary school, was developed to yield results useful to both schools and the military. The school testing program helps the military attract well qualified volunteers. Schools use ASVAB-14 test results to assist their students in identifying their aptitudes and developing future educational and career plans. The military services use the results to help determine the qualifications of young people for enlistment and to help place them in military occupational programs.

Test Subjects

The ASVAB consists of the following 10 subjects which are given in the order listed.

ORDER OF ADMINISTRATION	TEST SUBJECT
Subtest 1	General Science (GS)
Subtest 2	Arithmetic Reasoning (AR)
Subtest 3	Word Knowledge (WK)
Subtest 4	Paragraph Comprehension (PC)
Subtest 5	Numerical Operations (NO)
Subtest 6	Coding Speed (CS)
Subtest 7	Auto & Shop Information (AS)
Subtest 8	Mathematics Knowledge (MK)
Subtest 9	Mechanical Comprehension (MC)
Subtest 10	Electronics Information (EI)

Eight of these subtests allow for maximum performance with generous time limits. You will have enough time to answer every question. Two subtests (Subtest 5—Numerical Operations and Subtest 6—Coding Speed) are speeded subtests and generally can *not* be completed in the time allotted. Do not worry about not completing all items of a speeded test in the time allowed. However, do work as quickly and accurately as you can.

Figure 1 on page 9 presents the ASVAB subtests, the time allowed for the administration of each subtest, the number of items in each subtest, and a description of the abilities or knowledge measured. The subtests are designed to measure general abilities and acquired information in specific areas covered in the general high school program or acquired as an interest or a hobby.

COMPOSITES

ASVAB results are reported by composite scores which are combinations of subtest scores. ASVAB-14 yields three academic and four occupational composite scores.

The three academic composites—academic ability, verbal, and math—measure a student's potential for further formal education and predict performance in general areas requiring verbal and mathematical skills. The three academic composites along with the subtests that comprise them are presented in Figure 2 on page 10.

The four occupational composites measure a student's potential for performance in the following general career areas: Mechanical and Crafts; Business and Clerical; Electronics and Electrical; and Health, Social, and Technology.

The four occupational composites along with the subtests that comprise them and sample occupational groupings are presented in Figure 3 shown on page 11.

Although the military services use sets of composites and scoring slightly different from the ASVAB-14 school composites, most service composites have subtest content the same as or similar to that of ASVAB-14 occupational composites. While somewhat different from the service composites, ASVAB-14 school composites are similar to them in their ability to predict successful performance in military technical training courses.

With the replacement of the Armed Forces Qualification Test (AFQT) by the Armed Services Vocational Aptitude Battery (ASVAB), the AFQT is no longer a separate screening test but has become a composite of several ASVAB subtests. The AFQT is now formed from the following four ASVAB subtests:

Word Knowledge .... 35 items
Paragraph Comprehension .... 15 items
Arithmetic Reasoning .... 30 items
Mathematics Knowledge..................................... 25 items

The number correct on Word Knowledge + the number correct on Paragraph Comprehension + the number correct on Arithmetic Reasoning + the number correct on Mathematics Knowledge = AFQT raw score which is then converted into a percentile score.

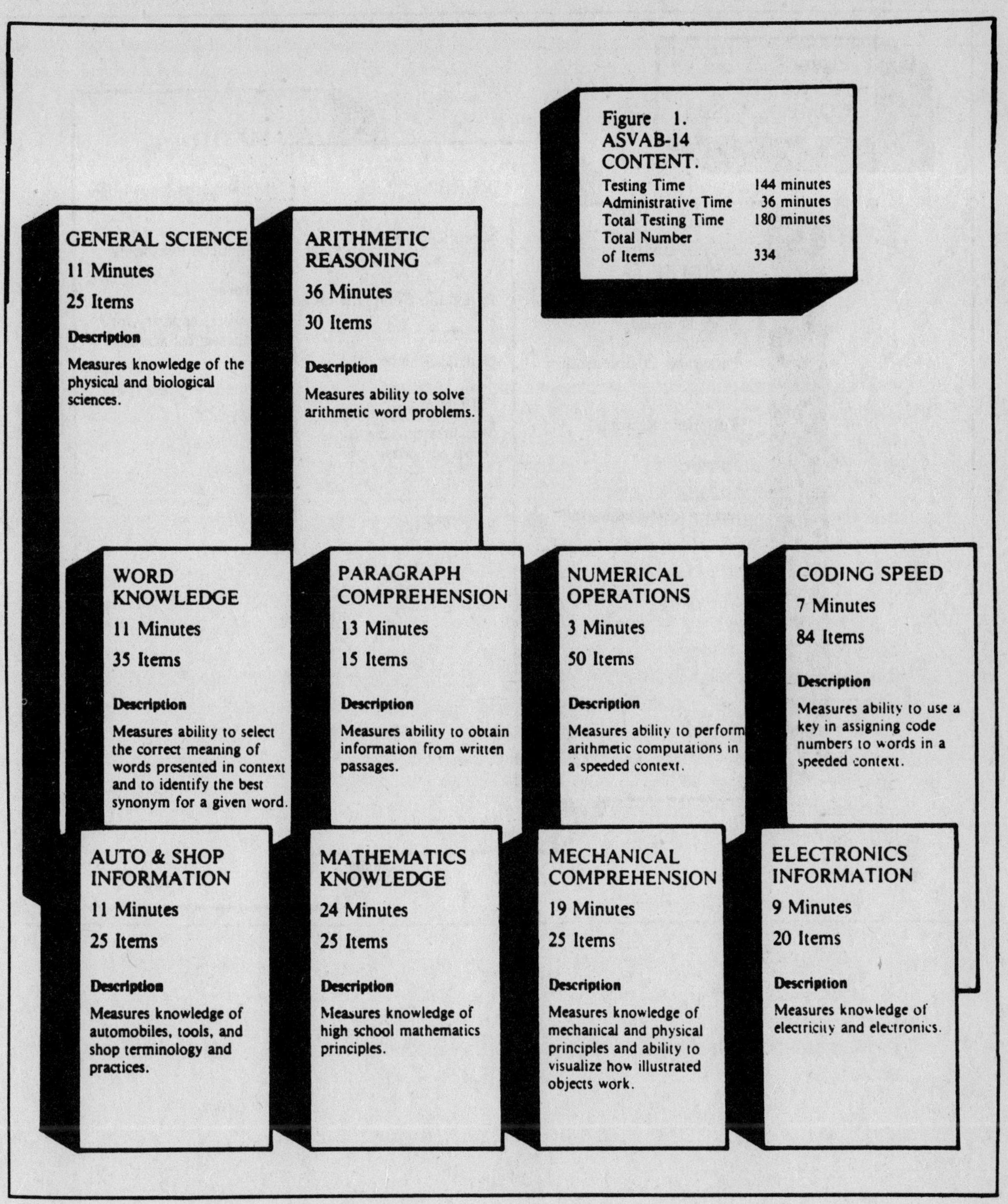

**Figure 1.
ASVAB-14
CONTENT.**

Testing Time	144 minutes
Administrative Time	36 minutes
Total Testing Time	180 minutes
Total Number of Items	334

GENERAL SCIENCE

11 Minutes

25 Items

Description

Measures knowledge of the physical and biological sciences.

ARITHMETIC REASONING

36 Minutes

30 Items

Description

Measures ability to solve arithmetic word problems.

WORD KNOWLEDGE

11 Minutes

35 Items

Description

Measures ability to select the correct meaning of words presented in context and to identify the best synonym for a given word.

PARAGRAPH COMPREHENSION

13 Minutes

15 Items

Description

Measures ability to obtain information from written passages.

NUMERICAL OPERATIONS

3 Minutes

50 Items

Description

Measures ability to perform arithmetic computations in a speeded context.

CODING SPEED

7 Minutes

84 Items

Description

Measures ability to use a key in assigning code numbers to words in a speeded context.

AUTO & SHOP INFORMATION

11 Minutes

25 Items

Description

Measures knowledge of automobiles, tools, and shop terminology and practices.

MATHEMATICS KNOWLEDGE

24 Minutes

25 Items

Description

Measures knowledge of high school mathematics principles.

MECHANICAL COMPREHENSION

19 Minutes

25 Items

Description

Measures knowledge of mechanical and physical principles and ability to visualize how illustrated objects work.

ELECTRONICS INFORMATION

9 Minutes

20 Items

Description

Measures knowledge of electricity and electronics.

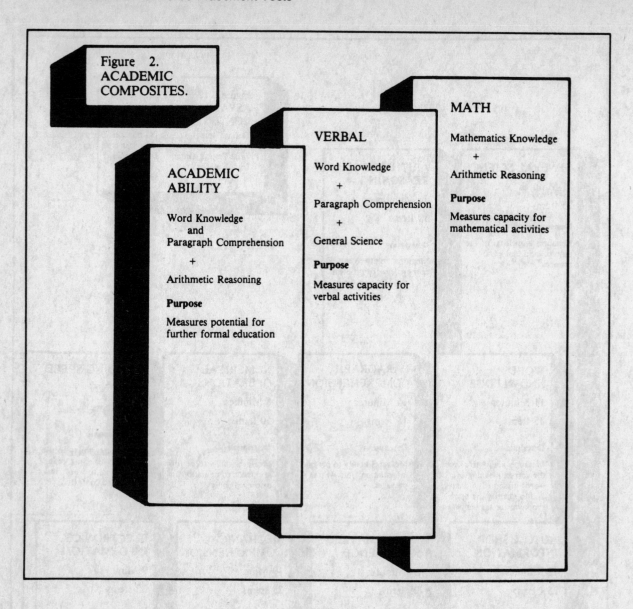

Figure 2.
ACADEMIC
COMPOSITES.

ACADEMIC ABILITY

Word Knowledge
    and
Paragraph Comprehension
    +
Arithmetic Reasoning

Purpose

Measures potential for
further formal education

VERBAL

Word Knowledge
    +
Paragraph Comprehension
    +
General Science

Purpose

Measures capacity for
verbal activities

MATH

Mathematics Knowledge
    +
Arithmetic Reasoning

Purpose

Measures capacity for
mathematical activities

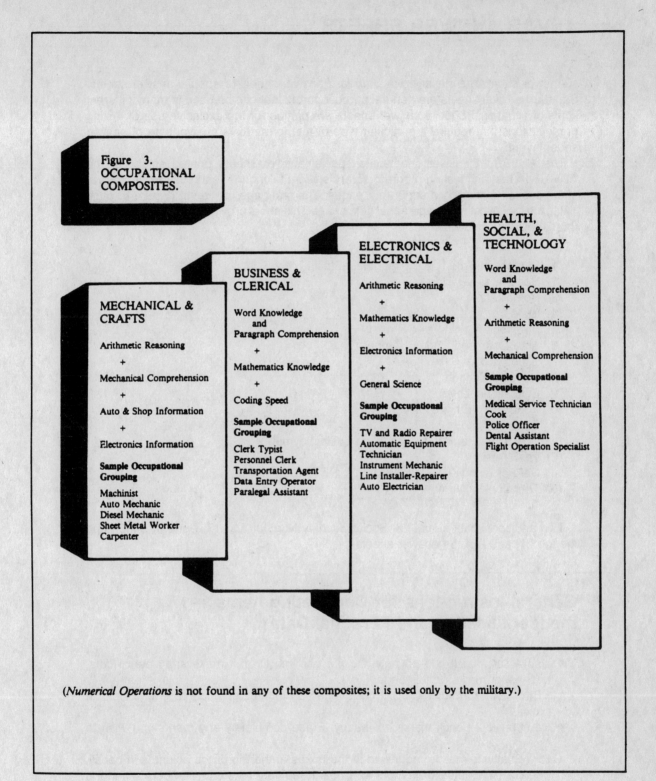

Figure 3.
OCCUPATIONAL COMPOSITES.

MECHANICAL & CRAFTS

Arithmetic Reasoning

+

Mechanical Comprehension

+

Auto & Shop Information

+

Electronics Information

Sample Occupational Grouping

Machinist
Auto Mechanic
Diesel Mechanic
Sheet Metal Worker
Carpenter

BUSINESS & CLERICAL

Word Knowledge
and
Paragraph Comprehension

+

Mathematics Knowledge

+

Coding Speed

Sample Occupational Grouping

Clerk Typist
Personnel Clerk
Transportation Agent
Data Entry Operator
Paralegal Assistant

ELECTRONICS & ELECTRICAL

Arithmetic Reasoning

+

Mathematics Knowledge

+

Electronics Information

+

General Science

Sample Occupational Grouping

TV and Radio Repairer
Automatic Equipment Technician
Instrument Mechanic
Line Installer-Repairer
Auto Electrician

HEALTH, SOCIAL, & TECHNOLOGY

Word Knowledge
and
Paragraph Comprehension

+

Arithmetic Reasoning

+

Mechanical Comprehension

Sample Occupational Grouping

Medical Service Technician
Cook
Police Officer
Dental Assistant
Flight Operation Specialist

(*Numerical Operations* is not found in any of these composites; it is used only by the military.)

ASVAB ANSWER SHEETS

Answer sheets are classified as *standard* answer sheets or *special* answer sheets. Standard answer sheets are general purpose forms that can be used in many different kinds of situations. Special answer sheets are printed for the exclusive use of testing organizations that require a particular type of test format or a special type of answer sheet layout.

The ASVAB-14 answer sheets are special answer sheets printed solely for the ASVAB-14 test and testing program. Every student taking the test receives an answer sheet packet containing a set of four pages. The first page of the set (Figure 4, page 14) is the identification and personal data sheet. This sheet provides space for recording (mark sensing) the following:

1. Student's Name (Last, First, Middle Initial)
2. Home Mailing Address
3. Home City
4. State
5. ZIP Code
6. Area Code and Phone Number
7. School Code
8. Name of School
9. Educational Level
10. Population (Ethnic) Group
11. Sex
12. Intentions (Re: Future Schooling or Employment)
13. Test Version
14. Date of Birth (Year, Month, Day)
15. Test Booklet Number

Two additional data items, 16. Social Security Number and 17. Code, are found on the top of page 2 of the answer sheets.

General Instructions for Completing Items 1–17, the Identification and Personal Data

- Use a soft pencil (No. 2) only. Do *not* use ink. Do *not* make stray pencil dots, dashes, or marks on this page.
- PRINT all information in CAPITAL letters or numbers (uppercase or block) in pencil.
- Be sure your pencil marks are heavy. Erase completely any marks you wish to change.
- PRINT all information requested in the boxes at the top of the columns in pencil, one CAPITAL letter or number to a box. Keep your letters or numbers within the box. In each column, darken (with pencil) the bracket containing the CAPITAL letter or number in the box at the top of the column. Fill in the bracket completely like this ■, but do *not* go outside the bracket with your pencil. Do *not* use X or check marks. Do *not* circle brackets. Be sure you are in the right column. Each column should have only one bracket darkened under a CAPITAL letter or number in the box at the top.

Figure 4

SCHEMATIC SAMPLE

**ANSWER SHEET
ARMED SERVICES VOCATIONAL
APTITUDE BATTERY**

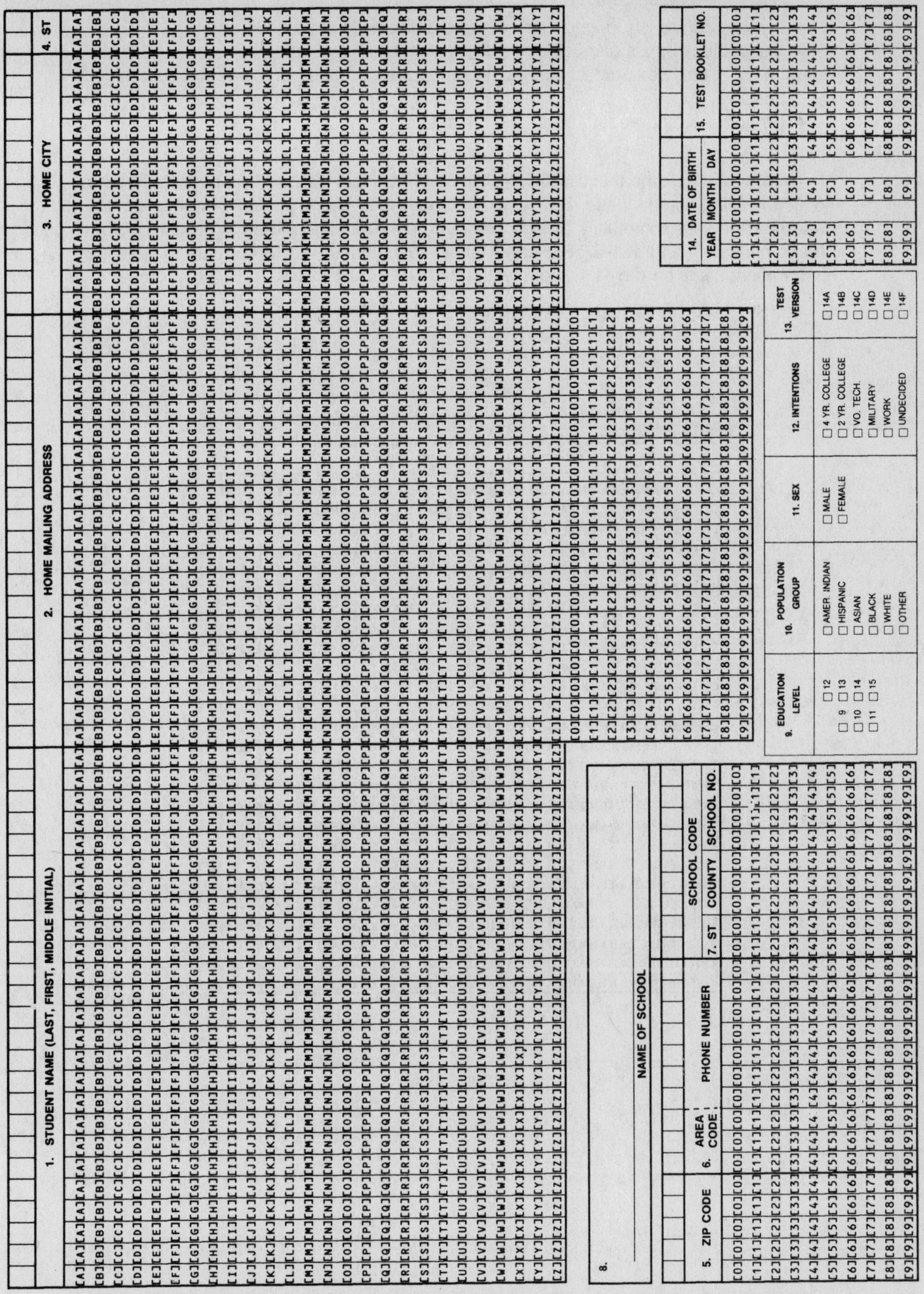

4. ST

3. HOME CITY

2. HOME MAILING ADDRESS

1. STUDENT NAME (LAST, FIRST, MIDDLE INITIAL)

8. NAME OF SCHOOL

5. ZIP CODE

6. AREA CODE | PHONE NUMBER

7. ST | COUNTY | SCHOOL NO. — SCHOOL CODE

9. EDUCATION LEVEL
□ 9 □ 10 □ 11 □ 12 □ 13 □ 14 □ 15

10. POPULATION GROUP
□ AMER. INDIAN □ HISPANIC □ ASIAN □ BLACK □ WHITE □ OTHER

11. SEX
□ MALE □ FEMALE

12. INTENTIONS
□ 4 YR. COLLEGE □ 2 YR. COLLEGE □ VO. TECH. □ MILITARY □ WORK □ UNDECIDED

13. TEST VERSION
□ 14A □ 14B □ 14C □ 14D □ 14E □ 14F

14. DATE OF BIRTH
YEAR | MONTH | DAY

15. TEST BOOKLET NO.

- Each of the items listed on the page should be completed in pencil in the order listed.
- If your address is too long, use standard abbreviations as necessary.
- Leave blank boxes and columns for any dashes in your address.
- Leave blank box and column between house number and street address, if possible.
- Be accurate and neat in filling out this data.

To illustrate, assume that Jane Q. Public of 415 Sunset Boulevard, Anytown, Illinois 60064 is filling out this page. She is an eleventh grade, white student who expects to attend a two-year community college program upon graduation from high school. Her home phone is (309) 421-6758. Her social security number is 123-45-6789.

Pertinent items on pages 1 and 2 would be filled out as follows:

1. Student's Name (Last, First, Middle Initial)

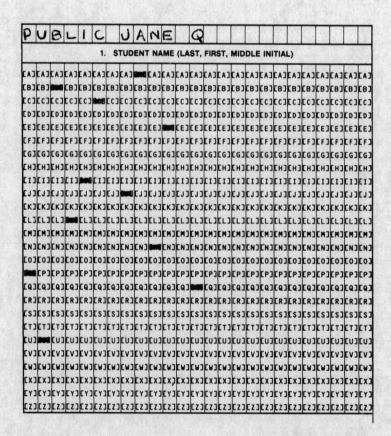

2. Home Mailing Address; 3. Home City; 4. State

```
415  SUNSET  BLVD         ANYTOWN      IL
```

2. HOME MAILING ADDRESS	3. HOME CITY	4. ST

5. ZIP Code; 6. Area Code and Phone Number

```
CCCC643094316758
```

5. ZIP CODE	6. AREA CODE	PHONE NUMBER	SCHOOL CODE		
			7. ST	COUNTY	SCHOOL NO.

9. Educational Level;   10. Population Group;   11. Sex;   12. Intentions

9. EDUCATION LEVEL	10. POPULATION GROUP	11. SEX	12. INTENTIONS	13. TEST VERSION
☐ 12	☐ AMER. INDIAN	☐ MALE	☐ 4 YR. COLLEGE	☐ 14A
☐ 9 ☐ 13	☐ HISPANIC	■ FEMALE	■ 2 YR. COLLEGE	☐ 14B
☐ 10 ☐ 14	☐ ASIAN		☐ VO. TECH.	☐ 14C
■ 11 ☐ 15	☐ BLACK		☐ MILITARY	☐ 14D
	■ WHITE		☐ WORK	☐ 14E
	☐ OTHER		☐ UNDECIDED	☐ 14F

16. Social Security Number

```
1 2 3 4 5 6 7 8 9
16  SOCIAL SECURITY NUMBER

[0][0][0][0][0][0][0][0][0]
[1][1][1][1][1][1][1][1][1]
[2][2][2][2][2][2][2][2][2]
[3][3][3][3][3][3][3][3][3]
[4][4][4][4][4][4][4][4][4]
[5][5][5][5][5][5][5][5][5]
[6][6][6][6][6][6][6][6][6]
[7][7][7][7][7][7][7][7][7]
[8][8][8][8][8][8][8][8][8]
[9][9][9][9][9][9][9][9][9]
```

The second page of the answer sheet packet provides space on the top of the page for recording (mark sensing) the following additional identification and personal data information, as well as the name of the test taker:

16. Social Security Number
17. Code (Alphabetic and Numerical)

The rest of the page provides space for recording the answers to the first five ASVAB subtests.

Part 1 is the section for recording your answers to the first subtest, General Science (GS), which consists of 25 four-option, multiple-choice questions. It also includes a practice column for three sample questions.

Part 2 is the section for recording your answers to the second subtest, Arithmetic Reasoning (AR), which consists of 30 four-option, multiple-choice questions.

Part 3 is the section for recording your answers to the third subtest, Word Knowledge (WK), which consists of 35 four-option, multiple-choice questions.

Part 4 is the section for recording your answers to the fourth subtest, Paragraph Comprehension (PC), which consists of 15 four-option, multiple-choice questions.

Part 5 is the section for recording your answers to the fifth subtest, Numerical Operations (NO), which consists of 50 four-option, multiple-choice questions.

A sample page 2 of the ASVAB answer sheet packet (Figure 5) is shown on page 18.

The third page of the answer sheet packet provides space for the name of the test taker and for recording the answers to ASVAB subtests 6–10.

Part 6 is the section for recording your answers to the sixth subtest, Coding Speed (CS), which consists of 84 five-option, multiple-choice questions.

Part 7 is the section for recording your answers to the seventh subtest, Auto & Shop Information, which consists of 25 four-option, multiple-choice questions.

Part 8 is the section for recording your answers to the eighth subtest, Mathematics Knowledge (MK), which consists of 25 four-option, multiple-choice questions.

Part 9 is the section for recording your answers to the ninth subtest, Mechanical Comprehension (MC), which consists of 25 four-option, multiple-choice questions.

Part 10 is the section for recording your answers to the tenth and last subtest, Electronics Information (EI), which consists of 20 four-option, multiple-choice questions.

A sample page 3 of the ASVAB answer sheet packet (Figure 6) is shown on page 19.

The last page of the ASVAB answer sheet packet (Figure 7) is a Privacy Act Statement. Students must sign this statement in order to receive their test results.

A sample Privacy Act Statement is shown below:

Figure 7

AUTHORITY: 10 USC 3012, 10 USC 5012, 10 USC 5013, 10 USC 8012

PRINCIPAL PURPOSE: For use by high schools for purposes of vocational/career counseling, curriculum planning and group assessment, and to assist in recruiting personnel for the armed services.

ROUTINE USE: For student vocational/career counseling, curriculum planning and group assessment; for preparation of service recruiting prospect cards and market analysis, research by DOD agencies and appropriate outside activities, recruiting and enlistment selection/qualification, and creation of computer listings for recruiting services. Collected data is retained for 2 additional school years. Any data retained past this time requires removal of name, social security number, street address, and telephone number from those records. Only data obtained from testing juniors, seniors, and post secondary students will be released to armed service recruiters.

DISCLOSURE: Student disclosure of social security number is voluntary. Student disclosure of test responses is also voluntary; however, failure to sign below acknowledging the intended uses and release of test scores will result in the test not being processed.

SIGNATURE _____

DATE _____

The ASVAB answer sheet packets used in the regular military enlistment program are similar to the ASVAB-14 answer sheet packets used in the school testing program.

One important difference in these programs is that students in the school testing program are permitted to take the ASVAB-14 although they may not have a social security number. In the regular enlistment program, all potential enlistees must have a social security number before they are permitted to take ASVAB, Forms 15, 16, or 17.

Figure 5

SCHEMATIC SAMPLE

**ANSWER SHEET
ARMED SERVICES VOCATIONAL
APTITUDE BATTERY**

17 CODE

[A][A][A] [B][B][B] [C][C][C] [D][D][D] [E][E][E] [F][F][F] [G][G][G] [H][H][H] [I][I][I] [J][J][J] [K][K][K] [L][L][L] [M][M][M] [N][N][N] [O][O][O] [P][P][P] [Q][Q][Q] [R][R][R] [S][S][S] [T][T][T] [U][U][U] [V][V][V] [W][W][W] [X][X][X] [Y][Y][Y] [Z][Z][Z] [0][0][0] [1][1][1] [2][2][2] [3][3][3] [4][4][4] [5][5][5] [6][6][6] [7][7][7] [8][8][8] [9][9][9]

16 SOCIAL SECURITY NUMBER

[0][0][0][0][0][0][0][0][0] [1][1][1][1][1][1][1][1][1] [2][2][2][2][2][2][2][2][2] [3][3][3][3][3][3][3][3][3] [4][4][4][4][4][4][4][4][4] [5][5][5][5][5][5][5][5][5] [6][6][6][6][6][6][6][6][6] [7][7][7][7][7][7][7][7][7] [8][8][8][8][8][8][8][8][8] [9][9][9][9][9][9][9][9][9]

MI / FIRST / LAST

PART 1—GS

PRACTICE
S1 A B ■ D
S2 A B C D
S3 A B C D

1–25 A B C D (answer rows)

PART 2—AR

1–30 A B C D

PART 3—WK

1–35 A B C D

PART 4—PC

1–15 A B C D

PART 5—NO

1–50 A B C D

Figure 6

SCHEMATIC SAMPLE

**ANSWER SHEET
ARMED SERVICES VOCATIONAL
APTITUDE BATTERY**

MI

FIRST

LAST

PART 6—CS

1 A B C D E	15 A B C D E	29 A B C D E	43 A B C D E	57 A B C D E	71 A B C D E
2 A B C D E	16 A B C D E	30 A B C D E	44 A B C D E	58 A B C D E	72 A B C D E
3 A B C D E	17 A B C D E	31 A B C D E	45 A B C D E	59 A B C D E	73 A B C D E
4 A B C D E	18 A B C D E	32 A B C D E	46 A B C D E	60 A B C D E	74 A B C D E
5 A B C D E	19 A B C D E	33 A B C D E	47 A B C D E	61 A B C D E	75 A B C D E
6 A B C D E	20 A B C D E	34 A B C D E	48 A B C D E	62 A B C D E	76 A B C D E
7 A B C D E	21 A B C D E	35 A B C D E	49 A B C D E	63 A B C D E	77 A B C D E
8 A B C D E	22 A B C D E	36 A B C D E	50 A B C D E	64 A B C D E	78 A B C D E
9 A B C D E	23 A B C D E	37 A B C D E	51 A B C D E	65 A B C D E	79 A B C D E
10 A B C D E	24 A B C D E	38 A B C D E	52 A B C D E	66 A B C D E	80 A B C D E
11 A B C D E	25 A B C D E	39 A B C D E	53 A B C D E	67 A B C D E	81 A B C D E
12 A B C D E	26 A B C D E	40 A B C D E	54 A B C D E	68 A B C D E	82 A B C D E
13 A B C D E	27 A B C D E	41 A B C D E	55 A B C D E	69 A B C D E	83 A B C D E
14 A B C D E	28 A B C D E	42 A B C D E	56 A B C D E	70 A B C D E	84 A B C D E

PART 7—AS

1 A B C D	5 A B C D	9 A B C D	13 A B C D	17 A B C D	21 A B C D	25 A B C D
2 A B C D	6 A B C D	10 A B C D	14 A B C D	18 A B C D	22 A B C D	
3 A B C D	7 A B C D	11 A B C D	15 A B C D	19 A B C D	23 A B C D	
4 A B C D	8 A B C D	12 A B C D	16 A B C D	20 A B C D	24 A B C D	

PART 8—MK

1 A B C D	5 A B C D	9 A B C D	13 A B C D	17 A B C D	21 A B C D	25 A B C D
2 A B C D	6 A B C D	10 A B C D	14 A B C D	18 A B C D	22 A B C D	
3 A B C D	7 A B C D	11 A B C D	15 A B C D	19 A B C D	23 A B C D	
4 A B C D	8 A B C D	12 A B C D	16 A B C D	20 A B C D	24 A B C D	

PART 9—MC

1 A B C D	5 A B C D	9 A B C D	13 A B C D	17 A B C D	21 A B C D	25 A B C D
2 A B C D	6 A B C D	10 A B C D	14 A B C D	18 A B C D	22 A B C D	
3 A B C D	7 A B C D	11 A B C D	15 A B C D	19 A B C D	23 A B C D	
4 A B C D	8 A B C D	12 A B C D	16 A B C D	20 A B C D	24 A B C D	

PART 10—EI

1 A B C D	4 A B C D	7 A B C D	10 A B C D	13 A B C D	16 A B C D	19 A B C D
2 A B C D	5 A B C D	8 A B C D	11 A B C D	14 A B C D	17 A B C D	20 A B C D
3 A B C D	6 A B C D	9 A B C D	12 A B C D	15 A B C D	18 A B C D	

MARKING THE ANSWER SHEET

Multiple-choice test items generally have either four or five options. The parts of the multiple-choice test items are illustrated below.

FOUR-OPTION ITEM

The portrait of the American president found on a $1 bill is that of ⎫ stem

A. Hamilton ⎫
B. Jefferson ⎬ distractors
C. Lincoln ⎭ or foils
D. Washington ←—key or correct answer ⎫ choices or options

Since the correct answer to this four-option item is (D), the test-taker should record this answer by marking the response position on the ASVAB answer sheet like this:

A B C ▮

NOT A B C Ⓓ

NOT A B C ✗

NOT A B C ✓

NOT A B C D *D*

NOT A B C D ▮

NOT A B C ✗

NOT A B ⬤

BUT A B C ▮

ASVAB SAMPLE QUESTIONS

This section illustrates the nature of the ASVAB test battery. By giving the general contents and/or purpose of the subtests, as well as a sampling of the various types of questions that appear on each of the ASVAB subtests, it shows applicants what to expect and provides them with a better understanding of the types of questions that appear on the official test battery and on the three specimen ASVAB test batteries.

SUBTEST 1
GENERAL SCIENCE (GS)

The General Science subtest consists of 25 items and covers the material generally taught in junior and senior high school science courses. Most of the questions deal with life science and physical science. There are also a few questions on earth science.

The life science items deal with basic biology, human nutrition, and health. The physical science items are concerned with elementary chemistry and physics. Geology, meteorology, and astronomy may be included in the earth science area.

Sample Test Items:

1. The chief nutrient in lean meat is

    1-A fat
    1-B starch
    1-C protein
    1-D carbohydrates

2. Which of the following is an invertebrate?

    2-A starfish
    2-B pigeon
    2-C gorilla
    2-D alligator

3. Substances which hasten chemical reaction time without themselves undergoing change are called

    3-A buffers
    3-B colloids
    3-C reducers
    3-D catalysts

4. The case of a compass would *not* be made of

    4-A brass
    4-B copper
    4-C plastic
    4-D steel

5. An eclipse of the sun throws the shadow of the

    5-A moon on the sun
    5-B moon on the earth
    5-C earth on the sun
    5-D earth on the moon

SUBTEST 2
ARITHMETIC REASONING (AR)

The Arithmetic Reasoning subtest consists of 30 items and covers basic mathematical problems generally encountered in everyday life. These questions are designed to measure general reasoning and the ability to solve mathematical problems.

Sample Test Items:

1. If three hoses of equal length connected together reach 24 feet, how long is each hose?

   1-A 6 feet
   1-B 7 feet
   1-C 8 feet
   1-D 9 feet

2. If 4′ is cut from a 12′ board, how much will be left?

   2-A 3′
   2-B 4′
   2-C 6′
   2-D 8′

3. A salesperson earns 30% commission on each sale made. How large a commission would the salesperson earn for selling $160.00 of merchandise?

   3-A $36.00
   3-B $40.00
   3-C $48.00
   3-D $50.00

4. It costs $0.50 per square yard to waterproof canvas. What will it cost to waterproof a canvas truck cover that is 15′ × 24′?

   4-A $6.67
   4-B $18.00
   4-C $20.00
   4-D $180.00

5. A floor that is 9′ wide and 12′ long measures how many square feet?

   5-A 21
   5-B 42
   5-C 108
   5-D 118

6. 30 inches is equal to

   6-A $2\frac{1}{2}$ feet
   6-B 3 feet
   6-C $2\frac{1}{2}$ yards
   6-D 3 yards

SUBTEST 3
WORD KNOWLEDGE (WK)

The Word Knowledge subtest consists of 35 items and is designed to test for ability to understand the meaning of words through synonyms—words having the same or nearly the same meaning as other words in the language. Vocabulary is one of many factors which characterizes reading comprehension, but it provides a "good" measure of verbal comprehension.

The words used in these synonym questions are those used in everyday language. The test questions may appear in either of two forms, as follows:

1. The key word appears in the stem and is followed by "most nearly means" (Sample test items 1–3).
2. The key word is used in a sentence (Sample test items 4–6).

Sample Test Items:

1. <u>Small</u> most nearly means

    1-A cheap
    1-B round
    1-C sturdy
    1-D little

2. <u>Impair</u> most nearly means

    2-A direct
    2-B weaken
    2-C improve
    2-D stimulate

3. <u>Cease</u> most nearly means

    3-A stop
    3-B start
    3-C change
    3-D continue

4. The wind is <u>variable</u> today.

    4-A mild
    4-B steady
    4-C shifting
    4-D chilling

5. The student <u>discovered</u> an error.

    5-A found
    5-B entered
    5-C searched
    5-D enlarged

6. Do not <u>obstruct</u> the entrance to the building.

    6-A block
    6-B enter
    6-C leave
    6-D cross

SUBTEST 4
PARAGRAPH COMPREHENSION (PC)

The Paragraph Comprehension subtest consists of 15 items and is designed to measure ability to obtain information from written material. The reading passages vary in length from one paragraph to several paragraphs and may be used for one or several questions. Each question should be answered solely on the basis of the information contained in the reading passage.

Sample Test Items:

1. In the relations of man to nature, the procuring of food and shelter is fundamental. With the migration of man to various climates, ever new adjustments to the food supply and to the climate became necessary.

   According to the passage, the means by which man supplies his material needs are

   1-A accidental
   1-B inadequate
   1-C limited
   1-D varied

2. From a building designer's standpoint, three things that make a home livable are the needs of the client, the building site, and the amount of money the client has to spend.

   According to the passage, to make a home livable,

   2-A it can be built on any piece of land
   2-B the design must fit the designer's income
   2-C the design must fit the owner's income and site
   2-D the prospective piece of land makes little difference

3. Twenty-five percent of all household burglaries can be attributed to unlocked windows or doors. Crime is the result of opportunity plus desire. To prevent crime, it is each individual's responsibility to

   3-A provide the desire
   3-B provide the opportunity
   3-C prevent the desire
   3-D prevent the opportunity

4. In certain areas water is so scarce that every attempt is made to conserve it. For instance, on one oasis in the Sahara Desert the amount of water necessary for each date palm has been carefully determined.

   How much water is each tree given?

   4-A no water at all
   4-B water on alternate days
   4-C exactly the amount required
   4-D water only if it is healthy

SUBTEST 5
NUMERICAL OPERATIONS (NO)

The Numerical Operations subtest contains 50 simple, two-number computations in addition, subtraction, multiplication, and division. All numbers are one or two digit whole numbers.

As this is a speed test, you should work as fast as you can without making mistakes.

Sample Test Items:

1. $3 + 6 =$

    1-A 3
    1-B 6
    1-C 9
    1-D 12

2. $18 - 6 =$

    2-A 3
    2-B 12
    2-C 15
    2-D 24

3. $3 \times 4 =$

    3-A 7
    3-B 12
    3-C 14
    3-D 34

4. $60 \div 15 =$

    4-A 4
    4-B 5
    4-C 6
    4-D 7

5. $18 - 11 =$

    5-A 7
    5-B 8
    5-C 9
    5-D 10

6. $7 \times 4 =$

    6-A 11
    6-B 21
    6-C 28
    6-D 38

7. $12 + 4 =$

    7-A 6
    7-B 7
    7-C 14
    7-D 16

8. $20 \div 4 =$

    8-A 2
    8-B 3
    8-C 4
    8-D 5

SUBTEST 6
CODING SPEED (CS)

The Coding Speed subtest contains 84 questions, each with five options, and is designed to ascertain how quickly and accurately you can find a number in a table. At the top of each section, there is a key which consists of a group of words with a code number for each word. Each question in the subtest is a word taken from the key at the top of that section. From among the options listed for each question, you must find the one that is the correct code number for that word.

As this is a speed test, you should work as fast as you can without making mistakes.

Sample Test Items:

Key

game 6456	hat 1413	man 3451	salt 4586
green 2715	house 2859	room 2864	tree 5972

QUESTION #			OPTIONS		
	A	**B**	**C**	**D**	**E**
1. room	1413	2715	2864	3451	4586
2. green	2715	2864	3451	4586	5972
3. tree	1413	2715	3451	4586	5972
4. hat	1413	2715	3451	4586	5972
5. room	1413	2864	3451	4586	5972
6. house	1413	2859	4586	5972	6456
7. man	2715	2864	3451	4586	5972
8. game	2859	2864	4586	5972	6456
9. salt	2859	2864	3451	4586	5972
10. tree	2864	3451	4586	5972	6456

SUBTEST 7
AUTO & SHOP INFORMATION (AS)

The Auto & Shop Information subtest consists of 25 items and covers the material generally taught in automobile mechanics in vocational-technical schools and in shop instruction. It is designed to measure knowledge of automobiles, tools, and shop terminology and practices.

The automotive information may also be acquired as a hobby or by working with automobiles. The questions generally pertain to diagnosing malfunctions of a car, the use of particular parts on a car, or meaning of terminology.

The shop information may also be acquired as a hobby or through shop experience using a variety of tools and materials.

Sample Test Items:

1. A fuel injection system on an automobile engine eliminates the necessity for

    1-A a manifold
    1-B a carburetor
    1-C spark plugs
    1-D a distributor

2. A car uses too much oil when which parts are worn?

    2-A pistons
    2-B piston rings
    2-C main bearings
    2-D connecting rods

3. The function of the rotor is to

    3-A distribute the electricity to the spark plugs
    3-B open and close the distributor points
    3-C rotate the distributor cam
    3-D rotate the distributor shaft

4. What happens if cylinder head torquing is not done in proper sequence?

    4-A It warps the piston rings.
    4-B It cracks the intake manifold.
    4-C It distorts the head.
    4-D It reduces valve clearance.

5. The saw shown above is used mainly to cut

    5-A across the grain of the wood
    5-B along the grain of the wood
    5-C plywood
    5-D odd-shaped holes in wood

6. Sheet metal should be cut with

    6-A household scissors
    6-B a hack saw
    6-C tin shears
    6-D a jig saw

7. A lathe would normally be used in making which of the following items?

    7-A a baseball bat
    7-B a bookcase
    7-C a hockey stick
    7-D a picture frame

SUBTEST 8
MATHEMATICS KNOWLEDGE (MK)

The Mathematics Knowledge subtest consists of 25 items and is designed to measure general mathematical knowledge. It is a test of your ability to solve problems using high school mathematics, including algebra and some basic geometry. Scratch paper is provided for any figuring you may wish to do.

Sample Test Items:

1. If $a + 6 = 7$, then a is equal to

   1-A 0
   1-B 1
   1-C -1
   1-D $\dfrac{7}{6}$

2. What is the area of this square?

   2-A 1 square foot
   2-B 5 square feet
   2-C 10 square feet
   2-D 25 square feet

3. If 50% of X = 66, then X =

   3-A 33
   3-B 66
   3-C 99
   3-D 132

4. In the triangle below, angle B is 90 degrees. Which line in the triangle is the longest?

   4-A AB
   4-B AC
   4-C neither
   4-D can't be determined from the information given

5. If $3X = -5$, then X =

   5-A $\dfrac{3}{5}$
   5-B $-\dfrac{5}{3}$
   5-C $-\dfrac{3}{5}$
   5-D -2

6. The first digit of the square root of 59043 is

   6-A 2
   6-B 3
   6-C 4
   6-D 5

7. If you multiply $x + 3$ by $2x + 5$, how many x's will there be in the product?

   7-A 3
   7-B 6
   7-C 9
   7-D 11

SUBTEST 9

MECHANICAL COMPREHENSION (MC)

The Mechanical Comprehension test consists of 25 items designed to measure your understanding of mechanical and physical principles. Many of the questions use drawings to illustrate specific principles. Understanding of these principles comes from observing the physical world, working with or operating mechanical devices, or reading and studying.

Sample Test Items:

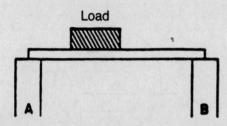

1. Which post holds up the greater part of the load?

    1-A post A
    1-B post B
    1-C both equal
    1-D not clear

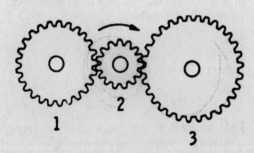

2. Which of the other gears is moving in the same direction as gear 2?

    2-A gear 1
    2-B gear 3
    2-C neither of the other gears
    2-D both of the other gears

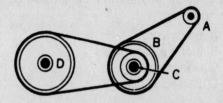

3. In this arrangement of pulleys, which pulley turns fastest?

    3-A A
    3-B B
    3-C C
    3-D D

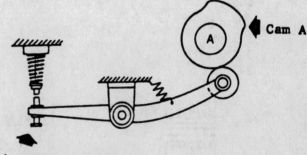

4. As cam A makes one complete turn, the setscrew will hit the contact point

    4-A once
    4-B twice
    4-C three times
    4-D not at all

SUBTEST 10
ELECTRONICS INFORMATION (EI)

The Electronics Information subtest consists of 20 items dealing with electricity, radio principles, and electronics. This information can be learned through working on radios, working on electrical equipment, reading books, or taking courses.

Sample Test Items:

1. The safest way to run an extension cord to a lamp is

    1-A under a rug
    1-B along a baseboard
    1-C under a sofa
    1-D behind a sofa

2. What does the abbreviation AC stand for?

    2-A additional charge
    2-B alternating coil
    2-C alternating current
    2-D ampere current

3. Which of the following has the *least* resistance?

    3-A rubber
    3-B silver
    3-C wood
    3-D iron

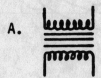 A.   B.

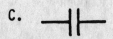 C.   D.

4. Which of the above is the symbol for a transformer?

    4-A A
    4-B B
    4-C C
    4-D D

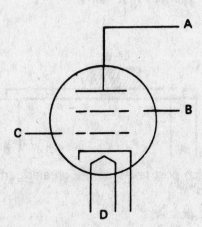

5. in the schematic vacuum tube illustrated, the cathode is element

    5-A A
    5-B B
    5-C C
    5-D D

6. Flux is used in the process of soldering together two conductors in order to

    6-A provide a luster finish
    6-B prevent oxidation when the connection is heated
    6-C maintain the temperature of the soldering iron
    6-D prevent the connection from becoming overheated

ANSWER KEY TO SAMPLE TEST QUESTIONS

SUBTEST 1—GENERAL SCIENCE

1. C   2. A   3. D   4. D   5. B

SUBTEST 2—ARITHMETIC REASONING

1. C   2. D   3. C   4. C   5. C   6. A

SUBTEST 3—WORD KNOWLEDGE

1. D   2. B   3. A   4. C   5. A   6. A

SUBTEST 4—PARAGRAPH COMPREHENSION

1. D   2. C   3. D   4. C

SUBTEST 5—NUMERICAL OPERATIONS

1. C   2. B   3. B   4. A   5. A   6. C   7. D   8. D

SUBTEST 6—CODING SPEED

1. C   2. A   3. E   4. A   5. B   6. B   7. C   8. E   9. D   10. D

SUBTEST 7—AUTO & SHOP INFORMATION

1. B   2. B   3. A   4. C   5. D   6. C   7. A

SUBTEST 8—MATHEMATICS KNOWLEDGE

1. B   2. D   3. D   4. B   5. B   6. A   7. D

SUBTEST 9—MECHANICAL COMPREHENSION

1. A   2. D   3. A   4. A

SUBTEST 10—ELECTRONICS INFORMATION

1. B   2. C   3. B   4. A   5. D   6. B

STRATEGIES FOR PREPARING FOR AND TAKING THE ASVAB

PREPARING FOR THE TEST

Whether it be studying subject matter, reviewing sample questions in practice exercises, or getting into condition for a strenuous physical test, the "test-wise" individual will begin *immediately* preparing for the tests ahead.

Become familiar with the format of multiple-choice test items. These items are used exclusively in the Armed Services Vocational Aptitude Battery.

Become familiar with the layout of machine-scored answer sheets. Know the proper way to record your answers in the spaces provided; whether they be brackets, bars, squares, ovals, or circles. These standard answer sheets are not complicated if you understand the layout and have practiced blackening the answer space in the correct manner.

Find out what the test will cover. This book, as well as your vocational advisor or school guidance counselor, is an excellent source for invaluable suggestions and guidance.

Review subject matter covered in the test. Books and other study materials may be borrowed from libraries or purchased in bookstores.

Take each Specimen Test under actual test conditions. Answer all questions in these practice tests.

Check your answers with the key answers and explanations at the end of each test. For those questions answered incorrectly, determine why your original answers are incorrect. Make certain that you understand the rationale for arriving at the correct answer. This is essential to broaden your background, increase your test sophistication, and prepare you for the real test.

Set aside definite hours each day for concentrated study. Adhere closely to this schedule. Don't fritter away your time with too many breaks. A cup of coffee, a piece of fruit, or a look out of the window is fine—but not too often.

Try to find a quiet, private room for your study. If necessary, use the library, which is generally free from the distractions at home.

Keep physically fit. You cannot study effectively when you are exhausted, ill, or tense. Guard you health by making sure you get

- Sufficient sleep
- Daily exercise and recreation
- A balanced diet

If possible, avoid taking the test when you are fatigued, ill, injured, or upset.

Go to bed early the night before the test and get a good night's sleep.

Eat a light meal before taking the test. Eating a heavy meal just before the test can make you sleepy and dull your senses.

Bring along all supplies you may need for the test—a pen, several no. 2 pencils, an eraser, etc. Be certain to bring eyeglasses if you need them for reading.

Bring a watch to help you budget your time. Be certain that you know the amount of time you have for each subtest. While taking the ASVAB, you will not be permitted to go back and check your answers on subtests that have already been completed.

Arrive at the test site well before the scheduled time for the test.

Refrain from drinking excessive amounts of liquids before the test. Going to the rest room during the test wastes valuable testing time. Use the rest room before or after the test, not during the test.

GUESSING

If you do not know the answer to a multiple-choice test item, should you guess? Emphatically, *yes!* There is no penalty for incorrect answers on the ASVAB so it is to your advantage to answer every question.

To obtain the maximum score possible by guessing, you should understand what is meant by *guessing "blindly," "educated" guessing,* and *probability.*

To guess "blindly" is to select at random the correct answer to the question from all the options given. To make an "educated" guess is first to eliminate those options that you know to be definitely incorrect and then to make your selection from among the remaining options.

Probability is the likelihood or chance of some event or series of events occurring. For example, when tossing a coin, the probability that it will land heads up is one out of two. Similarly, the probability of its landing tails up is also one out of two. Head and tail are equally likely. Such probability is expressed as $\frac{1}{2}$ or .50.

Probability ranges between *one* and *zero*. At *one,* the event will probably occur every time. At *zero,* the event will probably never occur. The probability of occurring plus the probability of not occurring always equals one.

Assume that there are three marbles in a jar and only one marble is red. What is the probability of picking the red marble strictly by chance? The probability is one out of three, expressed as $\frac{1}{3}$ or .33. Similarly, if there are four marbles in a jar and only one is red, the probability of picking the red marble strictly by chance is one out of four, expressed as $\frac{1}{4}$ or .25. If there are five marbles in a jar and only one is red, the probability of picking the red marble strictly by chance is one out of five, expressed as $\frac{1}{5}$ or .20.

With a true-false or two-option item, the probability of guessing the correct answer when the test-taker knows nothing about the item is one out of two ($\frac{1}{2}$). For a three-option multiple-choice item, the probability of guessing the correct answer strictly by chance is one out of three ($\frac{1}{3}$). For a four-option multiple-choice item, the probability of guessing the correct answer strictly by chance is one out of four ($\frac{1}{4}$). For a five-option multiple-choice item, the probability of guessing the correct answer strictly by chance is one out of five ($\frac{1}{5}$). Obviously, the probability of selecting the correct answer increases with every incorrect option eliminated before making that "educated" guess.

By guessing "blindly" or picking strictly by chance, the test-taker will probably answer correctly 50 percent of the test items in a true-false or two-option test, 33 percent of the test items in a three-option multiple-choice test, 25 percent of the test items in a four-option test, and 20 percent of the test items in a five-option test.

Is probability important for the test-taker? Definitely! Understanding and applying the principles of probability will increase the test score by several to many points. It can make the difference between passing or failing a test, and it may make the difference between being accepted or rejected, or getting more desirable vocational offers.

The following two examples illustrate how the principles of probability may influence test scores. In both examples we will assume that no deduction is made for incorrect answers and that only the number of correct answers determines the subtest score. In the first example, we will assume that the subtest consists of 84 five-option items. In the second example, we will assume that the subtest consists of 50 four-option items.

Example 1: Five-Option Items

Assume that you are taking an 84-item, five-option multiple-choice subtest and that subtest scores are based solely on the number of correct answers. Assume further that there are twenty answers of which you are uncertain or that there are twenty questions you are unable to answer because of lack of time. If you do not answer these twenty items, you will receive no credit for them. If you guess "blindly" by picking any option at random, you will probably answer four out of the twenty items correctly and earn four extra points.

If you are able to eliminate one option that you know is incorrect on each of the twenty items and then pick at random from the remaining four options, you will probably answer five of the twenty items correctly and earn five extra points.

If you are able to eliminate two options that you know are incorrect on each of the twenty items and then pick at random from the remaining three options, you will probably answer seven of the twenty items correctly and earn seven extra points.

If you are able to eliminate three options that you know are incorrect on each of the twenty items and then pick at random from the remaining two options, you will probably answer ten of the twenty items correctly and earn ten extra points.

Answer all items.
If you are unsure of the correct answer, first eliminate options that you know are incorrect and then pick at random from the remaining options.
Guessing "blindly" is better than not guessing at all.

Example 2: Four-Option Items

Assume that you are taking a 50-item, four-option multiple-choice subtest and that subtest scores are based solely on the number of correct answers. Assume further that there are twelve answers of which you are uncertain or that there are twelve questions you are unable to answer because of lack of time. If you do not answer these twelve items, you will receive no credit for them. If you guess "blindly" by picking any option at random, you will probably answer three out of the twelve items correctly and earn three extra points.

If you are able to eliminate one option that you know is incorrect on each of the twelve items and then pick at random from the remaining three options, you will probably answer four of the twelve items correctly and earn four extra points.

If you are able to eliminate two options that you know are incorrect on each of the twelve items and then pick at random from the remaining two options, you will probably answer six of the twelve items correctly and earn six extra points.

Answer all items.
An "educated" guess is better than guessing "blindly."
Guessing "blindly" is better than not guessing at all.

TAKING THE TEST

Arrive early at the test location.

If you have a choice, choose a comfortable seat with good lighting and away from possible distractions such as friends, the proctor's desk, the door, open windows, etc.

If you are left-handed or have any special physical problem, inform the proctor of your special needs and ask if some arrangements can be made to enable you to compete equally with the other candidates.

If the examination room is too cold, too warm, or not well ventilated, call these conditions to the attention to the person in charge.

Be confident and calm. A certain amount of anxiety is not only normal but is highly desirable. Test-takers will not be at their best when they are completely relaxed. If you have prepared faithfully, you will attain your true score—based on your ability, your degree of preparation for the test, and your test sophistication.

Watch your watch and apportion your time intelligently.

Give the test your complete attention. Blot out all other thoughts, pleasant or otherwise, and concentrate solely on the task before you.

Listen carefully to all oral instructions. Read carefully the directions for taking the test and marking the answer sheets. If you don't understand the instructions or directions, raise your hand and ask the proctor for clarification. Failure to follow instructions or misreading directions can only result in a loss of points.

When the signal is given to begin the test, start with the first question. Don't jump to conclusions. Carefully read the stem of the question and all the options before selecting the answer.

Answer the question as given in the test booklet and not what you believe the question should be.

Work steadily and quickly but not carelessly.

Do not spend too much time on any one question. If you can't figure out the answer in a few seconds, go on to the next question. If you skip a question, be sure to skip the answer space for that question on the answer sheet. Continue in this fashion through the subtest, answering only those easy questions that require relatively little time and of which you are sure.

Make certain that the number of the question you are working on in the test booklet corresponds to the number of the question you are answering on the answer sheet. It is a good idea to check the numbers of questions and answers frequently. If you skip a question but fail to skip the corresponding answer blank for that question, all your answers after that will be in the wrong place.

After you have answered every question you know, go back to the more difficult questions you skipped in the subtest and attempt to answer them. If you are still unsure of the correct answer, eliminate those options that you know are incorrect and make an "educated" guess as to which one of the remaining options is correct. If time does not permit "educated" guessing, guess "blindly" but be sure to answer all questions in the subtest within the alloted time.

If time permits, recheck your answers for errors. If you find that your initial response is incorrect, change it to the correct answer, making sure to erase your initial response completely on the answer sheet.

THE ASVAB TEST BOOKLET

INTRODUCTORY INFORMATION

The ASVAB test booklet consists of approximately 64 pages.

Based upon previous forms, the title page is followed by several pages of introductory information for general orientation, such as:

- the purpose of ASVAB
- testing time
- a listing of ASVAB subtests, working time, and number of items
- how the various academic and occupational composites are determined
- the basic skills each subtest is purported to measure

GENERAL DIRECTIONS

General directions for taking the actual test are then given.

An updated version of the general directions that appeared in a previous form of the ASVAB test booklet follows.

Do not write or mark in this booklet. Write your name and mark your answers on the separate answer forms. Use the scratch paper which was given you for any figuring you need to do. Return this scratch paper with your other papers when you finish the test.

This booklet contains 10 subtests. Each subtest has its own instructions and time limit. When you finish one subtest, do not turn the page to the next one until the examiner tells you to. Do not turn back to a previous subtest at any time.

Each subtest has a separate section on the answer forms. Be sure you mark your answers for each subtest in the section that belongs to that subtest.

For each question be sure to pick the best one of the possible answers listed. When you have decided which one of the choices given is the best answer to a question, blacken the space on your answer form which has the same number and letter as your choice. Mark only in the answer space. Make no stray marks.

Sample Question 1

1. A square has

    1-A 2 sides
    1-B 3 sides
    1-C 4 sides
    1-D 5 sides

```
┌─────────────────────────────────┐
│      SAMPLE ANSWER FORM          │
│                                  │
│   1   Ä   B̈   ▮   D̈             │
│                                  │
│   2   Ä   B̈   C̈   D̈             │
│                                  │
│   3   Ä   B̈   C̈   D̈             │
│                                  │
└─────────────────────────────────┘
```

The correct answer to Sample Question 1 is C. Note how space C opposite number 1 has been blackened above. Your marks should look like this and be placed in the space with the same number and letter as the correct answer to each question. Remember, there is only one best answer for each question. If you are not sure of the answer, make the best guess you can. If you want to change your answer, erase your first mark completely.

Answer as many questions as possible. Do not spend too much time on any one question. Work fast but work accurately.

THE TEST SECTION

The remainder of the test booklet contains the directions for answering each subtest and the actual questions for each of the 10 subtests which are called *parts* both in the test booklet and on the answer sheets.

DIAGNOSIS
FINDING YOUR STRENGTHS
AND WEAKNESSES

FIRST ASVAB SPECIMEN TEST

This section contains specimen answer sheets for use in answering the questions on each subtest, an actual specimen ASVAB test, key answers for determining your scores on these subtests, and the rationale or explanation for each key answer.

Remove (cut out) the specimen answer sheets on the following pages for use in recording your answers to the test questions. The ASVAB Specimen Test has the same format and content as the actual ASVAB test. Take this test under "real" test conditions. Time each subtest carefully.

Use the key answers to obtain your subtest scores and to evaluate your performance on each subtest. Record the number of items you answered correctly, as well as the number of each item you answered incorrectly or wish to review, in the space provided below the key answers for each subtest.

Be certain to review carefully and understand the explanations for the answers to all questions you answered incorrectly and for each of the questions which you answered correctly but are unsure of. This is absolutely essential in order to acquire the knowledge and expertise necessary to obtain the maximum scores possible on the real ASVAB subtests.

Transfer your scores for each part of the First ASVAB Specimen Test to the Self-Appraisal Chart appearing on page 275. This will enable you to see the progress made as you continue to prepare for the actual test.

Specimen Answer Sheet for Answering Parts 1–5

ANSWER SHEET
ARMED SERVICES VOCATIONAL
APTITUDE BATTERY

17 CODE

[A][A][A] [B][B][B] [C][C][C] [D][D][D] [E][E][E] [F][F][F] [G][G][G] [H][H][H] [I][I][I] [J][J][J] [K][K][K] [L][L][L] [M][M][M] [N][N][N] [O][O][O] [P][P][P] [Q][Q][Q] [R][R][R] [S][S][S] [T][T][T] [U][U][U] [V][V][V] [W][W][W] [X][X][X] [Y][Y][Y] [Z][Z][Z] [0][0][0] [1][1][1] [2][2][2] [3][3][3] [4][4][4] [5][5][5] [6][6][6] [7][7][7] [8][8][8] [9][9][9]

16 SOCIAL SECURITY NUMBER

[0][0][0][0][0][0][0][0][0] [1][1][1][1][1][1][1][1][1] [2][2][2][2][2][2][2][2][2] [3][3][3][3][3][3][3][3][3] [4][4][4][4][4][4][4][4][4] [5][5][5][5][5][5][5][5][5] [6][6][6][6][6][6][6][6][6] [7][7][7][7][7][7][7][7][7] [8][8][8][8][8][8][8][8][8] [9][9][9][9][9][9][9][9][9]

MI
FIRST
LAST

PART 1–GS

PRACTICE
S1 A B ■ D
S2 A B C D
S3 A B C D

1 A B C D 5 A B C D 9 A B C D 13 A B C D 17 A B C D 21 A B C D 25 A B C D
2 A B C D 6 A B C D 10 A B C D 14 A B C D 18 A B C D 22 A B C D
3 A B C D 7 A B C D 11 A B C D 15 A B C D 19 A B C D 23 A B C D
4 A B C D 8 A B C D 12 A B C D 16 A B C D 20 A B C D 24 A B C D

PART 2–AR

1 A B C D 5 A B C D 9 A B C D 13 A B C D 17 A B C D 21 A B C D 25 A B C D 29 A B C D
2 A B C D 6 A B C D 10 A B C D 14 A B C D 18 A B C D 22 A B C D 26 A B C D 30 A B C D
3 A B C D 7 A B C D 11 A B C D 15 A B C D 19 A B C D 23 A B C D 27 A B C D
4 A B C D 8 A B C D 12 A B C D 16 A B C D 20 A B C D 24 A B C D 28 A B C D

PART 3–WK

1 A B C D 6 A B C D 11 A B C D 16 A B C D 21 A B C D 26 A B C D 31 A B C D
2 A B C D 7 A B C D 12 A B C D 17 A B C D 22 A B C D 27 A B C D 32 A B C D
3 A B C D 8 A B C D 13 A B C D 18 A B C D 23 A B C D 28 A B C D 33 A B C D
4 A B C D 9 A B C D 14 A B C D 19 A B C D 24 A B C D 29 A B C D 34 A B C D
5 A B C D 10 A B C D 15 A B C D 20 A B C D 25 A B C D 30 A B C D 35 A B C D

PART 4–PC

1 A B C D 3 A B C D 5 A B C D 7 A B C D 9 A B C D 11 A B C D 13 A B C D 15 A B C D
2 A B C D 4 A B C D 6 A B C D 8 A B C D 10 A B C D 12 A B C D 14 A B C D

PART 5–NO

1 A B C D 8 A B C D 15 A B C D 22 A B C D 29 A B C D 36 A B C D 43 A B C D 50 A B C D
2 A B C D 9 A B C D 16 A B C D 23 A B C D 30 A B C D 37 A B C D 44 A B C D
3 A B C D 10 A B C D 17 A B C D 24 A B C D 31 A B C D 38 A B C D 45 A B C D
4 A B C D 11 A B C D 18 A B C D 25 A B C D 32 A B C D 39 A B C D 46 A B C D
5 A B C D 12 A B C D 19 A B C D 26 A B C D 33 A B C D 40 A B C D 47 A B C D
6 A B C D 13 A B C D 20 A B C D 27 A B C D 34 A B C D 41 A B C D 48 A B C D
7 A B C D 14 A B C D 21 A B C D 28 A B C D 35 A B C D 42 A B C D 49 A B C D

**Specimen Answer Sheet for
Answering Parts 6–10**

MI

FIRST

LAST

PART 6—CS

1 A B C D E	15 A B C D E	29 A B C D E	43 A B C D E	57 A B C D E	71 A B C D E
2 A B C D E	16 A B C D E	30 A B C D E	44 A B C D E	58 A B C D E	72 A B C D E
3 A B C D E	17 A B C D E	31 A B C D E	45 A B C D E	59 A B C D E	73 A B C D E
4 A B C D E	18 A B C D E	32 A B C D E	46 A B C D E	60 A B C D E	74 A B C D E
5 A B C D E	19 A B C D E	33 A B C D E	47 A B C D E	61 A B C D E	75 A B C D E
6 A B C D E	20 A B C D E	34 A B C D E	48 A B C D E	62 A B C D E	76 A B C D E
7 A B C D E	21 A B C D E	35 A B C D E	49 A B C D E	63 A B C D E	77 A B C D E
8 A B C D E	22 A B C D E	36 A B C D E	50 A B C D E	64 A B C D E	78 A B C D E
9 A B C D E	23 A B C D E	37 A B C D E	51 A B C D E	65 A B C D E	79 A B C D E
10 A B C D E	24 A B C D E	38 A B C D E	52 A B C D E	66 A B C D E	80 A B C D E
11 A B C D E	25 A B C D E	39 A B C D E	53 A B C D E	67 A B C D E	81 A B C D E
12 A B C D E	26 A B C D E	40 A B C D E	54 A B C D E	68 A B C D E	82 A B C D E
13 A B C D E	27 A B C D E	41 A B C D E	55 A B C D E	69 A B C D E	83 A B C D E
14 A B C D E	28 A B C D E	42 A B C D E	56 A B C D E	70 A B C D E	84 A B C D E

PART 7—AS

1 A B C D	5 A B C D	9 A B C D	13 A B C D	17 A B C D	21 A B C D	25 A B C D
2 A B C D	6 A B C D	10 A B C D	14 A B C D	18 A B C D	22 A B C D	
3 A B C D	7 A B C D	11 A B C D	15 A B C D	19 A B C D	23 A B C D	
4 A B C D	8 A B C D	12 A B C D	16 A B C D	20 A B C D	24 A B C D	

PART 8—MK

1 A B C D	5 A B C D	9 A B C D	13 A B C D	17 A B C D	21 A B C D	25 A B C D
2 A B C D	6 A B C D	10 A B C D	14 A B C D	18 A B C D	22 A B C D	
3 A B C D	7 A B C D	11 A B C D	15 A B C D	19 A B C D	23 A B C D	
4 A B C D	8 A B C D	12 A B C D	16 A B C D	20 A B C D	24 A B C D	

PART 9—MC

1 A B C D	5 A B C D	9 A B C D	13 A B C D	17 A B C D	21 A B C D	25 A B C D
2 A B C D	6 A B C D	10 A B C D	14 A B C D	18 A B C D	22 A B C D	
3 A B C D	7 A B C D	11 A B C D	15 A B C D	19 A B C D	23 A B C D	
4 A B C D	8 A B C D	12 A B C D	16 A B C D	20 A B C D	24 A B C D	

PART 10—EI

1 A B C D	4 A B C D	7 A B C D	10 A B C D	13 A B C D	16 A B C D	19 A B C D
2 A B C D	5 A B C D	8 A B C D	11 A B C D	14 A B C D	17 A B C D	20 A B C D
3 A B C D	6 A B C D	9 A B C D	12 A B C D	15 A B C D	18 A B C D	

First

ASVAB

Specimen Test

The introductory material for general orientation, as well as the general directions for taking the test, appears before the actual test questions in the ASVAB test booklet. However, because this material was covered previously in this book, it is not included in the specimen ASVAB test booklet.

GENERAL SCIENCE

Directions

This is a test of 25 questions to find out how much you know about general science as usually covered in high school courses. Pick the best answer for each question, then blacken the space on your answer form which has the same number and letter as your choice.

Here are three sample questions.

S1. Water is an example of a

S1-A solid
S1-B gas
S1-C liquid
S1-D crystal

Now look at the section of your answer sheet labeled Part 1, "Practice." Notice that answer space C has been marked for question 1. Now do practice questions 2 and 3 by yourself. Find the correct answer to the question, then mark the space on your answer form that has the same letter as the answer you picked. Do this now.

S2. Lack of iodine is often related to which of the following diseases?

S2-A beriberi
S2-B scurvey
S2-C rickets
S2-D goiter

S3. An eclipse of the sun throws the shadow of the

S3-A earth on the moon
S3-B moon on the earth
S3-C moon on the sun
S3-D earth on the sun.

You should have marked D for quesion 2 and B for question 3. If you made any mistakes, erase your mark carefully and blacken the correct answer space. Do this now.

Your score on this test will be based on the number of questions you answer correctly. You should try to answer every question. Do not spend too much time on any one question.

When you begin, be sure to start with question number 1 of Part 1 of your test booklet, and number 1 in Part 1 on your answer form.

DO NOT TURN THIS PAGE UNTIL TOLD TO DO SO.

GENERAL SCIENCE

TIME: 11 Minutes—25 Questions

1. Which of the following operates by suction?

   1-A a riveting hammer
   1-B a balloon
   1-C a vacuum cleaner
   1-D an electric fan

2. If a 33⅓ rpm phonograph record is played at a speed of 45 rpm, it will

   2-A sound lower-pitched
   2-B sound higher-pitched
   2-C give no sound
   2-D play louder

3. The chief nutrient in lean meat is

   3-A starch
   3-B protein
   3-C fat
   3-D carbohydrates

4. You are most likely to develop hypothermia when

   4-A it is very hot and you have nothing to drink
   4-B you are bitten by a rabid dog
   4-C you fall asleep in the sun
   4-D it is very cold and your clothes are wet

5. If you are caught away from home during a thunderstorm, the safest place to be is

   5-A in a car
   5-B under a tree
   5-C in an open field
   5-D at the top of a small hill

6. During a thunderstorm, we see a lightning bolt before we hear the sound of the accompanying thunder chiefly because

   6-A the eye is more sensitive than the ear
   6-B the wind interferes with the sound of the thunder
   6-C the storm may be very far away
   6-D the speed of light is much greater than the speed of sound

7. The process which is responsible for the continuous removal of carbon dioxide from the atmosphere is

   7-A respiration
   7-B oxidation
   7-C metabolism
   7-D photosynthesis

8. Ringworm is caused by a(n)

   8-A alga
   8-B fungus
   8-C bacterium
   8-D protozoan

9. Light passes through the crystalline lens in the eye and focuses on the

   9-A cornea
   9-B iris
   9-C pupil
   9-D retina

10. Of the following gases in the air, the most plentiful is

    10-A argon
    10-B oxygen
    10-C nitrogen
    10-D carbon dioxide

11. The time it takes for light from the sun to reach the earth is approximately

    11-A four years
    11-B eight minutes
    11-C four months
    11-D sixteen years

12. Of the following types of clouds, the ones which occur at the greatest altitude are called

    12-A cirrus
    12-B nimbus
    12-C cumulus
    12-D stratus

1

47   **GO ON TO THE NEXT PAGE.**

1

13. The smallest particle of gold that still retains the characteristics of gold is

    13-A a molecule
    13-B a proton
    13-C an electron
    13-D an atom

14. Narcotics may be dangerous if used without supervision, but they are useful in medicine because they

    14-A increase production of red blood cells
    14-B kill bacteria
    14-C relieve pain
    14-D stimulate the heart

15. The primary reason why fungi are often found growing in abundance deep in the forest is that there

    15-A it is cooler
    15-B it is warmer
    15-C they have little exposure to sunlight for photosynthesis
    15-D they have a plentiful supply of organic matter

16. The principle function of an air conditioner, aside from regulating heat, is to regulate the air's

    16-A speed of motion
    16-B moisture content
    16-C oxygen content
    16-D density

17. Lack of iodine is often related to which of the following diseases?

    17-A beriberi
    17-B scurvy
    17-C rickets
    17-D goiter

18. Why will a given quantity of steam always produce a more severe burn than that produced by the same quantity of boiling water?

    18-A Steam always penetrates the epidermis.
    18-B Steam causes the skin to contract and break.
    18-C Steam always releases more heat per gram than water.
    18-D Steam always covers more area of the skin.

19. A person is more buoyant when swimming in salt water than in fresh water because

    19-A he keeps his head out of salt water
    19-B salt coats his body with a floating membrane
    19-C salt water has greater tensile strength
    19-D salt water weighs more than an equal volume of fresh water.

20. A volcanic eruption is caused by

    20-A sunspots
    20-B pressure inside the earth
    20-C nuclear fallout
    20-D boiling lava

21. The vitamin manufactured by the skin with the help of the sun is

    21-A A
    21-B B_6
    21-C B_{12}
    21-D D

22. Nitrogen-fixing bacteria are found in nodules on the roots of the

    22-A beet
    22-B potato
    22-C carrot
    22-D clover

23. The vascular system of the body is concerned with

    23-A respiration
    23-B sense of touch
    23-C circulation of blood
    23-D enzymes

GO ON TO THE NEXT PAGE.

24. Of the following substances, the one which is nonmagnetic is

    24-A iron
    24-B aluminum
    24-C nickel
    24-D cobalt

25. If you wish to cut down on saturated fats and cholesterol in your diet, which of the following foods should you avoid?

    25-A fish
    25-B dry beans and peas
    25-C cheese
    25-D spaghetti

1

DO NOT TURN THIS PAGE UNTIL TOLD TO DO SO.
STOP! IF YOU FINISH BEFORE THE TIME IS UP, YOU
MAY CHECK OVER YOUR WORK ON THIS PART ONLY.

2

ARITHMETIC REASONING

2

Directions

This test has 30 questions about arithmetic. Each question is followed by four possible answers. Decide which answer is correct, then blacken the space on your answer form which has the same number and letter as your choice. Use your scratch paper for any figuring you wish to do.

Here are two sample questions.

S1. A person buys a sandwich for 90¢, soda for 55¢, and pie for 70¢. What is the total cost?

S1-A $2.00
S1-B $2.05
S1-C $2.15
S1-D $2.25

The total cost is $2.15; therefore, the C answer is the right one.

S2. If 8 workers are needed to run 4 machines, how many workers are needed to run 20 machines?

S2-A 16
S2-B 32
S2-C 36
S2-D 40

The number needed is 40; therefore, D is the proper answer.

Your score on this test will be based on the number of questions you answer correctly. You should try to answer every question. Do not spend too much time on any one question.

Notice that Part 2 begins with question number 1. When you begin, be sure to start with question number 1 in Part 2 of your test booklet and number 1 in Part 2 on your answer form.

DO NOT TURN THIS PAGE UNTIL TOLD TO DO SO.

2

ARITHMETIC REASONING

TIME: 36 Minutes—30 Questions

1. A man owned 75 shares of stock worth $50 each. The corporation declared a dividend of 8%, payable in stock. How many shares did he then own?

   1-A 81 shares
   1-B 90 shares
   1-C 91 shares
   1-D 95 shares

2. If a scow is towed at the rate of three miles an hour, how many hours will be needed to tow the scow 28 miles?

   2-A 10 hours 30 minutes
   2-B 9 hours 20 minutes
   2-C 12 hours
   2-D 9 hours 15 minutes

3. If a fire truck is 60 feet away from a hydrant, it is how many feet nearer to the hydrant than a truck that is 100 feet away?

   3-A 60 feet
   3-B 50 feet
   3-C 40 feet
   3-D 20 feet

4. A mechanic greased 168 cars in 28 days. What was his daily average of cars greased?

   4-A 5
   4-B 6
   4-C 7
   4-D 8

5. What is the fifth term in the series: 4½; 8¾; 13; 17¼; _____?

   5-A $20\frac{3}{4}$
   5-B 21
   5-C $21\frac{1}{2}$
   5-D $21\frac{3}{4}$

6. Three workers assemble 360 switches per hour, but 5% of the switches are defective. How many good (nondefective) switches will these 3 workers assemble in an 8-hour shift?

   6-A 2736
   6-B 2880
   6-C 2944
   6-D 3000

7. On a blueprint in which 2 inches represents 5 feet, the length of a room measures 7½ inches. The actual length of the room is

   7-A $12\frac{1}{2}$ feet
   7-B $17\frac{1}{2}$ feet
   7-C $15\frac{3}{4}$ feet
   7-D $18\frac{3}{4}$ feet

8. During a 25% off sale, an article sells for $375. What was the original price of this article?

   8-A $93.75
   8-B $468.75
   8-C $500
   8-D $575

9. The total length of fencing needed to enclose a rectangular area 46 feet by 34 feet is

   9-A 26 yards, 1 foot
   9-B $26\frac{2}{3}$ yards
   9-C 52 yards, 2 feet
   9-D $53\frac{1}{3}$ yards

2

53   **GO ON TO THE NEXT PAGE**

10. If 6 men can paint a fence in 2 days, how many men, working at the same uniform rate, can finish it in 1 day?

10-A 2
10-B 3
10-C 12
10-D 14

11. If 3 apples cost 48¢, how many dozen apples can be bought for $3.84?

11-A 1
11-B $1\frac{1}{2}$
11-C 2
11-D $5\frac{1}{3}$

2

12. How much time is there between 8:30 a.m. today and 3:15 a.m. tomorrow?

12-A $17\frac{3}{4}$ hrs.
12-B $18\frac{1}{3}$ hrs.
12-C $18\frac{1}{2}$ hrs.
12-D $18\frac{3}{4}$ hrs.

13. A change purse contained 3 half dollars, 8 quarters, 7 dimes, 6 nickels, and 9 pennies. Express in dollars and cents the total amount of money in the purse.

13-A $3.78
13-B $4.32
13-C $3.95
13-D $4.59

14. How much does a salesperson earn for selling $68 worth of writing paper if she is paid a commission of 40% on her sales?

14-A $20.40
14-B $25.60
14-C $22.80
14-D $27.20

15. If a certain job can be performed by 18 clerks in 26 days, the number of clerks need to perform the job in 12 days is

15-A 24
15-B 30
15-C 39
15-D 52

16. A delivery company employs 6 truck drivers. If each driver travels 250 miles a day, how many miles do all 6 drivers travel in a 5-day work week?

16-A 750
16-B 1500
16-C 7500
16-D 15,000

17. The minute hand fell off a watch but the watch continued to work accurately. What time was it when the hour hand was at the 17-minute mark?

17-A 3:02
17-B 3:17
17-C 3:24
17-D 4:17

18. A manufacturer has 3,375 yards of material on hand. If the average dress takes 3⅜ yards of material, how many dresses can he make?

18-A 844
18-B 1000
18-C 1125
18-D 1250

19. A car can travel 24 miles on a gallon of gasoline. How many gallons will be used on a 192-mile trip?

19-A 8
19-B 9
19-C 10
19-D 11

20. If an annual salary of $21,600 is increased by a bonus of $720 and by a service increment of $1,200, the total pay rate is

20-A $22,320
20-B $22,800
20-C $23,320
20-D $23,520

GO ON TO THE NEXT PAGE

21. A man takes out a $5,000 life insurance policy at a yearly rate of $29.62 per $1,000. What is the yearly premium?

   21-A $ 90.10
   21-B $100.10
   21-C $126.10
   21-D $148.10

22. The area of a room measuring 12 feet by 15 feet is

   22-A 9 square yards
   22-B 12 square yards
   22-C 15 square yards
   22-D 20 square yards

23. A woman purchased a blouse for $10.98. She returned the blouse the next day and selected a better one costing $12.50. She gave the clerk a five-dollar bill to pay for the difference in price. How much change should she receive?

   23-A $3.58
   23-B $3.48
   23-C $2.52
   23-D $1.52

24. The daily almanac report for one day during the summer stated that the sun rose at 6:14 a.m. and set at 6:06 p.m. Find the number of hours and minutes in the time between the rising and setting of the sun on that day.

   24-A 11 hours, 52 minutes
   24-B 11 hours, 2 minutes
   24-C 12 hours, 8 minutes
   24-D 12 hours, 48 minutes

25. An officer traveled 1,200 miles in 20 hours. How many miles per hour did she average?

   25-A 45
   25-B 60
   25-C 50
   25-D 65

26. A boy sold $88.50 worth of stationery. If he received a $33\frac{1}{3}$% commission, what was the amount of his commission?

   26-A $29.50
   26-B $40.00
   26-C $50.00
   26-D $62.50

27. What is the shortest board a man must buy in order to cut three sections from it each 4 feet 8 inches long?

   27-A 12 feet
   27-B 14 feet
   27-C 16 feet
   27-D 18 feet

28. An employee's net pay is equal to his total earnings less all deductions. If an employee's total earnings in a pay period are $497.05, what is his net pay if he has the following deductions: federal income tax, $90.32; FICA, $28.74; state tax, $18.79; city tax, $7.25; pension, $1.88?

   28-A $351.17
   28-B $351.07
   28-C $350.17
   28-D $350.07

2

29. The price of a radio is $31.29, which includes a 5% sales tax. What was the price of the radio before the tax was added?

   29-A $29.80
   29-B $29.85
   29-C $29.90
   29-D $29.95

30. At the rate of 40 words per minute, how long will it take a typist to type a 3,600-word article?

   30-A $1\frac{1}{2}$ hours

   30-B $1\frac{3}{4}$ hours

   30-C 2 hours

   30-D $2\frac{1}{4}$ hours

STOP! **DO NOT TURN THIS PAGE UNTIL TOLD TO DO SO. IF YOU FINISH BEFORE THE TIME IS UP, YOU MAY CHECK OVER YOUR WORK ON THIS PART ONLY. DO NOT GO ON TO THE NEXT PART UNTIL YOU ARE TOLD TO DO SO.**

3

WORD KNOWLEDGE

3

Directions

This test has 35 questions about the meanings of words. Each question has an underlined word. You are to decide which one of the four words in the choices most nearly means the same as the underlined word, then mark the space on your answer form which has the same number and letter as your choice.

Now look at the two sample questions below.

S1. <u>Mended</u> most nearly means

    S1-A repaired
    S1-B torn
    S1-C clean
    S1-D tied

A REPAIRED is the correct answer. *Mended* means *fixed* or *repaired*. *Torn* (B) might be the state of an object before it is mended. The repair might be made by *tying* (D), but not necessarily. *Clean* (C) is wrong.

S2. It was a <u>small</u> table.

    S1-A sturdy
    S2-B round
    S2-C cheap
    S2-D little

Little means the same as small so the D answer is the best one.

Your score on this test will be based on the number of questions you answer correctly. You should try to answer every question. Do not spend too much time on any one question.

When you begin, be sure to start with question number 1 in Part 3 of your test booklet and number 1 in Part 3 on your answer form.

DO NOT TURN THIS PAGE UNTIL TOLD TO DO SO.

3

WORD KNOWLEDGE

TIME: 11 Minutes—35 Questions

1. <u>Revenue</u> most nearly means

   1-A taxes
   1-B income
   1-C expenses
   1-D produce

2. <u>Convene</u> most nearly means

   2-A meet
   2-B debate
   2-C agree
   2-D drink

3. The machine has <u>manual</u> controls.

   3-A self-acting
   3-B simple
   3-C hand-operated
   3-D handmade

4. The packages were kept in a <u>secure</u> place.

   4-A distant
   4-B safe
   4-C convenient
   4-D secret

5. <u>Customary</u> most nearly means

   5-A curious
   5-B necessary
   5-C difficult
   5-D common

6. The clerk was criticized for his <u>slipshod</u> work.

   6-A slow
   6-B careful
   6-C careless
   6-D original

7. <u>Counterfeit</u> most nearly means.

   7-A mysterious
   7-B false
   7-C unreadable
   7-D priceless

8. <u>Expertly</u> most nearly means

   8-A awkwardly
   8-B quickly
   8-C skillfully
   8-D unexpectedly

9. <u>Marshy</u> most nearly means

   9-A swampy
   9-B sandy
   9-C wooded
   9-D rocky

10. <u>Relish</u> most nearly means

    10-A care
    10-B speed
    10-C amusement
    10-D enjoy

11. <u>Sufficient</u> most nearly means

    11-A durable
    11-B substitution
    11-C expendable
    11-D appropriate

12. She will return in a <u>fortnight</u>.

    12-A two weeks
    12-B one week
    12-C two months
    12-D one month

13. <u>Prevented</u> most nearly means

    13-A allowed
    13-B suggested
    13-C hindered
    13-D urged

14. Mail will be <u>forwarded</u> to our new address.

    14-A sent
    14-B returned
    14-C canceled
    14-D received

3

GO ON TO THE NEXT PAGE.

15. The room was <u>vacant</u> when we arrived.

15-A quiet
15-B dark
15-C available
15-D empty

16. <u>Juvenile</u> most nearly means

16-A delinquent
16-B lovesick
16-C youthful
16-D humorous

17. <u>Concisely</u> most nearly means

17-A accurately
17-B briefly
17-C fully
17-D officially

3

18. <u>Unite</u> most nearly means

18-A improve
18-B serve
18-C uphold
18-D combine

19. <u>Gratitude</u> most nearly means

19-A thankfulness
19-B excitement
19-C disappointment
19-D sympathy

20. <u>Familiar</u> most nearly means

20-A welcome
20-B dreaded
20-C rare
20-D well-known

21. He had an <u>acute</u> pain in his back.

21-A dull
21-B slight
21-C alarming
21-D sharp

22. <u>Stench</u> most nearly means

22-A puddle of slimy water
22-B pile of debris
22-C foul odor
22-D dead animal

23. <u>Sullen</u> most nearly means

23-A grayish yellow
23-B soaking wet
23-C very dirty
23-D angrily silent

24. <u>Rudiments</u> most nearly means

24-A basic procedures
24-B politics
24-C promotion opportunities
24-D minute details

25. <u>Alert</u> most nearly means

25-A watchful
25-B busy
25-C helpful
25-D honest

26. The computer did not <u>function</u> yesterday.

26-A finish
26-B stop
26-C operate
26-D overheat

27. <u>Hazard</u> most nearly means

27-A damage
27-B choice
27-C opportunity
27-D danger

28. <u>Self-sufficient</u> most nearly means

28-A independent
28-B conceited
28-C stubborn
28-D clever

29. In his hand the hiker carried a sturdy <u>staff</u>.

29-A pack
29-B stick
29-C loaf
29-D musical instrument

30. <u>Insignificant</u> most nearly means

30-A unimportant
30-B unpleasant
30-C secret
30-D thrilling

GO ON TO THE NEXT PAGE.

31. <u>Fatal</u> most nearly means

   31-A accidental
   31-B deadly
   31-C dangerous
   31-D beautiful

32. <u>Indigent</u> people are entitled to food stamps.

   32-A poor
   32-B lazy
   32-C angry
   32-D homeless

33. <u>Technique</u> most nearly means

   33-A computed
   33-B engineered
   33-C calculation
   33-D method

34. The judge ruled it to be <u>immaterial</u>.

   34-A unclear
   34-B unimportant
   34-C unpredictable
   34-D not debatable

35. We <u>misconstrued</u> what she had said.

   35-A followed directions
   35-B ingenious
   35-C acting to supervise
   35-D interpreted erroneously

3

DO NOT TURN THIS PAGE UNTIL TOLD TO DO SO.
STOP! IF YOU FINISH BEFORE THE TIME IS UP, YOU
MAY CHECK OVER YOUR WORK ON THIS PART ONLY.

4

PART 4

PARAGRAPH COMPREHENSION

4

Directions

This test contains 15 items measuring your ability to obtain information from written passages. You will find one or more paragraphs of reading material followed by incomplete statements or questions. You are to read the paragraph(s) and select one of the lettered choices which best completes the statement or answers the question.

Here are two sample questions.

S1. From a building designer's standpoint, three things that make a home livable are the needs of the client, the building site, and the amount of money the client has to spend.
According to the passage, to make a home livable

S1-A the prospective piece of land makes little difference
S1-B it can be built on any piece of land
S1-C the design must fit the owner's income and site
S1-D the design must fit the designer's income

The correct answer is that the designer must fit the owner's income and site, so C is the correct response.

S2. In certain areas water is so scarce that every attempt is made to conserve it. For instance, on one oasis in the Sahara Desert the amount of water necessary for each date palm tree has been carefully determined.
How much water is each tree given?

S2-A no water at all
S2-B exactly the amount required
S2-C water only if it is healthy
S2-D water on alternate days

The correct answer is exactly the amount required, so B is the correct response.

Your score on this test will be based on the number of questions you answer correctly. You should try to answer every question. Do not spend too much time on any one question.

When you begin be sure to start with question number 1 in Part 4 of your test booklet and number 1 in Part 4 on your answer form.

DO NOT TURN THIS PAGE UNTIL TOLD TO DO SO.

4

PART 4

PARAGRAPH COMPREHENSION

TIME: 13 Minutes—15 Questions

1. The prevention of accidents makes it necessary not only that safety devices be used to guard exposed machinery, but also that mechanics be instructed in safety rules that they must follow for their own protection.

The passage best supports the statement that industrial accidents

1-A are always avoidable
1-B may be due to ignorance
1-C usually result from inadequate machinery
1-D cannot be entirely overcome

2. Blood pressure, the force that the blood exerts against the walls of the vessels through which it flows, is commonly meant to be the pressure in the arteries. The pressure in the arteries varies with contraction (work period) and the relaxation (rest period) of the heart. When the heart contracts, the blood in the arteries is at its greatest or systolic pressure. When the heart relaxes, the blood in the arteries is at its lowest or diastolic pressure. The difference between these pressures is called the pulse pressure.

According to the passage, which one of the following statements is most accurate?

2-A The blood in the arteries is at its greatest pressure during contraction.
2-B Systolic pressure measures the blood in the arteries when the heart is relaxed.
2-C The difference between systolic and diastolic pressure determines the blood pressure.
2-D Pulse pressure is the same as blood pressure.

3. Complaints from the public are no longer regarded by government officials as mere nuisances. Instead, complaints are often welcomed because they frequently bring into the open conditions and faults in operation and service that should be corrected.

This passage means most nearly that

3-A government officials now realize that complaints from the public are necessary
3-B faulty operations and services are not brought into the open except by complaints from the public
3-C government officials now realize that complaints from the public are in reality a sign of a well-run agency
3-D complaints from the public can be useful in indicating needs for improvement in operation and service

4. The speed of a boat is measured in knots. One knot is equal to a speed of one nautical mile an hour. A nautical mile is equal to 6080 feet, while an ordinary mile is 5280 feet.

According to the passage, which of the following statements is true?

4-A A nautical mile is longer than an ordinary mile.
4-B A speed of 2 knots is the same as 2 miles per hour.
4-C A knot is the same as a mile.
4-D The distance a boat travels is measured in knots.

5. Scientists are taking a closer look at the recent boom in the use of wood for heating. Wood burning, it seems, releases high levels of pollutants. It is believed that burning wood produces a thousand times more CO, carbon monoxide, than natural gas does when it burns.

According to the passage, CO is

5-A natural gas
5-B wood
5-C carbon monoxide
5-D heat

65　　**GO ON TO THE NEXT PAGE.**

6. Both the high school and the college should take the responsibility for preparing the student to get a job. Since the ability to write a good application letter is one of the first steps toward this goal, every teacher should be willing to do what he can to help the student learn to write such letters.

The paragraph best supports the statement that

6-A inability to write a good letter often reduces one's job prospects
6-B the major responsibility of the school is to obtain jobs for its students
6-C success is largely a matter of the kind of work the student applies for first
6-D every teacher should teach a course in the writing of application letters

7. Any business not provided with capable substitutes to fill all important positions is a weak business. Therefore, a foreman should train each man not only to perform his own particular duties but also to do those of two or three positions.

The paragraph best supports the statement that

7-A dependence on substitutes is a sign of a weak organization
7-B training will improve the strongest organization
7-C the foreman should be the most expert at any particular job under him
7-D vacancies in vital positions should be provided for in advance

8. Iron is used in making our bridges and skyscrapers, subways and steamships, railroads and automobiles, and nearly all kinds of machinery—besides millions of small articles, from the farmer's scythe to the tailor's needle.

The paragraph best supports the statement that iron

8-A is the most abundant of the metals
8-B has many different uses
8-C is the strongest of all metals
8-D is the only material used in building skyscrapers and bridges

9. In almost every community, fortunately, there are certain men and women known to be public-spirited. Others, however, may be selfish and act only as their private interests seem to require.

The paragraph suggests that those citizens who disregard others are

9-A needed
9-B found only in small communities
9-C not known
9-D not public-spirited

10. In the relations of man to nature, the procuring of food and shelter is fundamental. With the migration of man to various climates, ever new adjustments to the food supply and to the climate became necessary.

According to the passage, the means by which man supplies his material needs are

10-A accidental
10-B inadequate
10-C limited
10-D varied

Questions 11 and 12 are based on the following passage.

Racketeers are primarily concerned with business affairs, legitimate or otherwise, and preferably those that are close to the margin of legitimacy. They get their best opportunities from business organizations that meet the needs of large sections of the public for goods and services that are defined as illegitimate by the same public, such as gambling, illicit drugs, etc. In contrast to the thief, the racketeer and the establishments he or she controls deliver goods and services for money received.

GO ON TO THE NEXT PAGE.

11. According to the above passage, racketeering, unlike theft, involves

   11-A payment for goods received
   11-B unlawful activities
   11-C organized gangs
   11-D objects of value

12. It can be deduced that suppression of racketeering is difficult because

   12-A many people want services which are not obtainable through legitimate sources
   12-B racketeers are generally engaged in fully legitimate enterprises
   12-C victims of racketeers are not guilty of violating the law
   12-D laws prohibiting gambling are unenforceable

Questions 13–15 are based on the passage shown below.

A large proportion of the people behind bars are not convicted criminals, but people who have been arrested and are being held until their trial in court. Experts have often pointed out that this detention system does not operate fairly. For instance, a person who can afford to pay bail usually will not get locked up. The person must show up in court when he is supposed to; otherwise, he will forfeit his bail. Sometimes, one who can show that he is a stable citizen with a job and a family will be released on "personal recognizance." The result is that the well-to-do, the employed, and the family men can often avoid the detention system. Those who do wind up in detention tend to be the poor, the unemployed, the single, and the young.

4

13. According to the passage above, people who are put behind bars

   13-A are almost always dangerous criminals
   13-B include many innocent people who have been arrested by mistake
   13-C are often people who have been arrested but have not yet come to trial
   13-D are all people who tend to be young and single

14. The passage says that the detention system works unfairly against people who are

   14-A rich
   14-B married
   14-C old
   14-D unemployed

15. When someone is released on "personal recognizance," this means that

   15-A the judge knows that he is innocent
   15-B he does not have to show up for a trial
   15-C he has a record of previous convictions
   15-D he does not have to pay bail

DO NOT TURN THIS PAGE UNTIL TOLD TO DO SO.
STOP! IF YOU FINISH BEFORE THE TIME IS UP, YOU
MAY CHECK OVER YOUR WORK ON THIS PART ONLY.

5

NUMERICAL OPERATIONS

5

Directions

This is a test to see how rapidly and accurately you can do 50 simple arithmetic computations. Each problem is followed by four answers, only one of which is correct. Decide which answer is correct, then blacken the space on your answer form which has the same number and letter as your choice.

Now look at the four example problems below.

S1. $3 \times 3 =$

S1-A 6
S1-B 0
S1-C 9
S1-D 1

The answer is 9, so the C answer is correct.

S2. $3 + 7 =$

S2-A 4
S2-B 6
S2-C 8
S2-D 10

The answer is 10, so the D answer is correct.

S3. $5 - 2 =$

S3-A 2
S3-B 3
S3-C 1
S3-D 4

The answer is 3, so the B answer is correct.

S4. $9 \div 3 =$

S4-A 3
S4-B 6
S4-C 9
S4-D 12

The answer is 3, so the A answer is correct.

This is a speed test, so work as fast as you can without making mistakes. Do each problem as it comes. If you finish before time is up, go back and check your work. When the signal is given, you will turn the page and begin with question 1 in Part 5 of your test booklet and answer space 1 in Part 5 of your answer form.

DO NOT TURN THIS PAGE UNTIL TOLD TO DO SO.

PART 5

NUMERICAL OPERATIONS

TIME: 3 Minutes—50 Questions

1. 60 ÷ 10 =

1-A 5
1-B 6
1-C 10
1-D 16

2. 5 − 2 =

2-A 3
2-B 6
2-C 7
2-D 9

3. 3 × 4 =

3-A 7
3-B 12
3-C 15
3-D 21

4. 4 ÷ 2 =

4-A 2
4-B 4
4-C 6
4-D 8

5. 7 × 3 =

5-A 4
5-B 10
5-C 12
5-D 21

6. 9 ÷ 1 =

6-A 10
6-B 9
6-C 8
6-D 7

7. 10 ÷ 5 =

7-A 5
7-B 15
7-C 2
7-D 25

8. 2 × 9 =

8-A 18
8-B 36
8-C 16
8-D 15

9. 8 + 3 =

9-A 13
9-B 12
9-C 11
9-D 15

10. 16 ÷ 2 =

10-A 8
10-B 12
10-C 9
10-D 6

11. 9 × 3 =

11-A 21
11-B 25
11-C 27
11-D 29

12. 3 + 4 =

12-A 1
12-B 7
12-C 9
12-D 11

13. 6 × 7 =

13-A 13
13-B 24
13-C 27
13-D 42

14. 7 + 6 =

14-A 11
14-B 13
14-C 14
14-D 21

15. 8 − 5 =

15-A 13
15-B 11
15-C 4
15-D 3

16. 10 ÷ 2 =

16-A 5
16-B 6
16-C 8
16-D 12

17. 17 − 4 =

17-A 13
17-B 18
17-C 21
17-C 23

18. 3 + 3 =

18-A 0
18-B 5
18-C 6
18-D 9

19. 2 − 1 =

19-A 2
19-B 3
19-C 0
19-D 1

20. 4 × 0 =

20-A 4
20-B 1
20-C 16
20-D 0

21. 9 − 1 =

21-A 10
21-B 11
21-C 9
21-D 8

22. 2 × 2 =

22-A 2
22-B 4
22-C 6
22-D 8

23. 6 ÷ 1 =

23-A 16
23-B 15
23-C 7
23-D 6

24. 6 ÷ 2 =

24-A 12
24-B 8
24-C 4
24-D 3

25. 4 × 6 =

25-A 21
25-B 24
25-C 26
25-D 28

26. 7 + 2 =

26-A 3
26-B 5
26-C 9
26-D 14

27. 8 − 8 =

27-A 0
27-B 1
27-C 8
27-D 16

28. 1 + 6 =

28-A 5
28-B 7
28-C 8
28-D 9

70   **GO ON TO THE NEXT PAGE.**

29. 4 × 5 =

    29-A 8
    29-B 10
    29-C 16
    29-D 20

30. 7 − 7 =

    30-A 14
    30-B 10
    30-C 1
    30-D 0

31. 40 ÷ 8 =

    31-A 4
    31-B 5
    31-C 6
    31-D 8

32. 7 × 6 =

    32-A 24
    32-B 36
    32-C 42
    32-D 48

33. 4 + 5 =

    33-A 9
    33-B 7
    33-C 11
    33-D 1

34. 6 + 8 =

    34-A 14
    34-B 15
    34-C 17
    34-D 19

35. 9 + 2 =

    35-A 10
    35-B 7
    35-C 11
    35-D 12

36. 1 × 5 =

    36-A 5
    36-B 1
    36-C 6
    36-D 10

37. 9 + 4 =

    37-A 11
    37-B 13
    37-C 15
    37-D 17

38. 3 × 8 =

    38-A 24
    38-B 32
    38-C 36
    38-D 42

39. 1 + 7 =

    39-A 6
    39-B 7
    39-C 8
    39-D 5

40. 10 × 2 =

    40-A 2
    40-B 5
    40-C 12
    40-D 20

41. 4 + 7 =

    41-A 3
    41-B 8
    41-C 11
    41-D 18

42. 8 ÷ 2 =

    42-A 4
    42-B 6
    42-C 8
    42-D 10

43. 2 × 7 =

    43-A 5
    43-B 9
    43-C 12
    43-D 14

44. 35 ÷ 7 =

    44-A 12
    44-B 7
    44-C 6
    44-D 5

45. 10 − 9 =

    45-A 11
    45-B 19
    45-C 1
    45-D 0

46. 10 − 4 =

    46-A 4
    46-B 6
    46-C 8
    46-D 14

47. 4 + 7 =

    47-A 3
    47-B 21
    47-C 12
    47-D 11

48. 9 × 5 =

    48-A 45
    48-B 47
    48-C 55
    48-D 36

49. 6 + 7 =

    49-A 11
    49-B 13
    49-C 15
    49-D 9

50. 9 ÷ 1 =

    50-A 8
    50-B 9
    50-C 10
    50-D 11

5

DO NOT TURN THIS PAGE UNTIL TOLD TO DO SO.
STOP! IF YOU FINISH BEFORE THE TIME IS UP, YOU
MAY CHECK OVER YOUR WORK ON THIS PART ONLY.

6

CODING SPEED

6

Directions

This is a test of 84 items to see how quickly and accurately you can find a number in a table. At the top of each section, there is a number table or "key." The key is a group of words with a code number for each word.

Each question in the test is a word taken from the key at the top. From among the possible answers listed for each question, find the one that is the correct code number for that word.

Look at the sample key and answer the five sample questions below. Note that each of the questions is one of the words in the key. To the right of each question are possible answers listed under the options A, B, C, D, and E.

Sample Questions

Key

green 2715	man 3451	salt 4586
hat 1413	room..... 2864	tree...... 5972

Sample Questions	Options				
	A	**B**	**C**	**D**	**E**
S-1. room	1413	2715	2864	3451	4586
S-2. green	2715	2864	3451	4586	5972
S-3. tree	2715	2864	3451	4596	5972
S-4. hat	1413	2715	2864	3451	4586
S-5. room	1413	2864	3451	4586	5972

By looking at the key you see that the code number for the first word, "room," is 2864. 2864 is listed under the letter C so C is the correct answer. The correct answers for the other four questions are A, E, A, and B.

This is a speed test, so work as fast as you can without making mistakes.

Notice that Part 6 begins at the top of the next answer form. When you begin, be sure to start with question number 1 in Part 6 of your test booklet and number 1 in Part 6 on your answer form.

DO NOT TURN THIS PAGE UNTIL TOLD TO DO SO.

CODING SPEED

TIME: 7 Minutes—84 Questions

Key

button...... 5266	dawn 9745	gold 8351	love........ 2456	pot 7007
chop....... 1817	flu 3838	iris......... 4658	mail........ 6234	puppy...... 6606

Questions		Options			
	A	**B**	**C**	**D**	**E**
1. button	2456	4658	5266	6234	8351
2. puppy	1817	2456	5266	6234	6606
3. gold	1817	3838	6234	8351	9745
4. mail	2456	4658	5266	6234	8351
5. flu	3838	5266	6234	6606	9745
6. iris	2456	4658	5266	6234	8351
7. pot	3838	5266	6606	7007	9745
8. chop	1817	3838	6234	6606	8351
9. love	2456	4658	5266	6234	9745
10. iris	1817	3838	4658	6234	7007
11. dawn	2456	3838	6234	6606	9745
12. mail	2456	4658	6234	8351	9745

Key

bank....... 3029	dinner...... 8002	farm 9564	husk 4488	mule....... 9984
candle 5605	eel......... 2270	hill......... 6883	luck........ 1654	tube 7240

Questions		Options			
	A	**B**	**C**	**D**	**E**
13. candle	2270	3029	4488	5605	7240
14. hill	1654	5605	6883	8002	9984
15. farm	3029	4488	6883	7240	9564
16. bank	2270	3029	5605	6883	8002
17. dinner	4488	7240	8002	9564	9984
18. luck	1654	3029	4488	6883	7240
19. husk	4488	6883	7240	8002	9564
20. mule	3029	4488	8002	9564	9984
21. eel	2270	3029	4488	6883	8002
22. dinner	3029	4488	6883	8002	9984
23. tube	5605	7240	8002	9564	9984
24. husk	1654	2270	3029	4488	6883

Key

costume.... 5019	guard 3776	knife 7916	officer...... 9391	ribbon...... 6591
dime 8117	jelly........ 4891	liquid....... 2011	pillow 1511	sword...... 1171

Questions			Options		
	A	**B**	**C**	**D**	**E**
25. knife	1171	2011	4891	5019	7916
26. guard	2011	3776	5019	8117	9391
27. costume	4891	5019	7916	8117	9391
28. liquid	1171	1511	2011	3776	4891
29. ribbon	3776	4891	5019	6591	7916
30. jelly	1511	2011	4891	5019	6591
31. officer	4891	5019	6591	7916	9391
32. sword	1171	2011	3776	4891	5019
33. dime	3776	4891	6591	7916	8117
34. costume	4891	5019	6591	8117	9391
35. pillow	1171	1511	2011	3776	4891
36. guard	3776	4891	6591	7916	8117

6

Key

art.......... 1066	down 5974	hood....... 7877	pants 2468	spoon...... 9060
clue........ 3682	flower...... 4003	ice.......... 8880	silence 6969	taxi 1001

Questions			Options		
	A	**B**	**C**	**D**	**E**
37. silence	3682	4003	6969	8880	9060
38. hood	1066	4003	5974	7877	9060
39. pants	1001	2468	3682	4003	6969
40. clue	3682	4003	6969	8880	9060
41. art	1001	1066	4003	7877	8880
42. down	2468	4003	5974	6969	7877
43. ice	1001	1066	4003	8880	9060
44. flower	4003	5974	6969	7877	8880
45. spoon	2468	3682	6969	8880	9060
46. down	1066	3682	4003	5974	6969
47. hood	1001	2468	6969	7877	9060
48. taxi	1001	1066	4003	8880	9060

GO ON TO THE NEXT PAGE.

Key

bed........ 4814	doll 9086	fence 2026	girl........ 8797	kick........ 7546
coat 3765	elbow 5511	gift......... 1683	index 6904	lump....... 2826

Questions	Options				
	A	**B**	**C**	**D**	**E**
49. index	2026	2826	3765	6904	9086
50. coat	1683	3765	4814	5511	7546
51. lump	2826	3765	6904	7546	8797
52. fence	1683	2026	4814	5511	6904
53. kick	1683	3765	6904	7546	8797
54. doll	2026	2826	6904	8797	9086
55. bed	4814	5511	7546	8797	9086
56. elbow	1683	4814	5511	6904	7546
57. gift	1683	2026	3765	4814	6904
58. girl	2826	3765	6904	7546	8797
59. coat	1683	2026	2826	3765	4814
60. kick	2026	2826	3765	4814	7546

6

Key

art......... 2679	crust....... 9911	gas........ 1499	music...... 6242	nature...... 7004
basket 4562	flag........ 4855	link 3964	nation...... 5897	razor....... 8282

Questions	Options				
	A	**B**	**C**	**D**	**E**
61. basket	1499	4562	4855	5897	6242
62. nation	1499	2679	3964	4855	5897
63. music	4562	6242	7004	8282	9911
64. nature	2679	3964	4855	6242	7004
65. gas	1499	3964	4562	4855	9911
66. link	1499	2679	3964	5897	6242
67. flag	4562	4855	5897	6242	8282
68. razor	2679	4562	6242	8282	9911
69. art	2679	3964	4855	5897	6242
70. crust	1499	4562	4855	7004	9911
71. nature	2679	5897	7004	8282	9911
72. flag	1499	2679	3964	4562	4855

GO ON TO THE NEXT PAGE.

Key

author......9451	donkey.....7611	liquid.......1152	rake.......3829	voice.......6284
branch.....4390	handle.....5497	native......5746	space......8392	wine.......2772

Questions			Options		
	A	**B**	**C**	**D**	**E**
73. branch	1152	2772	3829	4390	5746
74. wine	2772	4390	5497	6284	8392
75. voice	3829	5497	6284	8392	9451
76. rake	1152	2772	3829	7611	8392
77. native	4390	5746	6284	7611	9451
78. donkey	5746	6284	7611	8392	9451
79. liquid	1152	2772	3829	5497	6284
80. handle	3829	4390	5497	7611	8392
81. space	2772	3829	4390	8392	9451
82. author	1152	2772	3829	7611	9451
83. voice	2772	4390	5746	6284	7611
84. rake	3829	5746	7611	8392	9451

6

DO NOT TURN THIS PAGE UNTIL TOLD TO DO SO.
STOP! IF YOU FINISH BEFORE THE TIME IS UP, YOU
MAY CHECK OVER YOUR WORK ON THIS PART ONLY.

7

Directions

This test has 25 questions about automobiles, shop practices, and the use of tools. Pick the best answer for each question, then blacken the space on your answer form which has the same number and letter as your choice.

Here are four sample questions.

> **S1.** The most commonly used fuel for running automobile engines is
>
> S1-A kerosene
> S1-B benzine
> S1-C crude oil
> S1-D gasoline

Gasoline is the most commonly used fuel, so D is the correct answer.

> **S2.** A car uses too much oil when which parts are worn?
>
> S2-A pistons
> S2-B piston rings
> S2-C main bearings
> S2-D connecting rods

Worn piston rings causes the use of too much oil, so B is the correct answer.

> **S3.** The saw shown to the right is used mainly to cut
>
> S3-A plywood
> S3-B odd-shaped holes in wood
> S3-C along the grain of the wood
> S3-D across the grain of the wood

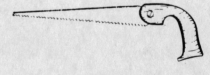

The compass saw is used to cut odd-shaped holes in wood, so B is the correct answer.

> **S4.** Thin sheet metal should be cut with
>
> S4-A ordinary scissors
> S4-B a hack saw
> S4-C tin shears
> S4-D a jig saw

Tin shears are used to cut thin sheet metal, so C is the correct answer.

Your score on this test will be based on the number of questions you answer correctly. You should try to answer every question. Do not spend too much time on any one question.

When you are told to begin, be sure to start with question number 1 in Part 7 of your test booklet and number 1 in Part 7 on your answer form.

DO NOT TURN THIS PAGE UNTIL TOLD TO DO SO.

7

PART 7

AUTO & SHOP INFORMATION

TIME: 11 Minutes—25 Questions

1. Which of the following devices prevents the generator/alternator from overcharging the battery in an automobile?

   1-A governor
   1-B solenoid switch
   1-C current regulator
   1-D voltage regulator

2. A torsion bar might be found in the

   2-A transmission
   2-B distributor
   2-C speedometer
   2-D suspension

3. A black gummy deposit in the end of the tail pipe of an automobile indicates that

   3-A the automobile "burns" oil
   3-B there is probably a leak in the exhaust manifold
   3-C the timing is late
   3-D there are leaks in the exhaust valves

4. A governor is used on an automobile primarily to limit its

   4-A rate of acceleration
   4-B maximum speed
   4-C fuel consumption
   4-D stopping distance

5. Automobile headlights are ordinarily connected in

   5-A parallel
   5-B series
   5-C diagonal
   5-D perpendicular

6. A fuel injection system on an automobile engine eliminates the necessity for

   6-A a manifold
   6-B a carburetor
   6-C spark plugs
   6-D a distributor

7. A mechanic sets the proper electrode gap on a spark plug most accurately if he uses a

   7-A dial gauge
   7-B round wire feeler gauge
   7-C square wire feeler gauge
   7-D conventional flat feeler gauge

8. When reference is made to the "compression ratio" of an automotive gasoline engine, this is best described as the

   8-A volume above the piston at top dead center
   8-B displacement volume as the piston moves down to bottom dead center
   8-C total volume of a cylinder divided by its clearance volume
   8-D displacement volume of a cylinder divided by its clearance volume

9. Reverse flushing of a clogged gasoline engine block and radiator cooling system is done properly by

   9-A not removing the thermostat from the engine block
   9-B connecting the flushing gun at the bottom of the engine block
   9-C using air and water
   9-D using low pressure steam

10. The automotive power train includes all of the following *except* the

   10-A clutch
   10-B differential
   10-C steering gear
   10-D transmission

11. An automobile handbrake is set tightly and the engine is idling at 30 mph road speed. If you shift into high gear, release the clutch, and the engine continues to run about the same, what would most likely need repair?

   11-A clutch
   11-B throttle
   11-C high gear
   11-D carburetor

GO ON TO THE NEXT PAGE.

7

12. The pistons of gasoline engines will some-times increase in size so that they "stick" in the cylinder. This is often caused by

   12-A low engine operating temperature
   12-B overheating of the engine
   12-C worn oil rings
   12-D worn compression rings

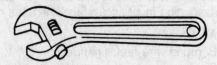

13. The tool shown above is a

   13-A crescent wrench
   13-B monkey wrench
   13-C pipe wrench
   13-D torque wrench

14. Concrete is usually made by mixing

   14-A only sand and water
   14-B only cement and water
   14-C lye, cement, and water
   14-D rock, sand, cement, and water

15. The set of a saw is the

   15-A angle at which the handle is set
   15-B amount of springiness of the blade
   15-C amount of sharpness of the teeth
   15-D distance the points stick out beyond the sides of the blade

16. A wood screw that can be tightened by a wrench is known as a

   16-A lag screw
   16-B carriage screw
   16-C Philips screw
   16-D monkey screw

17. The reason that a lubricant prevents rubbing surfaces from becoming hot is that the oil

   17-A is cold and cools off the rubbing metal surfaces
   17-B is sticky, preventing the surfaces from moving over each other too rapidly
   17-C forms a smooth layer between the two surfaces, preventing their coming into contact
   17-D makes the surfaces smooth so that they move easily over each other

18.

The tool shown above is used to

   18-A set nails
   18-B drill holes in concrete
   18-C cut a brick accurately
   18-D centerpunch for holes

19. What is used to fasten ceramic tiles to walls?

   19-A putty
   19-B caulking
   19-C plaster of paris
   19-D mastic

20. With which of these screw heads do you use an "Allen" wrench?

   20-A

   20-B

   20-C

   20-D

21. When sanding wood by hand, best results are usually obtained in finishing the surface when the sanding block is worked

   21-A across the grain
   21-B in a diagonal to the grain
   21-C in a circular motion
   21-D with the grain

GO ON TO THE NEXT PAGE.

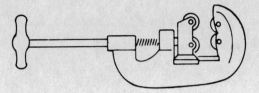

22. The tool above is a

    22-A marking gauge
    22-B knurling tool
    22-C thread cutter
    22-D pipe cutter

23. A high speed grinder operator will check the abrasive wheel before starting the machine because

    23-A it must be wetted properly before use
    23-B if cracked or chipped, it could injure someone
    23-C a dry wheel will produce excessive sparks
    23-D previous work may have clogged the wheel

7

24. When marking wood, an allowance of $\frac{1}{16}$ inch to $\frac{1}{8}$ inch should be made to allow for

    24-A drying of the wood
    24-B absorption of water by wood
    24-C the width of the saw
    24-D knots in the wood

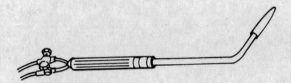

25. The tool shown above is used for

    25-A pressure lubricating
    25-B welding steel plate
    25-C drilling small holes in tight places
    25-D holding small parts for heat treating

DO NOT TURN THIS PAGE UNTIL TOLD TO DO SO.
STOP! IF YOU FINISH BEFORE THE TIME IS UP, YOU
MAY CHECK OVER YOUR WORK ON THIS PART ONLY.

8

PART 8

MATHEMATICS KNOWLEDGE

8

Directions

This is a test of your ability to solve 25 general mathematical problems. You are to select the correct response from the choices given. Then mark the space on your answer form which has the same number and letter as your choice. Use the scratch paper that has been given to you to do any figuring that you wish.

Now look at the two sample problems below.

S1. If $x + 6 = 7$, then x is equal to

S1-A 0
S1-B 1
S1-C -1
S1-D $\dfrac{7}{6}$

The correct answer is 1, so B is the correct response.

S2. What is the area of this square?

S2-A 1 square foot
S2-B 5 square feet
S2-C 10 square feet
S2-D 25 square feet

The correct answer is 25 square feet, so D is the correct response.

Your score on this test will be based on the number of questions you answer correctly. You should try to answer every question. Do not spend too much time on any one question.

When you are told to begin, be sure to start with question number 1 in Part 8 of your test booklet and number 1 in Part 8 on your answer form.

DO NOT TURN THIS PAGE UNTIL TOLD TO DO SO.

8

MATHEMATICS KNOWLEDGE

TIME: 24 Minutes—25 Questions

1. If you subtract $6a - 4b + 3c$ from a polynomial, you get $4a + 9b - 5c$. What is the polynomial?

   1-A $10a - 5b + 2c$
   1-B $10a + 5b - 2c$
   1-C $2a + 13b - 8c$
   1-D $2a + 5b + 8c$

2. If 50% of $x = 66$, then $x =$

   2-A 33
   2-B 99
   2-C 122
   2-D none of these

3. If $3x = -5$, then x equals

   3-A 3/5
   3-B $-5/3$
   3-C $-3/5$
   3-D -2

4. If $A^2 + B^2 = A^2 + X^2$, then B equals

   4-A X
   4-B $X^2 - 2A^2$
   4-C A
   4-D $A^2 + X^2$

5. If $6 + x + y = 20$, and $x + y = k$, then $20 - k =$

   5-A 6
   5-B 0
   5-C 14
   5-D 20

6. What is the maximum number of books each $\frac{1}{4}$ inch thick that can be placed standing on a shelf 4 feet long?

   6-A 16
   6-B 192
   6-C 48
   6-D 96

7. When $2x + 3$ is multiplied by 10, the result is 55. What is the value of x?

   7-A $1\frac{1}{4}$

   7-B $4\frac{1}{2}$

   7-C 2
   7-D 3

8.

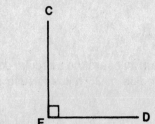

   In the diagram above, CE $\perp$ ED. If CE = 7 and ED = 6, what is the shortest distance from C to D?

   8-A 6
   8-B $4\sqrt{12}$
   8-C 7
   8-D $\sqrt{85}$

9. 5% of 5% of 100 is

   9-A 25
   9-B .25
   9-C 2.5
   9-D 10

10. A man has T dollars to invest; after he invests $1,000 how much money does he have remaining?

   10-A $T + 1,000$
   10-B $T - 1,000$
   10-C $1,000 - T$
   10-D $1,000T$

GO ON TO THE NEXT PAGE.

11. A rectangular field is 900 yards by 240 yards. What is the largest number of rectangular lots 120 yards by 60 yards that it can be divided into?

11-A 20
11-B 60
11-C 30
11-D 40

12. $\sqrt{\dfrac{9}{64} + \dfrac{16}{64}} =$

12-A $\dfrac{5}{8}$

12-B $\dfrac{7}{64}$

12-C $\dfrac{5}{64}$

12-D $\dfrac{25}{64}$

8

13. The distance in miles around a circular course that has a radius of 35 miles is (use pi = $^{22}/_7$)

13-A 156
13-B 220
13-C 440
13-D 880

14. The expression "3 factorial" equals

14-A $\dfrac{1}{9}$

14-B $\dfrac{1}{6}$

14-C 6
14-D 9

15. If a = 2b and 4b = 6c, then a =

15-A 3c
15-B 4c
15-C 9c
15-D 12c

16. A square is changed into a rectangle by increasing its length 10% and decreasing its width 10%. Its area

16-A remains the same
16-B decreases by 10%
16-C increases by 1%
16-D decreases by 1%

17. If all P are S and no S are Q, it necessarily follows that

17-A all Q are S
17-B all Q are P
17-C no P are Q
17-D no S are P

18. An angle that is greater than 0° and less than 90° is called

18-A a right angle
18-B a straight angle
18-C an acute angle
18-D an obtuse angle

19. If you multiply x + 3 by 2x + 5, how many x's will there be in the product?

19-A 3
19-B 6
19-C 9
19-D 11

20. A desk was listed at $90.00 and was bought for $75.00. What was the rate of discount?

20-A 15%
20-B $16\dfrac{2}{3}$%
20-C 18%
20-D 20%

21. The sum of − 24 and −3 is

21-A 8
21-B 21
21-C −8
21-D −27

22. 2.2 × .00001 =

22-A .0022
22-B .00022
22-C .000022
22-D .0000022

GO ON TO THE NEXT PAGE.

23. The figure on the right is a

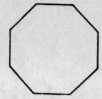

    23-A hexagon
    23-B octagon
    23-C pentagon
    23-D decahedron

24. $8! = 8 \times 7 \times 6 \times 5 \times 4 \times 3 \times 2 \times 1$
    $4! =$

    24-A 4^4
    24-B 32
    24-C 4^2
    24-D 24

25. If T tons of snow fall in 1 second, how many tons fall in M minutes?

    25-A 60 MT
    25-B MT + 60
    25-C MT
    25-D $\dfrac{60\,M}{T}$

8

DO NOT TURN THIS PAGE UNTIL TOLD TO DO SO.
STOP! IF YOU FINISH BEFORE THE TIME IS UP, YOU
MAY CHECK OVER YOUR WORK ON THIS PART ONLY.

9

MECHANICAL COMPREHENSION

9

Directions

This test has 25 questions about mechanical principles. Most of the questions use drawings to illustrate specific principles. Decide which answer is correct and mark the space on your separate answer form which has the same number and letter as your choice.

Here are two sample questions.

S1. Which bridge is the strongest?

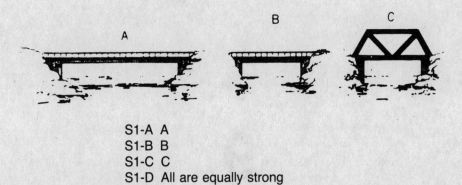

S1-A A
S1-B B
S1-C C
S1-D All are equally strong

Answer C is correct.

S2. If all of these objects are the same temperature, which will feel coldest?

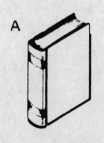 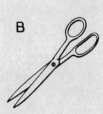  

S2-A A
S2-B B
S2-C C
S2-D D

Answer B is correct.

Your score on this test will be based on the number of questions you answer correctly. You should try to answer every question. Do not spend too much time on any one question.

When you are told to begin, be sure to start with question number 1 in Part 9 of your test booklet and number 1 in Part 9 on your answer form.

DO NOT TURN THIS PAGE UNTIL TOLD TO DO SO.

9

MECHANICAL COMPREHENSION

TIME: 19 Minutes—25 Questions

1. In the figure shown below, the weight held by the board and placed on the two identical scales will cause *each* scale to read

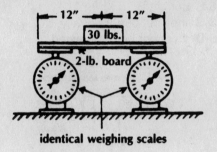

identical weighing scales

    1-A 8 pounds
    1-B 15 pounds
    1-C 16 pounds
    1-D 32 pounds

2. In the figure shown below, the pulley system consists of a fixed block and a movable block. The theoretical mechanical advantage is

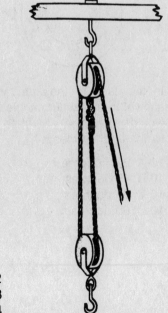

    2-A 1
    2-B 2
    2-C 3
    2-D 4

3. A single movable block is being used in the figure shown below. The person is lifting a 200-pound cask with approximately how great a pull (disregard friction, weight of pulley, and weight of line)?

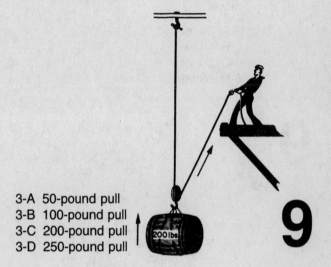

    3-A 50-pound pull
    3-B 100-pound pull
    3-C 200-pound pull
    3-D 250-pound pull

4.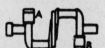

What is the function of A and B in the crankshaft shown in the drawing?

    4-A They strengthen the crankshaft by increasing its weight.
    4-B They make it easier to remove the crankshaft for repairs.
    4-C They are necessary to maintain the proper balance of the crankshaft.
    4-D They hold grease for continuous lubrication of the crankshaft.

5. Sweating usually occurs on pipes that

    5-A contain cold water
    5-B contain hot water
    5-C are chrome plated
    5-D require insulation

GO ON TO THE NEXT PAGE.

9

6.

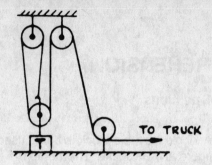

The tank T is to be raised as shown by attaching the pull rope to a truck. If the tank is to be raised ten feet, the truck will have to move

6-A 20 feet
6-B 40 feet
6-C 30 feet
6-D 50 feet

7.

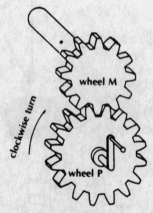

Study the gear wheels in the figure above, then determine which of the following statements is true.

7-A If you turn wheel M clockwise by means of the handle, wheel P will also turn clockwise.
7-B It will take the same time for a tooth of wheel P to make a full turn as it will for a tooth of wheel M.
7-C It will take less time for a tooth of wheel P to make a full turn than it will take a tooth of wheel M.
7-D It will take more time for a tooth of wheel P to make a full turn than it will for a tooth of wheel M.

8.

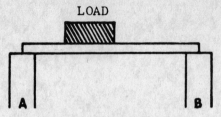

In the figure above which upright supports the greater part of the load?

8-A upright A
8-B upright B
8-C they support it equally
8-D it cannot be determined

9.

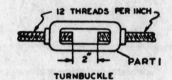

For the turnbuckle shown, the number of complete turns of Part 1 required to make the ends of the threaded rods meet is

9-A 6
9-B 18
9-C 12
9-D 24

10.

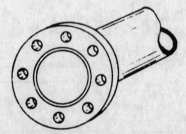

In the case of the standard flanged pipe shown, the maximum angle through which it would be necessary to rotate the pipe in order to line up the holes is

10-A 22.5 degrees
10-B 45 degrees
10-C 30 degrees
10-D 60 degrees

GO ON TO THE NEXT PAGE.

11.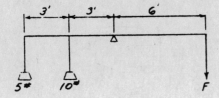

The force F needed to balance the lever is, in pounds, most nearly

11-A 7.5
11-B 12.5
11-C 10
11-D 15

12.

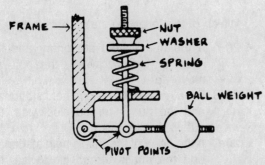

If the ball and spring mechanism are balanced in the position shown, the ball will move upward if

12-A the nut is loosened
12-B the ball is moved away from the frame
12-C the nut is loosened and the ball moved away from the frame
12-D the nut is tightened

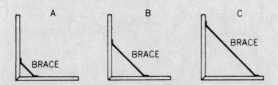

13. Which of the angles is braced most securely?

13-A A
13-B B
13-C C
13-D all equally braced

14. In order to keep down the inside temperature of an oil tank that is exposed to the sun, the outside of the tank should be painted

14-A black
14-B brown
14-C green
14-D white

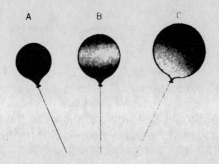

15. The amount of gas in the balloons is equal. The atmospheric pressure outside the balloons is highest on which balloon?

15-A A
15-B B
15-C C
15-D the pressure is equal on all balloons

9

16.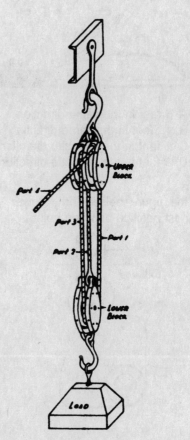

Determine which part of the rope is fastened directly to the block.

16-A Part 1
16-B Part 3
16-C Part 2
16-D Part 4

GO ON TO THE NEXT PAGE.

17.

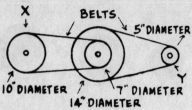

A double belt drive is shown in the figure above. If the pulley marked X is revolving at 100 rpm, the speed of pulley Y is

17-A 800 rpm
17-B 200 rpm
17-C 400 rpm
17-D 25 rpm

18. In the figure below, a 150-pound person jumps off a 500-pound raft to a point in the water 10 feet away. Theoretically, the raft will move

9

18-A 5 feet in the same direction
18-B 10 feet in the same direction
18-C 1 foot in the opposite direction
18-D 3 feet in the opposite direction

19. In the figure below, the follower is at its highest position between points

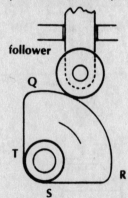

19-A Q and R
19-B R and S
19-C S and T
19-D T and Q

20.

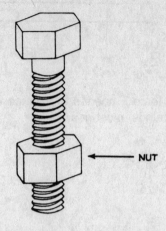

Which of the following statements is true?

20-A If the nut is held stationary and the head turned clockwise, the bolt will move up.
20-B If the head of the bolt is held stationary and the nut is turned clockwise, the nut will move down.
20-C If the head of the bolt is held stationary and the nut is turned clockwise, the nut will move up.
20-D If the nut is held stationary and the bolt is turned counterclockwise, the nut will move up.

21.

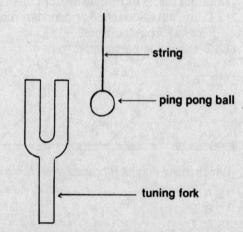

When the tuning fork is struck, the Ping-Pong ball will

21-A remain stationary
21-B bouce up and down
21-C hit the tuning fork
21-D swing away from the tuning fork

GO ON TO THE NEXT PAGE.

22.

If the block on which the lever is resting is moved closer to the brick, the brick will be

22-A easier to lift and will be lifted higher
22-B harder to lift and will be lifted higher
22-C easier to lift but will not be lifted as high
22-D harder to lift and will not be lifted as high

24. In the figure shown below, one complete revolution of the windlass drum will move the weight up

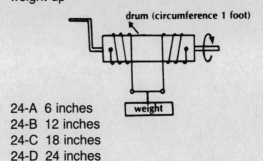

24-A 6 inches
24-B 12 inches
24-C 18 inches
24-D 24 inches

23.

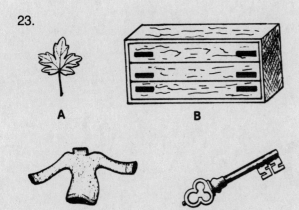
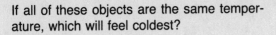

If all of these objects are the same temperature, which will feel coldest?

23-A A
23-B B
23-C C
23-D D

25.

If both cyclists pedal at the same rate on the same surface, the cyclist in front will

25-A travel at the same speed as the cyclist behind
25-B move faster than the cyclist behind
25-C move more slowly than the other cyclist
25-D have greater difficulty steering

9

DO NOT TURN THIS PAGE UNTIL TOLD TO DO SO.
STOP! IF YOU FINISH BEFORE THE TIME IS UP, YOU
MAY CHECK OVER YOUR WORK ON THIS PART ONLY.

10

PART 10

ELECTRONICS INFORMATION

10

Directions

This is a test of your knowledge of electrical, radio, and electronics information. There are 20 questions. You are to select the correct response from the choices given. Then mark the space on your answer form which has the same number and letter as your choice.

Now look at the two sample questions below.

1S. What does the abbreviation AC stand for?

1S-A additional charge
1S-B alternating coil
1S-C alternating current
1S-D ampere current

The correct answer is alternating current, so C is the correct response.

2S. Which of the following has the least resistance?

2S-A wood
2S-B silver
2S-C rubber
2S-D iron

The correct answer is silver, so B is the correct response.

Your score on this test will be based on the number of questions you answer correctly. You should try to answer every question. Do not spend too much time on any one question.

When you are told to begin, be sure to start with question number 1 in Part 10 of your test booklet and number 1 in Part 10 on your answer form.

DO NOT TURN THIS PAGE UNTIL TOLD TO DO SO.

10

ELECTRONICS INFORMATION

TIME: 9 Minutes—20 Questions

1. In lights controlled by three-way switches, the switches should be treated and put in as

   1-A flush switches
   1-B single pole switches
   1-C three double pole switches
   1-D three pole switches

2. When working on live 600-volt equipment where rubber gloves might be damaged, an electrician should

   2-A work without gloves
   2-B carry a spare pair of rubber gloves
   2-C reinforce the fingers of the rubber gloves with rubber tape
   2-D wear leather gloves over the rubber gloves

3. A "mil" measures

   3-A an eighth of an inch
   3-B a millionth of an inch
   3-C a thousandth of an inch
   3-D a ten-thousandth of an inch

4. Excessive resistance in the primary circuit will lessen the output of the ignition coil and cause the

   4-A battery to short out and the generator to run down
   4-B battery to short out and the plugs to wear out prematurely
   4-C generator to run down and the timing mechanism to slow down
   4-D engine to perform poorly and be hard to start

5. During a "short circuit," the

   5-A current flow becomes very large
   5-B resistance becomes very large
   5-C voltage applied becomes very small
   5-D power input becomes very small

6. The main reason for making wire stranded is

   6-A to make it easier to insulate
   6-B so that the insulation will not come off
   6-C to decrease its weight
   6-D to make it more flexible

7. Electrical contacts are opened or closed when the electrical current energizes the coils of a device called a

   7-A reactor
   7-B transtat
   7-C relay
   7-D thermostat

10

8. To determine directly whether finished wire installations possess resistance between conductors between conductors and ground, use

   8-A clamps
   8-B set screws
   8-C shields
   8-D a megger

9.

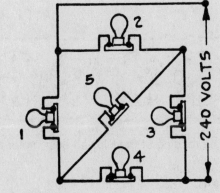

The five lamps shown are each rated at 120 volts, 60 watts. If all are good lamps, lamp 5 will be

   9-A much brighter than normal
   9-B about its normal brightness
   9-C much dimmer than normal
   9-D completely dark

GO ON TO THE NEXT PAGE.

10. If a condenser is connected across the make-and-break contact of an ordinary electric bell, the effect will be to

10-A speed up the action of the clapper
10-B reduce the amount of arcing at the contact
10-C slow down the action of the clapper
10-D reduce the load on the bell transformer or battery

11. A material *not* used in the make-up of lighting wires or cables is

11-A rubber
11-B paper
11-C lead
11-D cotton

12.

10

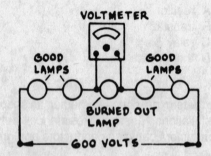

The reading of the voltmeter should be

12-A 600
12-B 300
12-C 120
12-D 0

13.

The reading of the kilowatt-hour meter is

13-A 7972
13-B 1786
13-C 2786
13-D 6872

14. Commutators are found on

14-A mercury rectifiers
14-B DC motors
14-C circuit breakers
14-D alternators

15. Neutral wire can be quickly recognized by the

15-A greenish color
15-B bluish color
15-C natural or whitish color
15-D black color

16. Which of the following devices converts heat energy directly into electrical energy?

16-A a piezoelectric crystal
16-B a photoelectric cell
16-C a steam driven generator
16-D a thermocouple

17. One use of a coaxial cable is to

17-A ground a signal
17-B pass a signal from the set to the antenna of a mobile unit
17-C carry the signal from a ballast tube
17-D carry grid signals in high altitude areas

18. Which of the following has the *least* resistance?

18-A silver
18-B aluminum
18-C copper
18-D steel

GO ON TO THE NEXT PAGE.

19.

The sketch shows a head-on view of a three-pronged plug used with portable electrical power tools. Considering the danger of shock when using such tools, it is evident that the function of the U-shaped prong is to

19-A insure that the other two prongs enter the outlet with the proper polarity

19-B provide a half-voltage connection when doing light work

19-C prevent accidental pulling of the plug from the outlet

19-D connect the metallic shell of the tool motor to ground

20. A compound motor usually has

20-A only a shunt field
20-B both a shunt and a series field
20-C only a series field
20-D no brushes

END OF EXAMINATION

10

IF YOU FINISH BEFORE TIME IS UP, YOU MAY CHECK YOUR WORK ON THIS PART ONLY. DO NOT GO BACK TO ANY PREVIOUS PART.

ANSWER KEY—FIRST ASVAB SPECIMEN TEST

Use these key answers to determine how many questions you answered correctly on each part and to list those items which you answered incorrectly or which you are not sure how to answer.

Be certain to review carefully and understand the rationale for arriving at the correct answer for all questions you answered incorrectly, as well as those you answered correctly but are unsure of. This is absolutely essential in order to acquire the knowledge and expertise necessary to obtain the maximum scores possible on the actual ASVAB subtests.

Transfer the scores you obtained on each part of the First ASVAB Specimen Test to the Self-Appraisal Chart appearing on page 275. This will enable you to see the progress made as you continue to prepare for the actual test.

PART 1—GENERAL SCIENCE

1. C	5. A	8. B	11. B	14. C	17. D	20. B	23. C
2. B	6. D	9. D	12. A	15. D	18. C	21. D	24. B
3. B	7. D	10. C	13. D	16. B	19. D	22. D	25. C
4. D							

Items
Answered
Incorrectly: ——; ——; ——; ——; ——; ——; ——; ——.

Items
Unsure
Of: ——; ——; ——; ——; ——; ——; ——; ——.

Total
Number
Answered
Correctly: _____

PART 2—ARITHMETIC REASONING

1. A	5. C	9. D	13. D	17. C	21. D	25. B	28. D
2. B	6. A	10. C	14. D	18. B	22. D	26. A	29. A
3. C	7. D	11. C	15. C	19. A	23. B	27. B	30. A
4. B	8. C	12. D	16. C	20. D	24. A		

104

Items
Answered
Incorrectly: ___; ___; ___; ___; ___; ___; ___; ___.

Items
Unsure
Of: ___; ___; ___; ___; ___; ___; ___; ___.

Total
Number
Answered
Correctly: _____

PART 3—WORD KNOWLEDGE

1. B	6. C	11. D	16. C	20. D	24. A	28. A	32. A
2. A	7. B	12. A	17. B	21. D	25. A	29. B	33. D
3. C	8. C	13. C	18. D	22. C	26. C	30. A	34. B
4. B	9. A	14. A	19. A	23. D	27. D	31. B	35. D
5. D	10. D	15. D					

Items
Answered
Incorrectly: ___; ___; ___; ___; ___; ___; ___; ___.

Items
Unsure
Of: ___; ___; ___; ___; ___; ___; ___; ___.

Total
Number
Answered
Correctly: _____

PART 4—PARAGRAPH COMPREHENSION

1. B	3. D	5. C	7. D	9. D	11. A	13. C	15. D
2. A	4. A	6. A	8. B	10. D	12. A	14. D	

Items
Answered
Incorrectly: ___; ___; ___; ___; ___; ___; ___; ___.

Items
Unsure
Of: ___; ___; ___; ___; ___; ___; ___; ___.

Total
Number
Answered
Correctly: _____

PART 5—NUMERICAL OPERATIONS

1. B	8. A	15. D	21. D	27. A	33. A	39. C	45. C
2. A	9. C	16. A	22. B	28. B	34. A	40. D	46. B
3. B	10. A	17. A	23. D	29. D	35. C	41. C	47. D
4. A	11. C	18. C	24. D	30. D	36. A	42. A	48. A
5. D	12. B	19. D	25. B	31. B	37. B	43. D	49. B
6. B	13. D	20. D	26. C	32. C	38. A	44. D	50. B
7. C	14. B						

Items
Answered
Incorrectly: ___; ___; ___; ___; ___; ___; ___; ___.

Items
Unsure
Of: ___; ___; ___; ___; ___; ___; ___; ___.

Total
Number
Answered
Correctly: _____

PART 6—CODING SPEED

1. C	12. C	23. B	34. B	45. E	55. A	65. A	75. C
2. E	13. D	24. D	35. B	46. D	56. C	66. C	76. C
3. D	14. C	25. E	36. A	47. D	57. A	67. B	77. B
4. D	15. E	26. B	37. C	48. A	58. E	68. D	78. C
5. A	16. B	27. B	38. D	49. D	59. D	69. A	79. A
6. B	17. C	28. C	39. B	50. B	60. E	70. E	80. C
7. D	18. A	29. D	40. A	51. A	61. B	71. C	81. D
8. A	19. A	30. C	41. B	52. B	62. E	72. E	82. E
9. A	20. E	31. E	42. C	53. D	63. B	73. D	83. D
10. C	21. A	32. A	43. D	54. E	64. E	74. A	84. A
11. E	22. D	33. E	44. A				

Items
Answered
Incorrectly: ___; ___; ___; ___; ___; ___; ___; ___.

Items
Unsure
Of: ___; ___; ___; ___; ___; ___; ___; ___.

Total
Number
Answered
Correctly: _____

PART 7—AUTO & SHOP INFORMATION

1. D	5. A	8. C	11. A	14. D	17. C	20. C	23. B
2. D	6. B	9. C	12. B	15. D	18. B	21. D	24. C
3. A	7. B	10. C	13. A	16. A	19. D	22. D	25. B
4. B							

Items
Answered
Incorrectly: ___; ___; ___; ___; ___; ___; ___; ___.

Items
Unsure
Of: ___; ___; ___; ___; ___; ___; ___; ___.

Total
Number
Answered
Correctly: _____

PART 8—MATHEMATICS KNOWLEDGE

1. B	5. A	8. D	11. C	14. C	17. C	20. B	23. B
2. D	6. B	9. B	12. A	15. A	18. C	21. D	24. D
3. B	7. A	10. B	13. B	16. D	19. D	22. C	25. A
4. A							

Items
Answered
Incorrectly: —— ; —— ; —— ; —— ; —— ; —— ; —— ; ——.

Items
Unsure
Of: —— ; —— ; —— ; —— ; —— ; —— ; —— ; ——.

Total
Number
Answered
Correctly: _____

PART 9—MECHANICAL COMPREHENSION

1. C	5. A	8. A	11. C	14. D	17. C	20. B	23. D
2. B	6. C	9. C	12. D	15. A	18. D	21. D	24. B
3. B	7. D	10. A	13. C	16. C	19. A	22. C	25. B
4. C							

Items
Answered
Incorrectly: —— ; —— ; —— ; —— ; —— ; —— ; —— ; ——.

Items
Unsure
Of: —— ; —— ; —— ; —— ; —— ; —— ; —— ; ——.

Total
Number
Answered
Correctly: _____

PART 10—ELECTRONICS INFORMATION

1. B	4. D	7. C	10. B	13. D	15. C	17. B	19. D
2. D	5. A	8. D	11. B	14. B	16. D	18. A	20. B
3. C	6. D	9. D	12. A				

Items
Answered
Incorrectly: —— ; —— ; —— ; —— ; —— ; —— ; —— ; ——.

Items
Unsure
Of: —— ; —— ; —— ; —— ; —— ; —— ; —— ; ——.

Total
Number
Answered
Correctly: _____

EXPLANATIONS—FIRST ASVAB SPECIMEN TEST

PART 1—GENERAL SCIENCE

1-C The vacuum cleaner is a device for cleaning floors, carpets, etc., by suction.

2-B The greater the number of vibrations per second produced by the sounding object, the higher will be the pitch produced. Playing a 33-1/3 rpm phonograph record at a faster speed (45 rpm) will produce a higher-pitched sound.

3-B Meat provides much essential protein in the form the body needs. Protein is the principal nutrient in lean meat.

4-D The prefix *hypo* means *below* or *abnormally deficient*. Hypothermia is a condition in which the body's temperature falls well below the normal 98.6° F. If it is very hot and you have nothing to drink, you may become dehydrated and might develop *hyper*thermia, *over*heating. Another name for rabies is hydrophobia.

5-A Lightning is most likely to strike the highest object in an area. if you are standing in an open field or at the top of a small hill, you are likely to be the highest object and a good target. If you stand under a tree, lightning might hit the tree and cause it to fall on you. A car is grounded. If you are inside a car that is hit by lightning you will only be frightened. The lightning will be transmitted into the ground by the car.

6-D The speed of light is about a million times that of sound.

7-D By the process of photosynthesis, green plants remove carbon dioxide from the atmosphere and replace it with oxygen.

8-B Ringworm is a skin disease caused by a fungus.

9-D Light enters the eye through the pupil (the opening in the center of the iris), travels through the transparent crystalline lens, then travels through the vitreous humor (eyeball), and finally focuses on the retina.

10-C Nitrogen constitutes about four-fifths of the atmosphere by volume.

11-B Light travels at the rate of 186,300 miles a second. The sun is 92,900,000 miles from the earth, so its light arrives here in just over 8 minutes.

12-A Cirrus clouds occur at 20,000 to 40,000 feet and are made up of ice crystals. Nimbus clouds are gray rain clouds; cumulus clouds are fluffy white clouds; stratus clouds are long, low clouds, generally at altitudes of 2,000 to 7,000 feet.

13-D An atom is the smallest part of an element that retains all the properties of the element.

14-C The action of narcotics is to deaden pain.

15-D Fungi do not contain chlorophyll so they cannot produce their own food through photosynthesis. Since fungi must rely for their food upon decaying organic matter, the forest is a hospitable home.

16-B The relative humidity is a very important factor in determining the comfort of the room's occupants. Relative humidity expresses the moisture (vapor) content of air as a fraction or percentage.

17-D Goiter is a disease of the thyroid gland, the body's storehouse for iodine. It may be caused by insufficient iodine in the diet.

18-C Steam at 212°F contains much more heat than does the same amount of water at 212°F.

19-D The weight of the salt water displaced by a human body is greater than the weight of fresh water displaced by that same body. Since the water displaced is heavier, the body is proportionally lighter and is more buoyant.

20-B Boiling lava erupts from a volcano. The force which causes the eruption is pressure inside the earth.

21-D Vitamin D can be found in fish liver oils and egg yolks. It can also be manufactured within skin that is exposed to sunlight.

22-D Clover serves to return nitrates to the soil through the action of nitrogen-fixing bacteria in nodules on its roots.

23-C The vascular system is the system of vessels for the circulation of blood. The respiratory system is concerned with respiration (breathing) and the endocrine system with enzymes.

24-B Aluminum is not magnetic. Cobalt and nickel are somewhat magnetic, while iron is highly magnetic.

25-C Milk and milk products such as cheese and butter are high in saturated fat and cholesterol.

PART 2—ARITHMETIC REASONING

1-A 8% of 75 = 6 shares; 75 shares + 6 shares = 81 shares

2-B 28 miles ÷ 3 mph = 9.33 hrs. = $9\frac{1}{3}$ hrs. = 9 hrs. 20 min.

3-C 100 ft. − 60 ft. = 40 ft.

4-B $\frac{168}{28}$ = 6 per day

5-C The interval between each member of the series is $4\frac{1}{4}$.
$$17\frac{1}{4} + 4\frac{1}{4} = 21\frac{1}{2}$$

6-A 360 × 8 = 2880 switches/8 hours
2880 × .05 = 144 defective switches
2880 − 144 = 2736 good switches

7-D 2 in. = 5 ft.; therefore, 1 in. = $2\frac{1}{2}$ ft.;
$$7\frac{1}{2} \times 2\frac{1}{2} = 18\frac{3}{4} \text{ ft.}$$

8-C $375 is 75% of the original price.

The original price = $375 ÷ 75%

= $375 ÷ .75

= $500

9-D Perimeter = 2l + 2w

= 2(46 ft) + 2(34 ft)

= 92 ft + 68 ft

= 160 ft

$160 ÷ 3 = 53\frac{1}{3}$ yd

10-C Common sense will tell you that twice as many men will paint the fence in half the time.

11-C 3 apples cost 48¢ so one apple costs 48 ÷ 3 = 16¢. $3.84 ÷ 16 = 24 apples; 24 = 2 dozen.

12-D

From 8:30 a.m.   12:00 = 11:60

until noon today: −8:30 =   8:30

                       3 hrs. 30 min.

From noon until midnight: + 12 hrs.

From midnight until 3:15 a.m.:   3 hrs. 15 min.

          Total time: 18 hrs. 45 min.

$= 18\frac{3}{4}$ hours

13-D $.50 × 3 = $1.50

.25 × 8 = $2.00

+.10 × 7 = $ .70

.05 × 6 = $ .30

.01 × 9 = $ .09

            $4.59

14-D $68 × 40% = $27.20

15-C 18 clerks can do the job in 26 days. Therefore, 1 clerk takes 18 × 26 = 468 days to do the job. To get the job done in 12 days will take 468 ÷ 12 = 39 clerks.

16-C 250 miles a day × 6 drivers = 1500 miles a day

1500 miles a day × 5 days = 7500 miles a week

17-C The 17-minute mark is ⅖ of the way between 3 and 4 o'clock. ⅖ of 60 = 24; 24 minutes past 3 o'clock = 3:24

18-B $3375 ÷ 3\frac{3}{8} = 3375 ÷ \frac{27}{8} = 3375 × \frac{8}{27}$

= 125 × 8 = 1000 dresses

19-A 192 ÷ 24 = 8 gal.

20-D $21,600 + $720 + $1,200 = $23,520

21-D $29.62 × 5 = $148.10

22-D 12 ft. × 15 ft. = 4 yd. × 5 yd. = 20 yd.²

23-B $12.50 − $10.98 = $1.52 cost to upgrade the blouse

$5.00 − $1.52 = $3.48 change

24-A If you look at the entire problem, you will see that the time between sunrise and sunset was just 8 minutes short of 12 hours (14 − 6 = 8).

    11 hrs. 60 min.

−   8 min.

    11 hrs. 52 min.

25-B Rate = Distance ÷ Time

1,200 miles ÷ 20 hours = 60 mph

26-A $33\frac{1}{3}\% = \frac{1}{3}$; $88.50 × $\frac{1}{3}$ = $29.50

27-B 4 ft. 8 in. × 3 = 12 ft. 24 in. = 14 ft.

28-D Total earnings in pay period = $497.05

Deduct:

federal income tax	$90.32
FICA	28.74
state tax	18.79
city tax	7.25
pension	1.88
	$146.98

      497.05

    −146.98

      $350.07

29-A Let x = price of radio before tax was added.

$$x + .05x = \$31.29$$
$$1.05x = 31.29$$
$$x = \frac{31.29}{1.05} = \$29.80$$

30-A $\frac{3600}{40}$ = 90 minutes = $1\frac{1}{2}$ hours

PART 3—WORD KNOWLEDGE

1-B *Revenue* means *income*. Taxes produce revenue but they are not in themselves revenue.

2-A To *convene* is to *assemble* or to *meet*. When people convene they often debate, agree, and/or drink.

3-C *Manual*, as opposed to automatic or mechanical, means *hand-operated*.

4-B *Secure* means *safe* as in *not exposed to danger*.

5-D That which is *customary* is *habitual* or established by *common* usage.

6-C *Slipshod* means *exceedingly slovenly* or *careless*.

7-B That which is *counterfeit* is an *imitation made with intent to defraud,* hence *false*.

8-C That which is done *expertly* is done *skillfully*. It might also be done quickly, but not necessarily so.

9-A *Marshy* means *boggy* or *swampy*.

10-D *Relish* means to like or enjoy.

11-D *Sufficient* means adequate, enough, or appropriate.

12-A The word *fortnight* means fourteen days or two weeks.

13-C To *prevent* is to *keep from happening* or to *hinder*.

14-A To *forward* is to *transmit* or to *send on*.

15-D *Vacant* means *unfilled* or *empty*.

16-C *Juvenile* means *youthful, young*, or *immature*.

17-B *Concisely* means *briefly*. The word that means "accurately" is "precisely."

18-D To *unite* is to *put together,* to *combine*, or to *join*.

19-A *Gratitude* is the *state of being grateful* or *thankfulness*.

20-D *Familiar* means *well-known*. (Think of the word "family.")

21-D An acute pain may well be alarming, but what makes it *acute* is its *sharpness*.

22-C *Stench* means an offensive smell or foul odor.

23-D *Sullen* means morose or angrily silent.

24-A *Rudiments* means basic principles or procedures.

25-A To be *alert* is to be *wide-awake* and *watchful*.

26-C To *function* is to *operate* or to *work*.

27-D A *hazard* is a *risk, peril,* or *danger.*

28-A One who is *self-sufficient* is able to accomplish his or her own aims without external aid and so is *independent.*

29-B The *staff* carried by a hiker is a *stick.* In music, a staff is the horizontal lines and spaces on which music is written.

30-A *Insignificant* means *meaningless* or *unimportant.* The prefix *in* means *not,* so the word literally means *not significant.*

31-B *Fatal* means *causing death* or *deadly.*

32-A *Indigent* means *needy* or *poor.* Indigent people might be lazy or homeless, but their indigence is their poverty. Indigent people might also become angry or *indignant.*

33-D The *technique* is *the method* by which something is done.

34-B The word *immaterial* means unimportant.

35-D The word *misconstrued* means misinterpreted or interpreted erroneously.

PART 4—PARAGRAPH COMPREHENSION

1-B The passage states that mechanics must be instructed in safety rules that they must follow for their own protection. This implies that industrial accidents may be due to ignorance of safety rules.

2-A The third sentence in the passage states that when the heart contracts, the blood in the arteries is at its greatest pressure.

3-D Complaints frequently bring into the open conditions and faults in operation and service that should be corrected.

4-A The last sentence states that a nautical mile is equal to 6080 feet while an ordinary mile is 5280 feet. Accordingly, a nautical mile is longer than an ordinary mile.

5-C The last sentence in the passage states that burning wood produces more CO, carbon monoxide, than natural gas does when it burns. CO is the chemical formula for carbon monoxide.

6-A Step one in the job application process is often the application letter. If the letter is not effective, the applicant will not move on to the

next step, and job prospects will be greatly lessened.

7-D The point of the passage is that a business should be prepared to fill unexpected vacancies with pretrained staff members.

8-B The passage lists many different uses for iron.

9-D The connective, "Others, however," with which the second sentence begins, implies the converse of the first sentence. Some citizens are public spirited; others, however, are not.

10-D The first three options are not supported by the passage. The correct answer is supported by the second sentence which states, "With the migration of man to various climates, ever new adjustments to the food supply and to the climate became necessary."

11-A See the last sentence in the reading passage.

12-A From the second sentence in the reading passage, it may be deduced that it is difficult to suppress racketeering because so many people want services which are not obtainable through legitimate sources.

13-C The first sentence states that a large proportion of the people behind bars are not criminals but people who are being held until their trial in court.

14-D The last sentence states that those who do wind up in detention tend to be the poor, the unemployed, the single, and the young.

15-D The passage states that one who can show that he is a stable citizen with a job and a family will be released on "personal recognizance" and can often avoid the detention system without paying bail.

PART 5—NUMERICAL OPERATIONS

1-B $60 \div 10 = 6$

2-A $5 - 2 = 3$

3-B $3 \times 4 = 12$

4-A $4 \div 2 = 2$

5-D $7 \times 3 = 21$

6-B $9 \div 1 = 9$

7-C $10 \div 5 = 2$

8-A $2 \times 9 = 18$

9-C $8 + 3 = 11$

10-A $16 \div 2 = 8$

11-C $9 \times 3 = 27$

12-B $3 + 4 = 7$

13-D $6 \times 7 = 42$

14-B $7 + 6 = 13$

15-D $8 - 5 = 3$

16-A $10 \div 2 = 5$

17-A $17 - 4 = 13$

18-C $3 + 3 = 6$

19-D $2 - 1 = 1$

20-D $4 \times 0 = 0$

21-D $9 - 1 = 8$

22-B $2 \times 2 = 4$

23-D $6 \div 1 = 6$

24-D $6 \div 2 = 3$

25-B $4 \times 6 = 24$

26-C $7 + 2 = 9$

27-A $8 - 8 = 0$

28-B $1 + 6 = 7$

29-D $4 \times 5 = 20$

30-D $7 - 7 = 0$

31-B $40 \div 8 = 5$

32-C $7 \times 6 = 42$

33-A $4 + 5 = 9$

34-A $6 + 8 = 14$

35-C $9 + 2 = 11$

36-A $1 \times 5 = 5$

37-B $9 + 4 = 13$

38-A $3 \times 8 = 24$

39-C $1 + 7 = 8$

40-D $10 \times 2 = 20$

41-C $4 + 7 = 11$

42-A $8 \div 2 = 4$

43-D $2 \times 7 = 14$

44-D $35 \div 7 = 5$

45-C $10 - 9 = 1$

46-B $10 - 4 = 6$ **48-A** $9 \times 5 = 45$ **50-B** $9 \div 1 = 9$

47-D $4 + 7 = 11$ **49-B** $6 + 7 = 13$

PART 6—CODING SPEED

There is no way to explain the answers to the Coding Speed questions. A few mistakes are inevitable. If you made many mistakes, look to see if they fall into any pattern. Slow down a bit on the next specimen test.

PART 7—AUTO & SHOP INFORMATION

1-D The voltage regulator prevents overcharging the battery by reducing current to the rotating electromagnet as the engine speeds up.

2-D Torsion bars are used in the suspension to absorb shock by twisting. Coil springs are actually coiled tension bars.

3-A When an automobile "burns" oil, it means that the engine oil consumption is excessive. This condition is manifested by the formation of a black gummy deposit in the end of the tail pipe.

4-B The governor is a device which is used to limit the maximum speed of an auto. It is used as a safety device.

5-A Headlights are connected in parallel. In a parallel circuit, if one headlight goes out, the other will still light.

6-B A fuel injection system eliminates the need for a carburetor by actually forcing the gasoline-air mixture into each one of the cylinders instead of having the gasoline combine with the air in the carburetor and then go through the intake manifold.

7-B The spark jumps across the arc at only one point on the electrode. A wire gauge gives the best spark plug gap at one point.

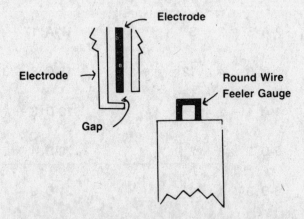

8-C The clearance volume is the space, at compression, between the top of the piston and the cylinder roof. The total volume is the total space in the cylinder when the piston is at the bottom of the intake stroke. To calculate the compression ratio, divide the total volume by the clearance volume. Many modern engines run at a compression ratio of 8 to 1.

9-C Choice C is the best answer. When the engine block and the radiator are clogged, a mechanic wants to remove any foreign material which prevents the antifreeze-water mixture from cooling the engine. Flushing with water and using compressed air remove the blockages. The other methods might not do the job adequately.

10-C The power train consists of the items used to conduct power from the pistons to the wheels.

11-A If the clutch slips, the full power of the engine is not transmitted. The clutch needs to be repaired or replaced.

12-B Pistons expand as the engine warms up. Pistons are so designed to fit the cylinders, regardless of whether the pistons are cold or at working temperature. However, when the engine is overheated, the pistons may increase in size to such an extent so that they "stick" in the cylinder.

13-A The tool is an adjustable open-end wrench. One jaw is fixed; the other moves along a slide with a thumbscrew adjustment. The tool shown is also called a crescent wrench.

14-D Concrete is made by mixing cement, sand, and broken rock with sufficient water to make the cement set and bind the entire mass.

15-D The set of a saw refers to how much the teeth are pushed out in opposite directions from the sides of the blade.

16-A The diagram below shows how a lag screw can fit into the head of a wrench.

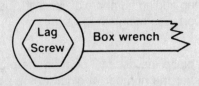

17-C When two pieces of metal rub together, the friction causes a great deal of heat. Oil reduces the friction between the two pieces of metal.

18-B The tool shown is a "star drill." It is hit with a hammer to make a hole in concrete.

19-D Mastic, a glue, is applied to a wall with a serrated applicator. Then the tiles are pressed into the mastic.

20-C An "Allen" wrench is hexagonal shaped and will fit into screw C.

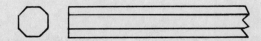

21-D The smoothest finish can be obtained by sanding the wood with the grain.

22-D The tool shown is a pipe cutter. Pipe cutters are used to cut pipe made of steel, brass, copper, wrought iron, and lead.

23-B The operator should check the abrasive wheel before starting the machine for safety reasons. A cracked or chipped wheel may injure someone.

24-C The allowance is made for the width of the saw.

25-B The tool is a welding torch used in making metal to metal joints. Welding is generally done with material made of steel.

PART 8—MATHEMATICS KNOWLEDGE

1-B Add: $6a - 4b + 3c$
$$\underline{4a + 9b - 5c}$$
$$10a + 5b - 2c$$

2-D $\frac{1}{2}$ of x = 66

$x = 66 \times 2$

$x = 132$

3-B $3x = -5$

$x = \dfrac{-5}{3} = -\dfrac{5}{3}$

4-A Subtract A^2 from both sides of the equation: $B^2 = X^2$, therefore $B = X$.

5-A $6 + x + y = 20$
$\quad\quad x + y = 14 = k$; now substitute
$\quad\quad 20 - 14 = 6$

6-B 4 feet = 48 inches
$48 \div \dfrac{1}{4} = 48 \times 4 = 192$ books

7-A $(2x + 3)(10) = 55$
$\quad\quad\quad 2x + 3 = 5.5$
$\quad\quad\quad\quad\quad 2x = 2.5$
$\quad\quad\quad\quad\quad\ x = 1.25 = 1\dfrac{1}{4}$

8-D CD is a hypotenuse, so use the Pythagorean Theorem:
$CD = \sqrt{CE^2 + ED^2}$
$CD = \sqrt{7^2 + 6^2} = \sqrt{49 + 36} = \sqrt{85}$

9-B $100 \times 5\% = 5$; $5 \times 5\% = .25$

10-B If the man uses $1,000 of his T dollars, he has remaining T − $1,000.

11-C The field is 900 yds. × 240 yds. = 216,000 sq. yds.
Each lot is 120 yds. × 60 yds. = 7,200 sq. yds.
216,000 ÷ 7,200 = 30 lots

12-A $\sqrt{\dfrac{9}{64} + \dfrac{16}{64}} = \sqrt{\dfrac{25}{64}} = \dfrac{5}{8}$

13-B If radius r = 35 miles, diameter = 70 miles.
Circumference $= \dfrac{22}{\overset{}{\underset{1}{7}}} \times \overset{10}{\cancel{70}} = 220$ miles

14-C $3! = 3 \times 2 \times 1 = 6$

15-A $a = 2b$; $2a = 4b = 6c$; $a = \dfrac{6c}{2} = 3c$

16-D Assign arbitrary values to solve this problem:
A square 10 ft. × 10 ft. = 100 sq. ft.
A rectangle 9 ft. × 11 ft. = 99 sq. ft.
$100 - 99 = 1$; $\dfrac{1}{100} = 1\%$

17-C Diagram this problem:

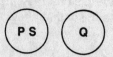

18-C An acute angle is an angle that is greater than 0° and less than 90°.

19-D
$$\begin{array}{r} x + 3 \\ \times\ 2x + 5 \\ \hline 2x^2 + \quad 6x \\ 5x + 15 \\ \hline 2x^2 + 11x + 15 \end{array}$$

20-B The amount of the discount was $90 − $75 = $15. The rate of discount or percent of change was $\dfrac{15}{90} = .1666 = 16\dfrac{2}{3}\%$

21-D When adding numbers of like sign, just add the numbers and maintain the sign.

22-C To place the decimal point in the product, add together the number of digits to the right of the decimal points in all of the multipliers. In this case, the answer requires 6 decimal places.

23-B An octagon has eight sides. A hexagon has six sides; a pentagon has five sides; a decahedron has ten sides.

24-D 4! (read "four prime") = $4 \times 3 \times 2 \times 1$ = 24

25-A To find how many tons fall in a given number of minutes, multiply the number of tons that fall in one minute by the number of minutes. There are 60 seconds in 1 minute, and T tons fall in 1 second. In M minutes, the amount of snow that falls is 60 MT.

PART 9—MECHANICAL COMPREHENSION

1-C 30 lbs. + 2 lbs. = 32 lbs., the total weight equally supported by two scales. $\frac{32}{2}$ = 16 lbs., the reading on each scale.

2-B The number of parts of the rope going to and from the movable block indicates the mechanical advantage. In this case, it is 2.

3-B The block is not fixed and the fall is doubled as it supports the 200-lb. cask. Each half of the fall carries one-half of the total load, or 100 lbs. The person is lifting a 200-lb. cask with a 100-lb. pull.

4-C The function of A and B in the crankshaft is to counterbalance the weight for smooth piston motion.

5-A The air surrounding a pipe contains water vapor at room temperature. This cold water cools the air in the immediate vicinity, reducing its ability to hold water vapor (warmer air will hold more water than cooler air). The water condenses on the cool pipe as sweat.

6-C Three ropes are supporting tank T. The mechanical advantage (the number of supporting wires holding the load) is 3. The distance must be 3 times the height raised, while the amount of force exerted by the truck will be $\frac{1}{3}$ of the weight of T.

7-D Wheel P has 16 teeth; wheel M has 12 teeth. When wheel M makes a full turn, wheel P will still have 4 more teeth to turn. So wheel P is slower, and will take more time to turn.

8-A Since the load is closer to upright A, it supports more of the load. If the load were directly over A, all of the weight would be supported by A; then upright B could be removed completely.

9-C The trick with this question is that both of the rods will be pulled in at the same time when the turnbuckle is turned. If it is turned 12 times (12 threads per inch), both rods will be pulled in 1 inch.

10-A There are 8 holes in the circular cross-section of the flanged pipe. All circles have 360°. Thus, each hole is separated by 360°/8 or 22.5°/hole.

11-C The sum of the moments must be zero. Summing around the fulcrum we have:
(6 ft. × 5 lbs.) + (3 ft. × 10 lbs.) = 6 ft. × F
Combining terms, we get:
60 (ft.–lbs) = 6 ft. × F dividing both sides by 6:
10 lbs = F

12-D The ball will move up if the arm holding it is pulled up. This will happen when the nut is tightened.

13-C As brace C has the greatest area support, it is the most secure.

14-D Of the colors listed, white will reflect the most solar heat thereby keeping down the inside temperature of the oil tank.

15-A The greater the pressure outside the balloon, the less expansion within the balloon.

16-C Begin with part 4, the line upon which the force is directed; part 1 is the next strand; then part 3; and finally, attached to the lower block, is part 2.

17-C *Step 1:* Pulley X revolves at 100 RPM (given). *Step 2:* Middle pulley (inner) rotates at 100 × 10/7. (Remember that a larger pulley causes a smaller one to travel faster by the ratio of their diameters.) *Step 3:* Pulley Y travels at (100 × 10/7) × (14/5) = 400.

18-D The raft will move in the opposite direction. Let x = theoretical distance moved.
10 × 150 = x × 500; 500x = 1500;
$x = \frac{1500}{500}$ = 3 feet.

18-D The raft will move in the opposite direction. Let x = theoretical distance moved.
10 × 150 = x × 500; 500x = 1500;
$x = \dfrac{1500}{500} = 3$ feet.

19-A Study the diagram on page 98 and note that the follower is at its highest position between points Q and R.

20-B Clockwise is left to right, so if the nut moves, it follows the threads of the bolt downward.

21-D When a tuning fork vibrates, it moves currents of air. This vibrating air would cause the ping-pong ball to be pushed away.

22-C If the block is moved toward the brick, the moment for a given force exerted will increase (being further from the force) making it easier to lift; the height will be made smaller, hardly raising the brick when moved to the limit (directly underneath it).

23-D The metal key has the highest conductivity. Metals are the best conductors of heat. The other choices can be used as insulators.

24-B One complete revolution will raise the weight 1 foot or 12 inches.

25-B The formula for circumference of a wheel is C = 2πr. The wheel radius of the bike in front is larger. One revolution of the larger wheel will cover a greater linear distance along the road in a given period of time.

PART 10—ELECTRONICS INFORMATION

1-B A three-way switch is a single-pole double-throw switch or two single-pole switches.

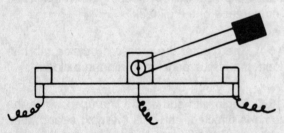

2-D Leather gloves offer the best protection over the rubber gloves. The leather can withstand severe conditions before it will tear. The rubber acts as insulation.

3-C A "mil" is short for milli or 1/1,000 of an inch.

4-D Resistance in the primary will reduce the current flow and reduce the voltage and current available at the spark plug. A "hot" spark with as high a voltage and current as possible is necessary for easy starting and smooth performance.

5-A The resistance of a short circuit usually consists of little more than the resistance of the circuit's copper wires since the load has been "shorted" or bypassed. This very low resistance results in very high current flow.

6-D Wires larger than No. 10 AWG are usually stranded because a solid wire of that diameter is too stiff to make good connections or to "fish" readily through raceways.

7-C A relay works on the principle of an energized coil or an electromagnet. Another device that works by an electromagnet is a solenoid.

8-D A megger (megohmmeter) is a portable device which produces a voltage. It is used to check for high voltage breakdown of insulation. In this case, it uses a resistance measurement to determine continuity.

9-D This is the Wheatstone bridge circuit with balanced loads in each of its arms. As there is no voltage across lamp No.5., it will not be lit.

10-B A condenser or capacitor is an electrical device that will store and discharge an electrical charge. When the bell is off, the condenser will store electricity. When the circuit is on, the condenser will discharge. This will eliminate arcing.

11-B Paper is not used in the make-up of a lighting wire because a small electrical charge could set it on fire.

12-A No electricity flows through a burned out bulb. However, the voltmeter acts as a bypass around the burned out bulb and is therefore connected in series. It measures all of the voltage in the circuit. The voltage is 600 volts.

13-D When reading an electric meter, you read the lower number just before the pointer. This meter would show 6872 kilowatt hours.

14-B In a DC motor, the commutators are the metal contact points that the brushes come into contact with.

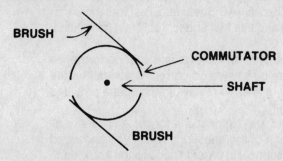

15-C The neutral wire is whitish in color; the hot lead is black; and the ground wire is green.

16-D Thermocouples usually consist of connections between wires of two dissimilar metals.

They are frequently calibrated so that the amount of voltage produced can be directly related to the temperature. They are thus capable of measuring temperatures.

17-B Coaxial cable consists of an inner conducting wire covered with insulation and run inside a concentric cylindrical outer conductor. TV antenna lead-in wires of the 75-ohm variety are examples of coaxial cables. Coaxial cables are used principally to minimize signal loss between antennas and either receiving or transmitting sets.

18-A All of the materials listed are conductors. Silver is the best although it is not often used because of its high cost. The moving contacts in motor starters, however, are often made of silver, and it is widely used where low resistance contacts are required.

19-D The third prong in the plug is the grounding wire.

20-B A compound motor has two sets of field coils. One is connected in series with the armature. The other is the shunt. It is connected in parallel across the armature.

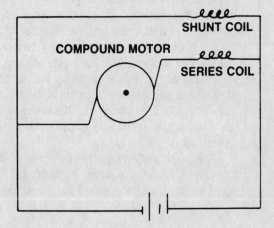

TEST YOURSELF AGAIN AND NOTE ANY IMPROVEMENT

SECOND ASVAB SPECIMEN TEST

This section contains specimen answer sheets for use in answering the questions on each subtest, an actual specimen ASVAB test, answer keys for determining your scores on these subtests, and the rationale or explanation for each answer.

Remove (cut out) the specimen answer sheets on the following pages and use them to record your answers to the test questions. The ASVAB Specimen Test has the same format and content as the actual ASVAB test. Take this test under "real" test conditions. Time each subtest carefully.

Use the answer keys to obtain your subtest scores and to evaluate your performance on each subtest. Record the number of items you answered correctly, as well as the number of each item you answered incorrectly or wish to review, in the space provided below the answer keys for each subtest.

Be certain to review carefully and understand the explanations for the answers to all questions you answered incorrectly and for each of the questions which you answered correctly but are unsure of. This is absolutely essential in order to acquire the knowledge and expertise necessary to obtain the maximum scores possible on the actual ASVAB subtests.

Transfer your scores for each part of the second ASVAB Specimen Test to the Self-Appraisal Chart appearing on page 275. This will enable you to see the progress made as you continue to prepare for the actual test.

**Specimen Answer Sheet for
Answering Parts 1–5**

**ANSWER SHEET
ARMED SERVICES VOCATIONAL
APTITUDE BATTERY**

17 CODE

[A][A][A] [B][B][B] [C][C][C] [D][D][D] [E][E][E] [F][F][F] [G][G][G] [H][H][H] [I][I][I] [J][J][J] [K][K][K] [L][L][L] [M][M][M] [N][N][N] [O][O][O] [P][P][P] [Q][Q][Q] [R][R][R] [S][S][S] [T][T][T] [U][U][U] [V][V][V] [W][W][W] [X][X][X] [Y][Y][Y] [Z][Z][Z] [0][0][0] [1][1][1] [2][2][2] [3][3][3] [4][4][4] [5][5][5] [6][6][6] [7][7][7] [8][8][8] [9][9][9]

16 SOCIAL SECURITY NUMBER

[0][0][0][0][0][0][0][0][0] [1][1][1][1][1][1][1][1][1] [2][2][2][2][2][2][2][2][2] [3][3][3][3][3][3][3][3][3] [4][4][4][4][4][4][4][4][4] [5][5][5][5][5][5][5][5][5] [6][6][6][6][6][6][6][6][6] [7][7][7][7][7][7][7][7][7] [8][8][8][8][8][8][8][8][8] [9][9][9][9][9][9][9][9][9]

MI / FIRST / LAST

PART 1—GS

PRACTICE
S1 A B ■ D
S2 A B C D
S3 A B C D

1–25 A B C D (each)

PART 2—AR 1–30 A B C D (each)

PART 3—WK 1–35 A B C D (each)

PART 4—PC 1–15 A B C D (each)

PART 5—NO 1–50 A B C D (each)

**Specimen Answer Sheet for
Answering Parts 6–10**

**ANSWER SHEET
ARMED SERVICES VOCATIONAL
APTITUDE BATTERY**

MI
FIRST
LAST

PART 6—CS

1 A B C D E	15 A B C D E	29 A B C D E	43 A B C D E	57 A B C D E	71 A B C D E
2 A B C D E	16 A B C D E	30 A B C D E	44 A B C D E	58 A B C D E	72 A B C D E
3 A B C D E	17 A B C D E	31 A B C D E	45 A B C D E	59 A B C D E	73 A B C D E
4 A B C D E	18 A B C D E	32 A B C D E	46 A B C D E	60 A B C D E	74 A B C D E
5 A B C D E	19 A B C D E	33 A B C D E	47 A B C D E	61 A B C D E	75 A B C D E
6 A B C D E	20 A B C D E	34 A B C D E	48 A B C D E	62 A B C D E	76 A B C D E
7 A B C D E	21 A B C D E	35 A B C D E	49 A B C D E	63 A B C D E	77 A B C D E
8 A B C D E	22 A B C D E	36 A B C D E	50 A B C D E	64 A B C D E	78 A B C D E
9 A B C D E	23 A B C D E	37 A B C D E	51 A B C D E	65 A B C D E	79 A B C D E
10 A B C D E	24 A B C D E	38 A B C D E	52 A B C D E	66 A B C D E	80 A B C D E
11 A B C D E	25 A B C D E	39 A B C D E	53 A B C D E	67 A B C D E	81 A B C D E
12 A B C D E	26 A B C D E	40 A B C D E	54 A B C D E	68 A B C D E	82 A B C D E
13 A B C D E	27 A B C D E	41 A B C D E	55 A B C D E	69 A B C D E	83 A B C D E
14 A B C D E	28 A B C D E	42 A B C D E	56 A B C D E	70 A B C D E	84 A B C D E

PART 7—AS

1 A B C D	5 A B C D	9 A B C D	13 A B C D	17 A B C D	21 A B C D	25 A B C D
2 A B C D	6 A B C D	10 A B C D	14 A B C D	18 A B C D	22 A B C D	
3 A B C D	7 A B C D	11 A B C D	15 A B C D	19 A B C D	23 A B C D	
4 A B C D	8 A B C D	12 A B C D	16 A B C D	20 A B C D	24 A B C D	

PART 8—MK

1 A B C D	5 A B C D	9 A B C D	13 A B C D	17 A B C D	21 A B C D	25 A B C D
2 A B C D	6 A B C D	10 A B C D	14 A B C D	18 A B C D	22 A B C D	
3 A B C D	7 A B C D	11 A B C D	15 A B C D	19 A B C D	23 A B C D	
4 A B C D	8 A B C D	12 A B C D	16 A B C D	20 A B C D	24 A B C D	

PART 9—MC

1 A B C D	5 A B C D	9 A B C D	13 A B C D	17 A B C D	21 A B C D	25 A B C D
2 A B C D	6 A B C D	10 A B C D	14 A B C D	18 A B C D	22 A B C D	
3 A B C D	7 A B C D	11 A B C D	15 A B C D	19 A B C D	23 A B C D	
4 A B C D	8 A B C D	12 A B C D	16 A B C D	20 A B C D	24 A B C D	

PART 10—EI

1 A B C D	4 A B C D	7 A B C D	10 A B C D	13 A B C D	16 A B C D	19 A B C D
2 A B C D	5 A B C D	8 A B C D	11 A B C D	14 A B C D	17 A B C D	20 A B C D
3 A B C D	6 A B C D	9 A B C D	12 A B C D	15 A B C D	18 A B C D	

Second

ASVAB

Specimen Test

The introductory material for general orientation, as well as the general directions for taking the test, appears before the actual test questions in the ASVAB test booklet. However, because this material was covered previously in this book, it is not included in the specimen ASVAB test booklet.

GENERAL SCIENCE

Directions

This is a test of 25 questions to find out how much you know about general science as usually covered in high school courses. Pick the best answer for each question, then blacken the space on your answer form which has the same number and letter as your choice.

Here are three sample questions.

S1. Water is an example of a

    S1-A solid
    S1-B gas
    S1-C liquid
    S1-D crystal

Now look at the section of your answer sheet labeled Part 1, "Practice." Notice that answer space C has been marked for question 1. Now do practice questions 2 and 3 by yourself. Find the correct answer to the question, then mark the space on your answer form that has the same letter as the answer you picked. Do this now.

S2. Lack of iodine is often related to which of the following diseases?

    S2-A beriberi
    S2-B scurvey
    S2-C rickets
    S2-D goiter

S3. An eclipse of the sun throws the shadow of the

    S3-A earth on the moon
    S3-B moon on the earth
    S3-C moon on the sun
    S3-D earth on the sun.

You should have marked D for question 2 and B for question 3. If you made any mistakes, erase your mark carefully and blacken the correct answer space. Do this now.

Your score on this test will be based on the number of questions you answer correctly. You should try to answer every question. Do not spend too much time on any one question.

When you begin, be sure to start with question number 1 of Part 1 of your test booklet, and number 1 in Part 1 on your answer form.

DO NOT TURN THIS PAGE UNTIL TOLD TO DO SO.

GENERAL SCIENCE

TIME: 11 Minutes—25 Questions

1. Citrus fruits include

   1-A apples
   1-B bananas
   1-C oranges
   1-D peaches

2. What temperature is shown on a Fahrenheit thermometer when a centigrade thermometer reads 0°?

   2-A −40°
   2-B −32°
   2-C 0°
   2-D +32°

3. The major chemical constituent of a cell (by weight) is

   3-A protein
   3-B ash
   3-C water
   3-D carbohydrates

4. Which one of the following metals is a liquid at room temperature?

   4-A mercury
   4-B molybdenum
   4-C cobalt
   4-D magnesium

5. The absence of any gravitational pull on an object is called

   5-A weightlessness
   5-B mass
   5-C kinetic energy
   5-D force

6. "Shooting stars" are

   6-A exploding stars
   6-B cosmic rays
   6-C planetoids
   6-D meteors

7. Of the following, a human blood disease which has been definitely shown to be due to a hereditary factor or factors is

   7-A pernicious anemia
   7-B polyscythemia
   7-C sickle cell anemia
   7-D leukemia

8. The number of degrees on the Fahrenheit thermometer between the freezing point and the boiling point of water is

   8-A 100 degrees
   8-B 212 degrees
   8-C 180 degrees
   8-D 273 degrees

9. An observer on earth sees the phases of the moon because the

   9-A moon revolves around the sun
   9-B moon revolves around the earth
   9-C earth revolves around the sun
   9-D moon rotates on its axis

10. Saliva contains an enzyme which acts on

    10-A carbohydrates
    10-B proteins
    10-C minerals
    10-D vitamins

11. The vitamin which helps coagulation of the blood is

    11-A C
    11-B E
    11-C D
    11-D K

12. Of the following, the part of a ship which gives it stability by lowering the center of gravity is the

    12-A bulkhead
    12-B keel
    12-C anchor
    12-D prow

126 **GO ON TO THE NEXT PAGE.**

13. The primary reason designers seek to lower the center of gravity in automobiles is to

13-A reduce wind resistance
13-B provide smoother riding
13-C increase stability
13-D reduce manufacturing costs

14. Substances which hasten a chemical reaction without themselves undergoing change are called

14-A buffers
14-B catalysts
14-C colloids
14-D reducers

15. The change from ice to water is

15-A a chemical change
15-B an elementary change
15-C a physical change
15-D a solid-state change

16. The type of joint that attaches the arm to the shoulder blade is known as a

16-A hinge
16-B pivot
16-C immovable
16-D ball and socket

17. Limes were eaten by British sailors in order to

17-A justify their nickname, "limeys"
17-B pucker their mouths to resist the wind
17-C satisfy their craving for something acid
17-D prevent scurvy

18. The time that it takes for the earth to rotate 45° is

18-A one hour
18-B four hours
18-C three hours
18-D ten hours

19. Vitamin C is also known as

19-A citric acid
19-B ascorbic acid
19-C lactic acid
19-D glutamic acid

20. The temperature of the air falls at night because the earth loses heat by

20-A radiation
20-B conduction
20-C convection
20-D rotation

21. The normal height of a mercury barometer at sea level is

21-A 15 inches
21-B 32 feet
21-C 30 inches
21-D 34 feet

22. A tumor is a

22-A cancer
22-B growth
22-C sore spot
22-D kind of mushroom

23. All types of steel contain

23-A iron
23-B chromium
23-C nickel
23-D tungsten

24. The *most important* provision for a hike in hot, dry countryside is

24-A dried meat
24-B raisins
24-C fresh fruit
24-D water

25. The moon is a

25-A star
25-B satellite
25-C planetoid
25-D planet

1

**DO NOT TURN THIS PAGE UNTIL TOLD TO DO SO.
STOP! IF YOU FINISH BEFORE THE TIME IS UP, YOU
MAY CHECK OVER YOUR WORK ON THIS PART ONLY.**

2

ARITHMETIC REASONING

2

Directions

This test has 30 questions about arithmetic. Each question is followed by four possible answers. Decide which answer is correct, then blacken the space on your answer form which has the same number and letter as your choice. Use your scratch paper for any figuring you wish to do.

Here are two sample questions.

S1. A person buys a sandwich for 90¢, soda for 55¢, and pie for 70¢. What is the total cost?

S1-A $2.00
S1-B $2.05
S1-C $2.15
S1-D $2.25

The total cost is $2.15, therefore, the C answer is the correct one.

S2. If 8 workers are needed to run 4 machines, how many workers are needed to run 20 machines?

S2-A 16
S2-B 32
S2-C 36
S2-D 40

The number needed is 40, therefore, D is the correct answer.

Your score on this test will be based on the number of questions you answer correctly. You should try to answer every question. Do not spend too much time on any one question.

Notice that Part 2 begins with question number 1. When you begin, be sure to start with question number 1 in Part 2 of your test booklet and number 1 in Part 2 on your answer form.

DO NOT TURN THIS PAGE UNTIL TOLD TO DO SO.

2

ARITHMETIC REASONING

TIME: 36 Minutes—30 Questions

1. If pencils are bought at 70 cents per dozen and sold at 3 for 20 cents, the total profit on 6 dozen is

   1-A 50 cents
   1-B 60 cents
   1-C 65 cents
   1-D 75 cents

2. A certain type of siding for a house costs $10.50 per square yard. What does it cost for the siding for a wall 4 yards wide and 60 feet long?

   2-A $800
   2-B $840
   2-C $2,520
   2-D $3,240

3. A parcel delivery service charges $9.26 for the first 4 pounds of package weight and an additional $1.06 for each half-pound over 4 pounds. What is the charge for a package weighing 6½ pounds?

   3-A $2.65
   3-B $6.89
   3-C $11.91
   3-D $14.56

4. At the rate of 4 peaches for a half dollar, 20 peaches will cost

   4-A $1.60
   4-B $2.00
   4-C $2.40
   4-D $2.50

5. A student deposited in his savings account the money he had saved during the week. Find the amount of his deposit if he had 10 one-dollar bills, 9 half dollars, 8 quarters, 16 dimes, and 25 nickels.

   5-A $16.20
   5-B $17.42
   5-C $18.60
   5-D $19.35.

6. How many minutes are there in 1 day?

   6-A 60
   6-B 1,440
   6-C 24
   6-D 1,440 × 60

7. Six gross of special drawing pencils were purchased for use in a department. If the pencils were used at the rate of 24 a week, the maximum number of weeks that the six gross of pencils would last is

   7-A 6 weeks
   7-B 24 weeks
   7-C 12 weeks
   7-D 36 weeks

8. A stock clerk had 600 pads on hand. He then issued ⅜ of his supply of pads to Division X, ¼ to Division Y, and ⅙ to Division Z. The number of pads remaining in stock is

   8-A 48
   8-B 240
   8-C 125
   8-D 475

9. During a sale, records which normally cost $6.98 each were priced at 2 for $12.50. Pete bought 4 records at the sale price. How much money did he save by buying the four records on sale?

   9-A $2.98
   9-B $2.92
   9-C $2.50
   9-D $1.46

10. A student must walk 2 miles to get to school. If she walks at an average of 3 miles per hour, how many minutes should it take her to walk to school?

    10-A 40
    10-B 20
    10-C 50
    10-D 45

2

GO ON TO THE NEXT PAGE.

2

11. Two sailors traveled by bus from one point to another. The trip took 15 hours, and they left their point of origin at 8 a.m. What time did they arrive at their destination?

    11-A 11 a.m.
    11-B 10 p.m.
    11-C 11 p.m.
    11-D 12 a.m.

12. A team won 8 of the 24 games it played in one season. What percent of the games did it win?

    12-A $66\frac{2}{3}$%

    12-B $33\frac{1}{3}$%

    12-C 50%
    12-D 16%

13. A clerk is asked to file 800 cards. If he can file cards at the rate of 80 cards an hour, the number of cards remaining to be filed after 7 hours of work is

    13-A 140
    13-B 240
    13-C 250
    14-D 260

14. A woman's weekly salary is increased from $350 to $380. The percent of increase is, most nearly,

    14-A 6 percent

    14-B $8\frac{1}{2}$ percent

    14-C 10 percent

    14-D $12\frac{1}{2}$ percent

15. A truck going at a rate of 20 miles an hour will reach a town 40 miles away in how many hours?

    15-A 3 hours
    15-B 4 hours
    15-C 1 hour
    15-D 2 hours

16. If a barrel has a capacity of 100 gallons, how many gallons will it contain when it is two-fifths full?

    16-A 20
    16-B 40
    16-C 60
    16-D 80

17. If a salary of $20,000 is subject to a 20 percent deduction, the net salary is

    17-A $14,000
    17-B $15,500
    17-C $16,000
    17-D $18,000

18. If $2,000 is the cost of repairing 100 square yards of pavement, the cost of repairing one square yard is

    18-A $20
    18-B $100
    18-C $150
    18-D $200

19. A man paid $42.30 for gasoline in May, $38.60 in June, and $43.00 in July. What was his average monthly cost for gasoline?

    19-A $40.45
    19-B $41.30
    19-C $61.95
    19-D $123.90

20. A skier started a fire in the fireplace. Each log she put on burned for a half-hour. If she started with a supply of 10 logs, for how many hours could the fire burn?

    20-A 5 hours

    20-B $8\frac{1}{2}$ hours

    20-C 10 hours
    20-D 7 hours

21. To go from Poughkeepsie, New York, to West Palm Beach, Florida, you must travel 1,400 miles. If you can average a driving speed of 50 miles an hour, how many hours must you drive to make this trip?

GO ON TO THE NEXT PAGE.

21-A 25

21-B 28

21-C 30

21-D $27\frac{1}{2}$

22. After an article is discounted at 25%, it sells for $112.50. The original price of the article was

22-A $28.12

22-B $84.37

22-C $150.00

22-D $152.50

23. A checking account has a balance of $627.04. After writing three checks for $241.75, $13.24, and $102.97, what is the balance remaining in the account?

23-A $257.88

23-B $269.08

23-C $357.96

23-D $369.96

24. If erasers cost 8¢ each for the first 250, 7¢ each for the next 250, and 5¢ for every eraser thereafter, how many erasers may be purchased for $50?

24-A 600

24-B 750

24-C 850

24-D 1000

25. An inch on a map represents 200 miles. On the same map a distance of 375 miles is represented by

25-A $1\frac{1}{2}$ inches

25-B $1\frac{7}{8}$ inches

25-C $2\frac{1}{4}$ inches

25-D $2\frac{3}{4}$ inches

26. The number of half-pound packages of tea that can be made up from a box which holds 10¼ pounds of tea is

26-A 5

26-B $10\frac{1}{2}$

26-C 20

26-D $20\frac{1}{2}$

27. A pile of magazines is 4 feet high. If each magazine is ¾ of an inch thick, the number of magazines in the pile is

27-A 36

27-B 48

27-C 64

27-D 96

28. If ½ cup of spinach contains 80 calories and the same amount of peas contains 300 calories, how many cups of spinach have the same caloric content as ⅔ cup of peas?

28-A $\frac{2}{5}$

28-B $1\frac{1}{3}$

28-C 2

28-D $2\frac{1}{2}$

29. If it takes 30 minutes to type 6 pages, how many hours will it take to type 126 pages at the same rate?

29-A 6.3

29-B 10.5

29-C 15

29-D 25

30. A night watchman must check a certain storage area every 45 minutes. If he first checks the area as he begins a 9-hour tour of duty, how many times will he have checked this storage area?

30-A 10

30-B 11

30-C 12

30-D 13

2

STOP! **IF YOU FINISH BEFORE THE TIME IS UP, YOU MAY CHECK OVER YOUR WORK ON THIS PART ONLY. DO NOT RETURN TO PART ONE. DO NOT TURN THE PAGE UNTIL YOU ARE TOLD TO DO SO.**

3

WORD KNOWLEDGE

3

Directions

This test has 35 questions about the meanings of words. Each question has an underlined word. You are to decide which one of the four words in the choices most nearly means the same as the underlined word, then mark the space on your answer form which has the same number and letter as your choice.

Now look at the two sample questions below.

     S1. <u>Mended</u> most nearly means

         S1-A repaired
         S1-B torn
         S1-C clean
         S1-D tied

A REPAIRED is the correct answer. *Mended* means *fixed* or *repaired*. *Torn* (B) might be the state of an object before it is mended. The repair might be made by *tying* (D), but not necessarily. *Clean* (C) is wrong.

     S2. It was a <u>small</u> table.

         S2-A sturdy
         S2-B round
         S2-C cheap
         S2-D little

Little means the same as small so D is the best answer.

Your score on this test will be based on the number of questions you answer correctly. You should try to answer every question. Do not spend too much time on any one question.

When you begin, be sure to start with question number 1 in Part 3 of your test booklet and number 1 in Part 3 on your answer form.

DO NOT TURN THIS PAGE UNTIL TOLD TO DO SO.

3

3

WORD KNOWLEDGE

TIME: 11 Minutes—35 Questions

1. <u>Superiority</u> most nearly means

   1-A abundance
   1-B popularity
   1-C permanence
   1-D excellence

2. <u>Absurd</u> most nearly means

   2-A disgusting
   2-B foolish
   2-C reasonable
   2-D very old

3. Be careful, that liquid is <u>inflammable</u>!

   3-A poisonous
   3-B valuable
   3-C explosive
   3-D likely to give off fumes

4. The fog horn sounded <u>intermittently</u>.

   4-A constantly
   4-B annually
   4-C using intermediaries
   4-D at irregular intervals

5. He told us about a strange <u>occurrence</u>.

   5-A event
   5-B place
   5-C occupation
   5-D opinion

6. <u>Deception</u> most nearly means

   6-A secrets
   6-B fraud
   6-C mistrust
   6-D hatred

7. The <u>captive</u> was treated kindly.

   7-A savage
   7-B jailer
   7-C spy
   7-D prisoner

8. <u>Vegetation</u> most nearly means

   8-A food
   8-B plant life
   8-C moisture
   8-D bird life

9. <u>Fictitious</u> most nearly means

   9-A imaginary
   9-B well-known
   9-C odd
   9-D easy to remember

10. All service was <u>suspended</u> during the emergency.

    10-A turned back
    10-B checked carefully
    10-C regulated strictly
    10-D stopped temporarily

11. The <u>territory</u> is too large for one platoon to defend.

    11-A region
    11-B swamp
    11-C ranch
    11-D beach

12. <u>Huge</u> most nearly means

    12-A ugly
    12-B tall
    12-C wide
    12-D immense

13. The driver <u>heeded</u> the traffic signals.

    13-A worried about
    13-B ignored
    13-C disagreed with
    13-D took notice of

14. <u>Vigorously</u> most nearly means

    14-A sleepily
    14-B thoughtfully
    14-C energetically
    14-D sadly

3

GO ON TO THE NEXT PAGE.

15. <u>Imitate</u> most nearly means

15-A copy
15-B attract
15-C study
15-D appreciate

16. <u>Alias</u> most nearly means

16-A enemy
16-B sidekick
16-C hero
16-D other name

17. <u>Impair</u> most nearly means

17-A direct
17-B improve
17-C weaken
17-D stimulate

3 18. <u>Itinerant</u> most nearly means

18-A traveling
18-B shrewd
18-C ignorant
18-D aggressive

19. The foreman <u>defended</u> the striking workers.

19-A delayed
19-B shot at
19-C protected
19-D informed on

20. The <u>aim</u> of the enlistee was to join the navy.

20-A bullseye
20-B goal
20-C duty
20-D promise

21. <u>Assemble</u> most nearly means

21-A bring together
21-B examine carefully
21-C locate
21-D fill

22. <u>Instructor</u> most nearly means

22-A expert
22-B assistant
22-C teacher
22-D foreman

23. <u>Commended</u> most nearly means

23-A reprimanded
23-B praised
23-C promoted
23-D blamed

24. <u>Revolving</u> most nearly means

24-A rocking
24-B working
24-C vibrating
24-D turning

25. <u>Nonessential</u> most nearly means

25-A damaged
25-B unnecessary
25-C expensive
25-D foreign-made

26. <u>Amplified</u> most nearly means

26-A expanded
26-B summarized
26-C analyzed
26-D shouted

27. The vase remained <u>intact</u> after it was dropped.

27-A unattended
27-B undamaged
27-C a total loss
27-D unmoved

28. We admired the exquisite <u>tapestry</u>.

28-A fabric of woven designs
28-B tent
28-C piece of elaborate jewelry
28-D exquisite painting

29. <u>Terse</u> most nearly means

29-A concise
29-B trivial
29-C oral
29-D lengthy

30. She prepared a delicious <u>concoction</u> for us.

30-A combination of ingredients
30-B appetizer
30-C drink made of wine and spices
30-D relish tray

GO ON TO THE NEXT PAGE.

31. <u>Acquired</u> most nearly means

    31-A sold
    31-B plowed
    31-C desired
    31-D obtained

32. <u>Exhaustion</u> most nearly means

    32-A fear
    32-B overconfidence
    32-C extreme tiredness
    32-D unsteadiness

33. The door was left <u>ajar</u>.

    33-A blocked
    33-B locked
    33-C unlocked
    33-D open

34. We heard the <u>steady</u> ticking of the clock.

    34-A noisy
    34-B eerie
    34-C tiresome
    34-D regular

35. The letter <u>emphasized</u> two important ideas.

    35-A introduced
    35-B overlooked
    35-C contrasted
    35-D stressed

3

DO NOT TURN THIS PAGE UNTIL TOLD TO DO SO.
STOP! IF YOU FINISH BEFORE THE TIME IS UP, YOU
MAY CHECK OVER YOUR WORK ON THIS PART ONLY.

4

PARAGRAPH COMPREHENSION

4

Directions

This test contains 15 items measuring your ability to obtain information from written passages. You will find one or more paragraphs of reading material followed by incomplete statements or questions. You are to read the paragraph(s) and select one of the lettered choices which best completes the statement or answers the question.

Here are two sample questions.

S1. From a building designer's standpoint, three things that make a home livable are the needs of the client, the building site, and the amount of money the client has to spend.

According to the passage, to make a home livable

S1-A the prospective piece of land makes little difference

S1-B it can be built on any piece of land

S1-C the design must fit the owner's income and site

S1-D the design must fit the designer's income

The correct answer is that the designer must fit the owner's income and site, so C is the correct response.

S2. In certain areas water is so scarce that every attempt is made to conserve it. For instance, on one oasis in the Sahara Desert the amount of water necessary for each date palm tree has been carefully determined.

How much water is each tree given?

S2-A no water at all

S2-B exactly the amount required

S2-C water only if it is healthy

S2-D water on alternate days

The correct answer is exactly the amount required, so B is the correct response.

Your score on this test will be based on the number of questions you answer correctly. You should try to answer every question. Do not spend too much time on any one question.

When you begin be sure to start with question number 1 in Part 4 of your test booklet and number 1 in Part 4 on your answer form.

DO NOT TURN THIS PAGE UNTIL TOLD TO DO SO.

4

PARAGRAPH COMPREHENSION

TIME: 13 Minutes—15 Questions

1. Numerous benefits to the employer as well as to the worker have resulted from physical examinations of employees. Such examinations are intended primarily as a means of increasing efficiency and production, and they have been found to accomplish these ends.

   The passage best supports the statement that physical examinations

   1-A may serve to increase output
   1-B are required in some plants
   1-C often reveal serious defects previously unknown
   1-D always are worth more than they cost

2. A good or service has value only because people want it. Value is an extrinsic quality wholly created in the minds of people, and is not intrinsic in the property itself.

   According to this passage, it is correct to say that an object will be valuable if it is

   2-A beautiful
   2-B not plentiful
   2-C sought after
   2-D useful

3. The rights of an individual should properly be considered of greatest importance in a democracy until the activities of an individual come in conflict with the community interest or with the interest of society.

   According to this passage, in a democracy

   3-A there is nothing of greater importance than the rights of the individual
   3-B there must be no conflict between the interest of the community and the rights of the individual
   3-C the rights of the individual are secondary to the interest of the community
   3-D the rights of the individual are generally incompatible with the interest of society

4. The Supreme Court was established by Article 3 of the Constitution. Since 1869 it has been made up of nine members—the chief justice and eight associate justices—who are appointed for life. Supreme Court justices are named by the President and must be confirmed by the Senate.

   The Supreme Court

   4-A was established in 1869
   4-B consists of nine justices
   4-C consists of justices appointed by the Senate
   4-D changes with each Presidential election

5. When gas is leaking, any spark or sudden flame can ignite it. This can create a "flashback," which burns off the gas in a quick puff of smoke and flame. But the real danger is in a large leak, which can cause an explosion.

   According to the passage, the real danger from leaking gas is

   5-A a flashback
   5-B a puff of smoke and flame
   5-C an explosion
   5-D a spark

6. It is a common assumption that city directories are prepared and published by the cities concerned. However, the directory business is as much a private business as is the publishing of dictionaries and encyclopedias. The companies financing the publication make their profits through the sales of the directories themselves and through the advertising in them.

   The paragraph best supports the statement that

   6-A the publication of a city directory is a commercial enterprise
   6-B the size of a city directory limits the space devoted to advertising
   6-C many city directories are published by dictionary and encyclopedia concerns
   6-D city directories are sold at cost to local residents and businessmen

4

GO ON TO THE NEXT PAGE.

7. A survey to determine the subjects that have helped students most in their jobs shows that typewriting leads all other subjects in the business group. It also leads among the subjects college students consider most valuable and would take again if they were to return to high school.

The paragraph best supports the statement that

7-A the ability to type is an asset in business and in school

7-B students who return to night school take typing

7-C students with a knowledge of typing do superior work in college

7-D success in business is assured those who can type

4

8. The X-ray has gone into business. Developed primarily to aid in diagnosing human ills, the machine now works in packing plants, in foundries, in service stations, and in a dozen ways contributes to precision and accuracy in industry.

The X-ray

8-A was first developed to aid business

8-B is being used to improve the functioning of industry

8-C is more accurate in packing plants than in foundries

8-D increases the output of such industries as service stations

9. The increasing size of business organizations has resulted in less personal contact between superior and subordinate. Consequently, business executives today depend more upon records and reports to secure information and exercise control over the operations of various departments.

The increasing size of business organizations

9-A has caused a complete cleavage between employer and employee

9-B has resulted in less personal contact between superior and subordinate

9-C has tended toward class distinctions in large organizations

9-D has resulted in a better means of controlling the operations of various departments

10. Twenty-five percent of all household burglaries can be attributed to unlocked windows or doors. Crime is the result of opportunity plus desire.

To prevent crime, it is each individual's responsibility to

10-A provide the desire

10-B provide the opportunity

10-C prevent the desire

10-D prevent the opportunity

Questions 11 and 12 are based on the following passage.

Because electric drills run at high speed, the cutting edges of a twist drill are heated quickly. If the metal is thick, the drill point must be withdrawn from the hole frequently to cool it and clear out chips. Forcing the drill continuously into a deep hole will heat it, thereby spoiling its temper and cutting edges. A portable electric drill can be used to drill holes in material too large to handle in a drill press.

11. According to the above passage, overheating a twist drill will

11-A slow down the work

11-B cause excessive drill breakage

11-C dull the drill

11-D spoil the accuracy of the work

12. One method of preventing overheating of a twist drill, according to the above passage, is to

12-A use cooling oil

12-B drill a smaller pilot hole first

12-C use a drill press

12-D remove the drill from the work frequently

GO ON TO THE NEXT PAGE.

Questions 13–15 are based on the passage shown below.

Arsonists are persons who set fires deliberately. They don't look like criminals, but they cost the nation millions of dollars in property loss and sometimes loss of life. Arsonists set fires for many different reasons. Sometimes a shopkeeper sees no way out of losing his business, and sets fire to it to collect the insurance. Another type of arsonist wants revenge, and sets fire to the home or shop of someone he feels has treated him unfairly. Some arsonists just like the excitement of seeing the fire burn and watching the firefighters at work; arsonists of this type have even been known to help fight the fire.

13. According to the passage above, an arsonist is a person who

13-A intentionally sets a fire
13-B enjoys watching fires
13-C wants revenge
13-D needs money

14. Arsonists have been known to help fight fires because they

14-A felt guilty
14-B enjoyed the excitement
14-C wanted to earn money
14-D didn't want anyone hurt

15. According to the passage above, we may conclude that arsonists

15-A would make good firefighters
15-B are not criminals
15-C are mentally ill
15-D are not all alike

4

DO NOT TURN THIS PAGE UNTIL TOLD TO DO SO.
STOP! IF YOU FINISH BEFORE THE TIME IS UP, YOU
MAY CHECK OVER YOUR WORK ON THIS PART ONLY.

5

NUMERICAL OPERATIONS

5

Directions

This is a test to see how rapidly and accurately you can do 50 simple arithmetic computations. Each problem is followed by four answers, only one of which is correct. Decide which answer is correct, then blacken the space on your answer form which has the same number and letter as your choice.

Now look at the four example problems below.

S1. $3 \times 3 =$

    S1-A 6
    S1-B 0
    S1-C 9
    S1-D 1

The answer is 9, so C is correct.

S3. $5 - 2 =$

    S3-A 2
    S3-B 3
    S3-C 4
    S3-D 4

The answer is 3, so B is correct.

S2. $3 + 7 =$

    S2-A 4
    S2-B 6
    S2-C 8
    S2-D 10

The answer is 10, so D is correct.

S4. $9 \div 3 =$

    S4-A 3
    S4-B 6
    S4-C 9
    S4-D 12

The answer is 3, so A is correct.

This is a speed test, so work as fast as you can without making mistakes. Do each problem as it comes. If you finish before time is up, go back and check your work. When the signal is given, you will turn the page and begin with question 1 in Part 5 of your test booklet and answer space 1 in Part 5 of your answer form.

DO NOT TURN THIS PAGE UNTIL TOLD TO DO SO.

PART 5

NUMERICAL OPERATIONS

TIME: 3 Minutes—50 Questions

5

1. $2 + 3 =$

1-A 1
1-B 4
1-C 5
1-D 6

2. $8 - 5 =$

2-A 4
2-B 3
2-C 2
2-D 1

3. $9 \div 3 =$

3-A 2
3-B 3
3-C 6
3-D 4

4. $4 + 6 =$

4-A 12
4-B 10
4-C 3
4-D 2

5. $6 \times 3 =$

5-A 3
5-B 9
5-C 12
5-D 18

6. $9 + 5 =$

6-A 14
6-B 4
6-C 13
6-D 16

7. $3 + 9 =$

7-A 12
7-B 11
7-C 13
7-D 14

8. $7 + 8 =$

8-A 12
8-B 15
8-C 17
8-D 19

9. $3 \times 8 =$

9-A 5
9-B 13
9-C 24
9-D 32

10. $3 \times 2 =$

10-A 1
10-B 4
10-C 5
10-D 6

11. $1 - 1 =$

11-A 2
11-B 3
11-C 0
11-D 1

12. $2 \times 9 =$

12-A 16
12-B 17
12-C 18
12-D 20

13. $9 + 3 =$

13-A 3
13-B 7
13-C 11
13-D 12

14. $8 + 16 =$

14-A 12
14-B 24
14-C 26
14-D 28

15. $9 - 4 =$

15-A 3
15-B 5
15-C 6
15-D 7

16. $6 + 8 =$

16-A 2
16-B 10
16-C 12
16-D 14

17. $4 \times 6 =$

17-A 12
17-B 16
17-C 24
17-D 28

18. $3 \div 3 =$

18-A 3
18-B 1
18-C 0
18-D 2

19. $5 + 8 =$

19-A 11
19-B 12
19-C 13
19-D 15

20. $7 - 6 =$

20-A 5
20-B 1
20-C 11
20-D 13

21. $8 - 3 =$

21-A 5
21-B 11
21-C 12
21-D 13

22. $5 + 8 =$

22-A 3
22-B 7
22-C 12
22-D 13

23. $20 \div 2 =$

23-A 6
23-B 8
23-C 10
23-D 12

24. $15 - 7 =$

24-A 5
24-B 8
24-C 10
24-D 12

25. $6 \div 2 =$

25-A 3
25-B 4
25-C 5
25-D 8

26. $7 - 2 =$

26-A 2
26-B 5
26-C 6
26-D 9

27. $10 \div 2 =$

27-A 8
27-B 7
27-C 5
27-D 4

28. $15 \div 3 =$

28-A 5
28-B 3
28-C 12
28-D 45

148   **GO ON TO THE NEXT PAGE.**

29. 2 × 8 =

29-A 6
29-B 16
29-C 18
29-D 36

30. 1 + 6 =

30-A 16
30-B 12
30-C 7
30-D 6

31. 2 × 9 =

31-A 17
31-B 19
31-C 18
31-D 16

32. 7 + 3 =

32-A 4
32-B 10
32-C 13
32-D 11

33. 30 ÷ 3 =

33-A 33
33-B 11
33-C 12
33-D 10

34. 7 + 9 =

34-A 2
34-B 13
34-C 16
34-D 18

35. 15 × 5 =

35-A 45
35-B 55
35-C 65
35-D 75

36. 4 − 3 =

36-A 1
36-B 5
36-C 7
36-D 9

37. 7 + 5 =

37-A 2
37-B 4
37-C 8
37-D 12

38. 27 ÷ 9 =

38-A 3
38-B 6
38-C 12
38-D 13

39. 6 + 4 =

39-A 10
39-B 12
39-C 14
39-D 16

40. 6 × 6 =

40-A 12
40-B 18
40-C 36
40-D 66

41. 8 + 9 =

41-A 15
41-B 17
41-C 19
41-D 21

42. 1 + 3 =

42-A 1
42-B 2
42-C 3
42-D 4

43. 16 ÷ 4 =

43-A 4
43-B 8
43-C 12
43-D 20

44. 9 × 9 =

44-A 99
44-B 0
44-C 72
44-D 81

45. 5 + 7 =

45-A 11
45-B 2
45-C 12
45-D 13

46. 30 ÷ 15 =

46-A 2
46-B 6
46-C 15
46-D 45

47. 7 + 5 =

47-A 12
47-B 13
47-C 14
47-D 15

48. 3 × 6 =

48-A 3
48-B 9
48-C 15
48-D 18

49. 9 − 6 =

49-A 3
49-B 7
49-C 14
49-D 15

50. 4 × 6 =

50-A 10
50-B 20
50-C 24
50-D 26

5

DO NOT TURN THIS PAGE UNTIL TOLD TO DO SO.
STOP! IF YOU FINISH BEFORE THE TIME IS UP, YOU
MAY CHECK OVER YOUR WORK ON THIS PART ONLY.

6

CODING SPEED

6

Directions

This is a test of 84 items to see how quickly and accurately you can find a number in a table. At the top of each section, there is a number table or "key." The key is a group of words with a code number for each word.

Each question in the test is a word taken from the key at the top. From among the possible answers listed for each question, find the one that is the correct code number for that word.

Look at the sample key and answer the five sample questions below. Note that each of the questions is one of the words in the key. To the right of each question are possible answers listed under the options A, B, C, D, and E.

Sample Questions

Key

green 2715	man 3451	salt 4586
hat 1413	room. 2864	tree 5972

Questions   **Options**

Questions	A	B	C	D	E
S-1 room	1413	2715	2864	3451	4586
S-2 green	2715	2864	3451	4586	5972
S-3 tree	2715	2864	3451	4596	5972
S-4 hat	1413	2715	2864	3451	4586
S-5 room	1413	2864	3451	4586	5972

By looking at the key you see that the code number for the first word, "room," is 2864. 2864 is listed under the letter C so C is the correct answer. The correct answers for the other four questions are A, E, A, and B.

This is a speed test, so work as fast as you can without making mistakes.

Notice that Part 6 begins at the top of the next answer form. When you begin, be sure to start with question number 1 in Part 6 of your test booklet and number 1 in Part 6 on your answer form.

DO NOT TURN THIS PAGE UNTIL TOLD TO DO SO.

CODING SPEED

TIME: 7 Minutes—84 Questions

Key

apron 4341	canoe 1936	earth 9229	germ 8606	knot 6157
bridge 3636	date 2024	face 5678	jet 7699	lizard 5163

Questions		Options			

6

		A	B	C	D	E
1.	lizard	2024	3636	4341	5163	7699
2.	jet	1936	5163	5678	6157	7699
3.	bridge	1936	3636	4341	7699	8606
4.	face	5678	6157	7699	8606	9229
5.	knot	1936	2024	4341	5163	6157
6.	apron	2024	4341	5163	6157	9229
7.	canoe	1936	3636	4341	5163	5678
8.	date	2024	5163	6157	7699	8606
9.	germ	2024	3636	6157	7699	8606
10.	earth	1936	4341	5163	6157	9229
11.	face	2024	3636	4341	5163	5678
12.	knot	1936	4341	6157	8606	9229

Key

figure 3341	harvest 6400	nature 6445	ruler 8791	tennis 4166
gang 1921	manager ... 2797	peach 7070	signal 9761	wrist 5961

Questions		Options			

		A	B	C	D	E
13.	ruler	3341	5961	6400	8791	9761
14.	gang	1921	6445	7070	8791	9761
15.	manager	1921	2797	3341	5961	7070
16.	tennis	3341	4166	6400	7070	8791
17.	wrist	4166	5961	6445	8791	9761
18.	figure	1921	2797	3341	4166	5961
19.	harvest	5961	6400	7070	8791	9761
20.	nature	1921	3341	4166	5961	6445
21.	signal	2797	4166	5961	6445	9761
22.	peach	3341	5961	6400	7070	8791
23.	tennis	1921	3341	4166	5961	6400
24.	manager	2797	4166	5961	8791	9761

GO ON TO THE NEXT PAGE.

Key

aunt 7959	deer 8812	hail 1929	judge 5761	mark 6776
couch 4790	dove 1918	iron 2458	ladle 3344	pistol 9434

Questions	Options				
	A	**B**	**C**	**D**	**E**
25. pistol	1918	1929	4790	7959	9434
26. iron	1929	2458	3344	6776	7959
27. mark	3344	4790	5761	6776	7959
28. judge	1918	1929	2458	4790	5761
29. ladle	2458	3344	6776	7959	9434
30. couch	4790	5761	6776	8812	9434
31. deer	1918	2458	5761	7959	8812
32. aunt	3344	5761	7959	8812	9434
33. pistol	1929	3344	4790	7959	9434
34. dove	1918	1929	2458	3344	4790
35. mark	4790	6776	7959	8812	9434
36. hail	1929	2458	5761	6776	7959

6

Key

author 6509	cake 2988	fire 1886	hunter 4141	shore 5135
blood 3348	card 7074	frog 9492	pin 8768	time 6852

Questions	Options				
	A	**B**	**C**	**D**	**E**
37. hunter	1886	2988	4141	5135	8768
38. shore	2988	3348	5135	6509	7074
39. frog	3348	4141	6852	8768	9492
40. author	2988	5135	6509	6852	8768
41. blood	1886	3348	4141	6852	7074
42. cake	2988	3348	5135	6509	6852
43. card	1886	4141	7074	8768	9492
44. pin	2988	3348	5135	6852	8768
45. fire	1886	2988	4141	6509	7074
46. time	3348	4141	5135	6509	6852
47. author	1886	3348	4141	6509	6852
48. shore	5135	6509	6852	7074	9492

GO ON TO THE NEXT PAGE.

Key

angel 7717	eye 6943	gown 3232	joke........ 8614	nut 9089
brick 1492	flood 5846	ink......... 4921	llama 2573	red 5487

Questions			Options		
	A	**B**	**C**	**D**	**E**
49. flood	1492	4921	5487	5846	6943
50. gown	2573	3232	6943	8614	9089
51. joke	1492	4921	5846	7717	8614
52. nut	1492	2573	3232	8614	9089
53. angel	2573	4921	6943	7717	8614
54. ink	1492	4921	6943	7715	8614
55. red	1492	4912	5487	5846	6943
56. eye	4921	6943	7717	8614	9089
57. brick	1492	4912	5846	6943	8614
58. llama	2573	3232	4921	6943	9089
59. eye	1492	2573	3232	5846	6943
60. ink	2573	3232	4921	7717	8614

Key

auto 9619	energy 3117	herd 7519	lawn 9451	shovel 8321
copper 6010	fork........ 1492	judge 4787	oven 5881	village....... 2588

Questions			Options		
	A	**B**	**C**	**D**	**E**
61. copper	3117	4787	5881	6010	7519
62. energy	1492	2588	3117	8321	9619
63. herd	4787	6010	7519	9451	9619
64. judge	2588	4787	5881	6010	8321
65. village	1492	2588	3117	5881	6010
66. lawn	2588	3117	4787	7519	9451
67. shovel	3117	5881	6010	7519	8321
68. oven	3117	4787	5881	8321	9619
69. auto	5881	6010	7519	8321	9619
70. fork	1492	2588	3117	4787	5881
71. energy	2588	3117	4787	6010	7519
72. judge	4787	5881	7519	9451	9619

GO ON TO THE NEXT PAGE.

6

Key

bell 5458	dash 4844	fuss 4363	iron 9100	mug 7613
cable 1058	echo 1978	height 2984	jewel 6877	tub 3439

Questions			Options		
	A	**B**	**C**	**D**	**E**
73. height	1058	1978	2984	7613	9100
74. jewel	1978	4844	5458	6877	7613
75. bell	2984	3439	4363	4844	5458
76. dash	2984	3439	4363	4844	6877
77. cable	1058	1978	6877	7613	9100
78. fuss	3439	4363	4844	5458	7613
79. mug	2984	4363	5458	6877	7613
80. echo	1978	2984	5458	7613	9100
81. tub	3439	4363	4844	6877	7613
82. iron	1058	1978	4363	7613	9100
83. bell	1978	2984	5458	6877	7613
84. dash	4363	4844	5458	7613	9100

6

DO NOT TURN THIS PAGE UNTIL TOLD TO DO SO.
STOP! IF YOU FINISH BEFORE THE TIME IS UP, YOU
MAY CHECK OVER YOUR WORK ON THIS PART ONLY.

7

AUTO & SHOP INFORMATION

7

Directions

This test has 25 questions about automobiles, shop practices, and the use of tools. Pick the best answer for each question, then blacken the space on your answer form which has the same number and letter as your choice.

Here are four sample questions.

S1. The most commonly used fuel for running automobile engines is

S1-A kerosene
S1-B benzine
S1-C crude oil
S1-D gasoline

Gasoline is the most commonly used fuel, so D is the correct answer.

S2. A car uses too much oil when which parts are worn?

S2-A pistons
S2-B piston rings
S2-C main bearings
S2-D connecting rods

Worn piston rings causes the use of too much oil, so B is the correct answer.

S3. The saw shown to the right is used mainly to cut

S3-A plywood
S3-B odd-shaped holes in wood
S3-C along the grain of the wood
S3-D across the grain of the wood

The compass saw is used to cut odd-shaped holes in wood, so B is the correct answer.

S4. Thin sheet metal should be cut with

S4-A ordinary scissors
S4-B a hack saw
S4-C tin shears
S4-D a jig saw

Tin shears are used to cut thin sheet metal, so C is the correct answer.

Your score on this test will be based on the number of questions you answer correctly. You should try to answer every question. Do not spend too much time on any one question.

When you are told to begin, be sure to start with question number 1 in Part 7 of your test booklet and number 1 in Part 7 on your answer form.

DO NOT TURN THIS PAGE UNTIL TOLD TO DO SO.

7

AUTO & SHOP INFORMATION

TIME: 11 Minutes—25 Questions

1. An engine, such as is most often used in automobiles, is called a(n)

   1-A diesel engine
   1-B external-combustion engine
   1-C internal-combustion engine
   1-D three cycle engine

2. In the four stroke cycle gasoline engine, the sequence of the steps in each cylinder to complete a cycle is which one of the following?

   2-A intake stroke, power stroke, compression stroke, exhaust stroke
   2-B intake stroke, compression stroke, exhaust stroke, power stroke
   2-C intake stroke, exhaust stroke, compression stroke, power stroke
   2-D intake stroke, compression stroke, power stroke, exhaust stroke

3. Vapor-lock in a gasoline engine is most likely due to

   3-A an over-rich gas-air mixture
   3-B fuel forming bubbles in the gas line
   3-C a tear in the fuel pump diaphragm
   3-D the carburetor being clogged with dirt

4. What would be the most probable cause if an automobile has a weak spark at the plugs, "turns over" very slowly, and has dim headlights?

   4-A weak battery
   4-B faulty condenser
   4-C faulty ignition cable
   4-D worn contact breaker points

5. An automobile engine won't "turn over." If the battery charge is found to be normal, the next test would normally be for

   5-A defective starter motor
   5-B short-circuited switches
   5-C faulty battery cable connections
   5-D defective generator

6. The generator or alternator of an automobile engine is usually driven by the

   6-A camshaft
   6-B flywheel
   6-C fan belt
   6-D cranking motor

7. Setting the spark plug gap opening closer than normally required would probably result in

   7-A smoother idling and increase in top engine speed
   7-B rougher idling and decrease in top engine speed
   7-C smoother idling and decrease in top engine speed
   7-D rougher idling and increase in top engine speed

8. If a gasoline engine is continued in operation with a voltage regulator unable to check the output voltage of the alternator, the result would most likely be to

   8-A "run down" the battery
   8-B reverse the current through the voltage coils
   8-C demagnetize the relay iron core
   8-D overcharge the battery

9. Upon dismantling a gasoline engine, it was found that the piston rings were stuck in the grooves, not being free to rotate. This was most likely caused by

   9-A operating the engine with spark setting in advanced position
   9-B the thermostat maintaining too low an engine temperature
   9-C dirty or contaminated lubricating oil
   9-D using the wrong type of spark plugs in the engine

7

GO ON TO THE NEXT PAGE.

7

10. Alcohol is put into the radiator of an automobile in cold weather because it

10-A lowers the boiling point of the mixture
10-B lowers the freezing point of the mixture
10-C raises the boiling point of the mixture
10-D raises the freezing point of the mixture

11. The purpose of the ignition coil in a gasoline engine is primarily to

11-A raise the current
11-B raise the voltage
11-C smooth the current
11-D smooth the voltage

12. The tool that is best suited for use with a wood chisel is

12-A

12-B

12-C

12-D

13. The type of screwdriver that will develop the greatest turning force is a

13-A screwdriver-bit and brace
13-B straight handle with ratchet
13-C standard straight handle
13-D spiral push-type

14.

The tool shown above is used to

14-A ream holes in wood
14-B countersink holes in soft metals
14-C turn Philips-head screws
14-D drill holes in concrete

15. A jointer plane is

15-A used for making close fits
15-B used for heavy rough work
15-C usualy less than 12 inches long
15-D used for squaring of end-stock

16. The principal reason for "tempering" or "drawing" steel is to

16-A reduce strength
16-B reduce hardness
16-C increase strength
16-D increase maleability

17. Sheet metal is dipped in sulphuric acid to

17-A clean it
17-B soften it
17-C harden it
17-D prevent it from rusting

18. The cut of a file refers to the

18-A shape of its handle
18-B shape of its edge
18-C kind of metal it is made of
18-D kind of teeth it has

19. Wood ladders should not be painted because

19-A paint will wear off rapidly due to the conditions under which ladders are used
19-B ladders are slippery when painted
19-C it is more effective to store the ladder in a dry place
19-D paint will hide defects in the ladder

GO ON TO THE NEXT PAGE.

20.

The tool shown above is used to measure

20-A clearances
20-B wire thickness
20-C inside slots
20-D screw pitch

21. A lathe would normally be used in making which of the following items?

21-A a hockey stick
21-B a picture frame
21-C a bookcase
21-D a baseball bat

22. The term "whipping" when applied to rope means

22-A binding the ends with cord to prevent unraveling
22-B coiling the rope in as tight a ball as possible
22-C lubricating the strands with tallow
22-D wetting the rope with water to cure it

23. The set in the teeth of a hand saw primarily

23-A prevents the saw from binding
23-B makes the saw cut true
23-C gives the saw a sharper edge
23-D removes the sawdust

24. Lacquer thinner would most likely be used to

24-A clean oil paint from a brush immediately after use
24-B rinse a new paint brush before using it
24-C clean a paint brush upon which paint has hardened
24-D remove paint from the hands

25. The tool used to measure the depth of a hole is

25-A

25-B

25-C

25-D

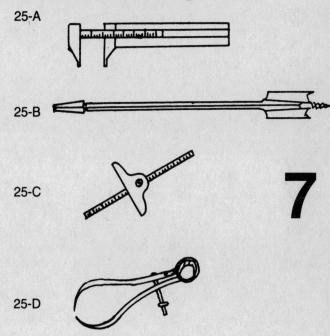

7

DO NOT TURN THIS PAGE UNTIL TOLD TO DO SO.
STOP! IF YOU FINISH BEFORE THE TIME IS UP, YOU
MAY CHECK OVER YOUR WORK ON THIS PART ONLY.

8

PART 8

MATHEMATICS KNOWLEDGE

8

Directions

This is a test of your ability to solve 25 general mathematical problems. You are to select the correct response from the choices given. Then mark the space on your answer form which has the same number and letter as your choice. Use the scratch paper that has been given to you to do any figuring that you wish.

Now look at the two sample problems below.

S1. If x + 6 = 7, then x is equal to

S1-A 0
S1-B 1
S1-C −1
S1-D $\frac{7}{6}$

The correct answer is 1, so B is the correct response.

S2. What is the area of this square?

S2-A 1 square foot
S2-B 5 square feet
S2-C 10 square feet
S2-D 25 square feet

The correct answer is 25 square feet, so D is the correct response.

Your score on this test will be based on the number of questions you answer correctly. You should try to answer every question. Do not spend too much time on any one question.

When you are told to begin, be sure to start with question number 1 in Part 8 of your test booklet and number 1 in Part 8 on your answer form.

DO NOT TURN THIS PAGE UNTIL TOLD TO DO SO.

8

MATHEMATICS KNOWLEDGE

TIME: 24 Minutes—25 Questions

1. The product of $(-4)(-3)$ is

    1-A +7
    1-B −7
    1-C +12
    1-D −12

2. When $2x - 1$ is multiplied by 10 the result is 70. What is the value of x?

    2-A 2
    2-B 12
    2-C 3
    2-D 4

3. If the circumference of a circle has the same numbered value as its area, then the radius of the circle must be

    3-A 1
    3-B 5
    3-C 2
    3-D 0

4. In the formula $I = p + prt$, what does I equal when $p = 500$, $r = 20\%$, $t = 2$?

    4-A 10,000
    4-B 700
    4-C 8,000
    4-D 12,000

5. If 5 pints of water are needed to water each square foot of lawn, the minimum gallons of water needed for a lawn 8′ by 12′ is

    5-A 5
    5-B 20
    5-C 40
    5-D 60

6. $25.726 \times .04 =$

    6-A 102.904
    6-B 10.2904
    6-C .0102904
    6-D 1.02904

7. $\sqrt{960}$ is a number between

    7-A 20 and 30
    7-B 60 and 70
    7-C 80 and 90
    7-D 30 and 40

8. $(6 + 8) - (21 - 4) =$

    8-A 14×17
    8-B $14 - 3$
    8-C $14 + 17$
    8-D $14 - 17$

9. If 50% of X = 66, then X =

    9-A 33
    9-B 66
    9-C 99
    9-D 132

10. If $\frac{3}{8}$ of a number is 96, the number is

    10-A 132
    10-B 36
    10-C 256
    10-D 156

11. A line of print in a magazine article contains an average of 6 words. There are 5 lines to the inch. If 8 inches are available for an article which contains 270 words, how must the article be changed?

    11-A Add 30 words.
    11-B Delete 30 words.
    11-C Delete 40 words.
    11-D Add 60 words.

12. $9\overline{)111111111} =$

    12-A 12345678
    12-B 11111119
    12-C 11191119
    12-D 12345679

GO ON TO THE NEXT PAGE.

8

13. If $\frac{3}{4}$ of a class is absent and $\frac{2}{3}$ of those present leave the room, what fraction of the original class remains in the room?

13-A $\frac{1}{24}$

13-B $\frac{1}{4}$

13-C $\frac{1}{12}$

13-D $\frac{1}{8}$

14. If $a = 3$, then $a^a \cdot a =$

14-A 9
14-B 51
14-C 18
14-D 81

15. A group left on a trip at 8:50 a.m. and reached its destination at 3:30 p.m. How long, in hours and minutes, did the trip take?

15-A 3 hours 10 minutes
15-B 4 hours 40 minutes
15-C 5 hours 10 minutes
15-D 6 hours 40 minutes

16. Solve for x: $\frac{2x}{7} = 2x^2$

16-A 1/7
16-B 2/7
16-C 2
16-D 7

17. Solve the following equation for C:

$$A^2 = \frac{B^2}{C + D}$$

17-A $C = \frac{B^2 - A^2D}{A^2B}$

17-B $C = \frac{A^2}{B^2} - D$

17-C $C = \frac{A^2 + D}{B^2 - D}$

17-D $C = \frac{B^2}{A^2} - D$

18. The expression, $-1 (3 - 2)$, is equal to

18-A $-3 + 2$
18-B $-3 - 2$
18-C $3 - 2$
18-D $3 + 2$

19. If $\frac{5}{4}x = \frac{5}{4}$, then $1 - x =$

19-A $-\frac{5}{4}$
19-B 1
19-C 0
19-D -1

20. If a piece of wood measuring 4 feet 2 inches is divided into three equal parts, each part is

20-A 1 foot, $4\frac{2}{3}$ inches

20-B 1 foot, $2\frac{1}{3}$ inches

20-C 1 foot, 4 inches

20-D 1 foot, $\frac{7}{18}$ inch

21. When 5.1 is divided by 0.017, the quotient is

21-A 30
21-B 300
21-C 3,000
21-D 30,000

22. The area of the figure shown can be determined by the formula

22-A $ac \div b$

22-B $\frac{1}{2}bh$

22-C $bc \div a$

22-D bh^2

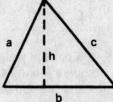

23. If psychological studies of college students show K percent to be emotionally unstable, the number of college students not emotionally unstable per one hundred college students is

23-A 100 minus K
23-B 1 minus K
23-C K minus 1
23-D 100 ÷ K

GO ON TO THE NEXT PAGE.

24. A cog wheel having 8 cogs plays into another cog wheel having 24 cogs. When the small wheel has made 42 revolutions, how many has the larger wheel made?

24-A 14
24-B 16
24-C 20
24-D 10

25. Angle ABD is

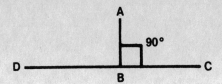

25-A a straight angle and contains 180°
25-B an acute angle and contains 35°
25-C a right angle and contains 90°
25-D a right angle and contains 45°

8

DO NOT TURN THIS PAGE UNTIL TOLD TO DO SO.
STOP! IF YOU FINISH BEFORE THE TIME IS UP, YOU
MAY CHECK OVER YOUR WORK ON THIS PART ONLY.

9

MECHANICAL COMPREHENSION

9

Directions

This test has 25 questions about mechanical principles. Most of the questions use drawings to illustrate specific principles. Decide which answer is correct and mark the space on your answer form which has the same number and letter as your choice.

Here are two sample questions.

S1. Which bridge is the strongest?

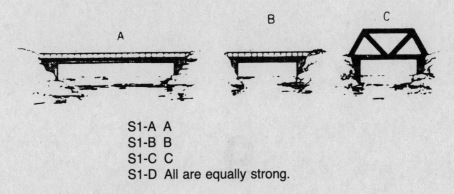

S1-A A
S1-B B
S1-C C
S1-D All are equally strong.

Answer C is correct.

S2. If all of these objects are the same temperature, which will feel coldest?

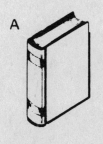 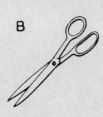  

S2-A A
S2-B B
S2-C C
S2-D D

Answer B is correct.

Your score on this test will be based on the number of questions you answer correctly. You should try to answer every question. Do not spend too much time on any one question.

When you are told to begin, be sure to start with question number 1 in Part 9 of your test booklet and number 1 in Part 9 on your answer form.

DO NOT TURN THIS PAGE UNTIL TOLD TO DO SO.

9

9

MECHANICAL COMPREHENSION

TIME: 19 Minutes—25 Questions

1.

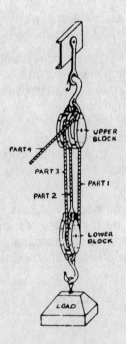

When a load is hoisted by means of the tackle shown above, the part that remains stationary is

1-A the load
1-B the lower block
1-C the lower hook
1-D the upper block

2.

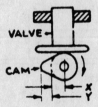

The figure above shows a cam and a valve. For each cam revolution, the vertical valve rise equals distance

2-A Y
2-B X
2-C X plus Y
2-D twice X

3.

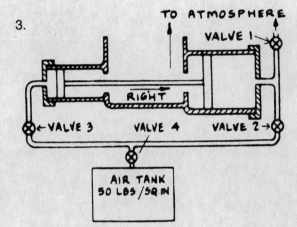

If all valves are closed at the start, in order to have air pressure from the tank move the pistons to the right, the valves to be opened are

3-A 2 and 4
3-B 2, 3, and 4
3-C 1 and 2
3-D 1, 3, and 4

4. In the figure shown below, one complete revolution of the sprocket wheel will bring weight W2 higher than weight W1 by

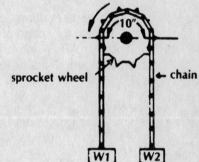

4-A 20 inches
4-B 30 inches
4-C 40 inches
4-D 50 inches

5. The figure below shows a worm and gear. If the worm rotates slowly on its shaft, the gear will

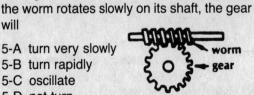

5-A turn very slowly
5-B turn rapidly
5-C oscillate
5-D not turn

GO ON TO THE NEXT PAGE.

9

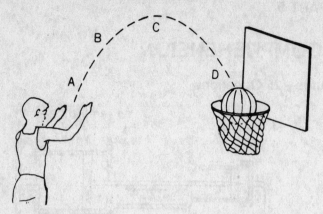

6. At which point was the basketball moving slowly?

6-A A
6-B B
6-C C
6-D D

7.

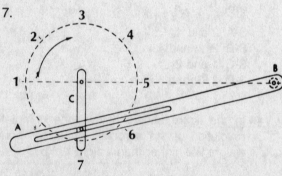

In the diagram above, crank arm C revolves at a constant speed of 400 rpm and drives the lever AB. When lever AB is moving the fastest, arm C will be in position

7-A 1
7-B 6
7-C 5
7-D 7

8. Assume that the color of the flame from a gas stove is bright yellow. To correct this, you should

8-A close the air flap
8-B increase the size of the gas opening
8-C increase the gas pressure
8-D open the air flap

9.

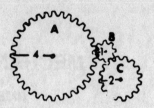

If gear A makes one clockwise revolution per minute, which of the following is true?

9-A Gear B makes one counterclockwise revolution every 4 minutes.
9-B Gear C makes two clockwise revolutions every minute.
9-C Gear B makes four clockwise revolutions every minute.
9-D Gear C makes one counterclockwise revolution every 8 minutes.

10. When the 100-pound weight is being slowly hoisted up by the pulley, as shown in the figure below, the downward pull on the ceiling to which the pulley is attached is

10-A 50 pounds
10-B 100 pounds
10-C 150 pounds
10-D 200 pounds

11.

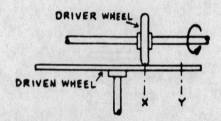

When the driver wheel is moved from location X to location Y, the driven wheel will

11-A reverse its direction of rotation
11-B turn slower
11-C not change its speed of rotation
11-D turn faster

GO ON TO THE NEXT PAGE.

12.

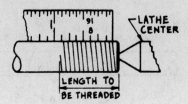

In the diagram above, the axle 8 inches in diameter has attached a handle 28 inches in diameter. If a force of 50 pounds is applied to the handle, the axle will lift a weight of

12-A 224 lbs.
12-B 175 lbs.
12-C 200 lbs.
12-D 88 lbs.

15.

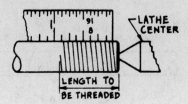

A very light cut (trace) is being measured as a check before cutting the thread on the lathe. The number of threads per inch shown is

15-A 12
15-B 14
15-C 13
15-D 15

9

16. The difference between the boiling point and the freezing point of water on the Celsius scale is

16-A 0°
16-B 100°
16-C 112°
16-D 180°

13.

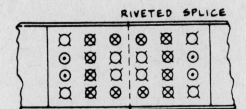

In the structural steel splice the different types of rivets are shown by different symbols. The number of different types of rivets is

13-A 6
13-B 4
13-C 5
13-D 3

14. The main purpose of baffle plates in a furnace is to

14-A change the direction of flow of heated gases
14-B retard the burning of gases
14-C increase combustion rate of the fuel
14-D prevent escape of flue gases through furnace openings

17. Liquid is being transferred from the barrel to the bucket by

17-A suction in the hose
17-B fluid pressure in the hose
17-C air pressure on top of the liquid
17-D capillary action

GO ON TO THE NEXT PAGE.

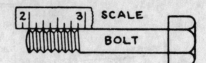

coupling
pipe A
pipe B
8 threads per inch

18. In the figure above, if pipe A is held in a vise and pipe B is turned 4 revolutions with a wrench, the overall length of the pipes and coupling will decrease

18-A $\frac{1}{8}$ inch

18-B $\frac{1}{4}$ inch

18-C $\frac{3}{8}$ inch

18-D $\frac{1}{2}$ inch

9

19.

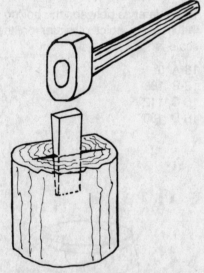

The simple machine pictured above is a form of

19-A inclined plane
19-B pulley
19-C spur gear
19-D torque

20.

SCALE

BOLT

The number of threads per inch on the bolt is

20-A 16
20-B 8
20-C 10
20-D 7

21. In order to open the valve in the figure below once every second, the wheel must rotate at

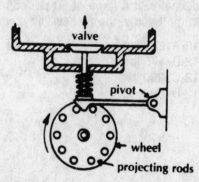

valve

pivot

wheel

projecting rods

21-A 6 rpm
21-B 10 rpm
21-C 20 rpm
21-D 30 rpm

22.

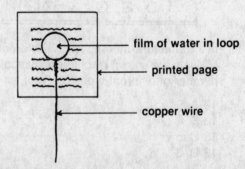

film of water in loop

printed page

copper wire

The print looked at through the film of water will

22-A be too blurred to read
22-B look the same as the surrounding print
22-C be enlarged
22-D appear smaller

GO ON TO THE NEXT PAGE.

23.

In the illustration above, if the man backs to the end of the seesaw, the woman will

23-A remain stationary
23-B rise in the air
23-C hit the ground hard
23-D slide to its end of the seesaw

24. Condensation on cold water pipes is frequently prevented by

24-A insulating the pipe
24-B keeping the temperature of cold water at least 10° above the freezing point
24-C keeping the cold water lines near the hot water lines
24-D oiling or greasing the outside of the pipe

25.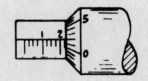

The micrometer above reads

25-A .2270
25-B .2120
25-C .2252
25-D .2020

9

DO NOT TURN THIS PAGE UNTIL TOLD TO DO SO.
STOP! IF YOU FINISH BEFORE THE TIME IS UP, YOU
MAY CHECK OVER YOUR WORK ON THIS PART ONLY.

10

ELECTRONICS INFORMATION

10

Directions

This is a test of your knowledge of electrical, radio, and electronics information. There are 20 questions. Your are to select the correct response from the choices given. Then mark the space on your answer form which has the same number and letter as your choice.

Now look at the two sample questions below.

S1. What does the abbreviation AC stand for?

S1-A additional charge
S1-B alternating coil
S1-C alternating current
S1-D ampere current

The correct answer is alternating current, so C is the correct response.

S2. Which of the following has the least resistance?

S2-A wood
S2-B silver
S2-C rubber
S2-D iron

The correct answer is silver, so B is the correct response.

Your score on this test will be based on the number of questions you answer correctly. You should try to answer every question. Do not spend too much time on any one question.

When you are told to begin, be sure to start with question number 1 in Part 10 of your test booklet and number 1 in Part 10 on your answer form.

DO NOT TURN THIS PAGE UNTIL TOLD TO DO SO.

10

ELECTRONICS INFORMATION

TIME: 9 Minutes—20 Questions

1. Boxes and fittings intended for outdoor use should be of

    1-A weatherproof type
    1-B stamped steel of not less than No. 16
    1-C standard gauge
    1-D stamped steel plated with cadmium

2. A direct-current supply may be obtained from an alternating-current source by means of

    2-A a frequency changer set
    2-B an inductance-capacitance filter
    2-C a silicon diode rectifier
    2-D none of the devices mentioned above

3. Fuses protecting motor circuits have to be selected to permit a momentary surge of

    3-A voltage when the motor starts
    3-B voltage when the motor stops
    3-C current when the motor starts
    3-D current when the motor stops

4. The device used to change AC to DC is a

    4-A frequency changer
    4-B transformer
    4-C regulator
    4-D rectifier

5.

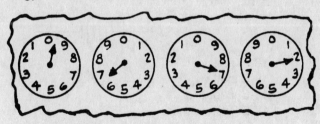

    The reading of the kilowatt-hour meter is

    5-A 9672
    5-B 1779
    5-C 2770
    5-D 0762

6. The device that is often used to change the voltage in alternating current circuits is the

    6-A contactor
    6-B converter
    6-C rectifier
    6-D transformer

7. The following equipment is required for a "2-line return-call" electric bell circuit:

    7-A 2 bells, 2 metallic lines, 2 ordinary push buttons, and one set of batteries
    7-B 2 bells, 2 metallic lines, 2 return-call push buttons, and 2 sets of batteries
    7-C 2 bells, 2 metallic lines, 2 return-call push buttons, and one set of batteries
    7-D 2 bells, 2 metallic lines, one ordinary push button, one return-call push button, and one set of batteries

10

8.

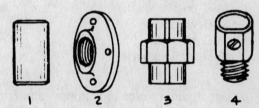

    The standard coupling for rigid electrical conduit is

    8-A 1
    8-B 2
    8-C 3
    8-D 4

9. Metal cabinets used for lighting circuits are grounded to

    9-A eliminate electrolysis
    9-B assure that the fuse in a defective circuit will blow
    9-C reduce shock hazard
    9-D simplify wiring

GO ON TO THE NEXT PAGE.

10

10. The one of the following devices that will store an electric charge is the

10-A capacitor
10-B inductor
10-C thyristor
10-D resistor

11. Of the nonmetallic elements listed below, which one is the best conductor of electricity?

11-A mica
11-B carbon
11-C formica
11-D hard rubber

12. If an electric motor designed for use on AC is plugged into a DC source, what will probably happen?

12-A Excessive heat will be produced.
12-B It will operate the same as usual.
12-C It will continue to operate, but will not get so warm.
12-D It cannot be predicted what will happen.

13. Silver is a better conductor of electricity than copper; however, copper is generally used for electrical conductors. The main reason for using copper instead of silver is its

13-A cost
13-B weight
13-C strength
13-D melting point

14. Direct current arcs are "hotter" and harder to extinguish than alternating current arcs, so that electrical appliances which include a thermostat are frequently marked for use on "AC only." One appliance which might be so marked because it includes a thermostat is a

14-A soldering iron
14-B floor waxer
14-C vacuum cleaner
14-D household iron

15. An alternator is

15-A an AC generator
15-B a frequency meter
15-C a ground detector device
15-D a choke coil

16.

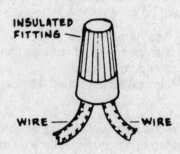

Wires are often spliced by the use of a fitting like the one shown above. The use of this fitting does away with the need for

16-A skinning
16-B cleaning
16-C twisting
16-D soldering

17. in order to control a lamp from two different positions it is necessary to use

17-A two single-pole switches
17-B one single-pole switch and one four-way switch
17-C two three-way switches
17-D one single-pole switch and two four-way switches

18. In electronic circuits, the symbol shown below usually represents a

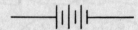

18-A resistor
18-B battery
18-C capacitor
18-D transformer

GO ON TO THE NEXT PAGE.

19. Rosin is a material generally used

19-A in batteries
19-B for high voltage insulation
19-C as a dielectric
19-D as a soldering flux

20. The letters RHW when applied to electrical wire indicate the wire

20-A has a solid conductor
20-B has rubber insulation
20-C is insulated with paper
20-D has lead sheath

END OF EXAMINATION

10

IF YOU FINISH BEFORE TIME IS UP, YOU MAY CHECK OVER YOUR WORK ON THIS PART ONLY. DO NOT GO BACK TO ANY PREVIOUS PART.

ANSWER KEY—SECOND ASVAB SPECIMEN TEST

Use these answer keys to determine how many questions you answered correctly on each part and to list those items which you answered incorrectly or which you are not sure how to answer.

Be certain to review carefully and understand the rationale for arriving at the correct answer for all questions you answered incorrectly, as well as those you answered correctly but are unsure of. This is absolutely essential in order to acquire the knowledge and expertise necessary to obtain the maximum scores possible on the actual ASVAB subtests.

Transfer the scores you obtained on each part of the Second ASVAB Specimen Test to the Self-Appraisal Chart appearing on page 275. This will enable you to see the progress made as you continue to prepare for the actual test.

PART 1—GENERAL SCIENCE

1. C	5. A	8. C	11. D	14. B	17. D	20. A	23. A
2. D	6. D	9. B	12. B	15. C	18. C	21. C	24. D
3. C	7. C	10. A	13. C	16. D	19. B	22. B	25. B
4. A							

Items
Answered
Incorrectly: ___; ___; ___; ___; ___; ___; ___; ___.

Items
Unsure
Of: ___; ___; ___; ___; ___; ___; ___; ___.

Total
Number
Answered
Correctly: _____

PART 2—ARITHMETIC REASONING

1. B	5. D	9. B	13. B	17. C	21. B	25. B	28. D
2. B	6. B	10. A	14. B	18. A	22. C	26. D	29. B
3. D	7. D	11. C	15. D	19. B	23. B	27. C	30. D
4. D	8. C	12. B	16. B	20. A	24. B		

Items
Answered
Incorrectly: ____; ____; ____; ____; ____; ____; ____; ____.

Items
Unsure
Of: ____; ____; ____; ____; ____; ____; ____; ____.

Total
Number
Answered
Correctly: _____

PART 3—WORD KNOWLEDGE

1. D	6. B	11. A	16. D	20. B	24. D	28. A	32. C
2. B	7. D	12. D	17. C	21. A	25. B	29. A	33. D
3. C	8. B	13. D	18. A	22. C	26. A	30. A	34. D
4. D	9. A	14. C	19. C	23. B	27. B	31. D	35. D
5. A	10. D	15. A					

Items
Answered
Incorrectly: ____; ____; ____; ____; ____; ____; ____; ____.

Items
Unsure
Of: ____; ____; ____; ____; ____; ____; ____; ____.

Total
Number
Answered
Correctly: _____

PART 4—PARAGRAPH COMPREHENSION

1. A	3. C	5. C	7. A	9. B	11. C	13. A	15. D
2. C	4. B	6. A	8. B	10. D	12. D	14. B	

Items
Answered
Incorrectly: ____; ____; ____; ____; ____; ____; ____; ____.

Items
Unsure
Of: ____; ____; ____; ____; ____; ____; ____; ____.

Total
Number
Answered
Correctly: _____

PART 5—NUMERICAL OPERATIONS

1. C	8. B	15. B	21. A	27. C	33. D	39. A	45. C
2. B	9. C	16. D	22. D	28. A	34. C	40. C	46. A
3. B	10. D	17. C	23. C	29. B	35. D	41. B	47. A
4. B	11. C	18. B	24. B	30. C	36. A	42. D	48. D
5. D	12. C	19. C	25. A	31. C	37. D	43. A	49. A
6. A	13. D	20. B	26. B	32. B	38. A	44. D	50. C
7. A	14. B						

Items
Answered
Incorrectly: ___; ___; ___; ___; ___; ___; ___; ___.

Items
Unsure
Of: ___; ___; ___; ___; ___; ___; ___; ___.

Total
Number
Answered
Correctly: _____

PART 6—CODING SPEED

1. D	12. C	23. C	34. A	45. A	55. C	65. B	75. E
2. E	13. D	24. A	35. B	46. E	56. B	66. E	76. D
3. B	14. A	25. E	36. A	47. D	57. A	67. E	77. A
4. A	15. B	26. B	37. C	48. A	58. A	68. C	78. B
5. E	16. B	27. D	38. C	49. D	59. E	69. E	79. E
6. B	17. B	28. E	39. E	50. B	60. C	70. A	80. A
7. A	18. C	29. B	40. C	51. E	61. D	71. B	81. A
8. A	19. B	30. A	41. B	52. E	62. C	72. A	82. E
9. E	20. E	31. E	42. A	53. D	63. C	73. C	83. C
10. E	21. E	32. C	43. C	54. B	64. B	74. D	84. B
11. E	22. D	33. E	44. E				

Items
Answered
Incorrectly: ___; ___; ___; ___; ___; ___; ___; ___.

Items
Unsure
Of: ___; ___; ___; ___; ___; ___; ___; ___.

Total
Number
Answered
Correctly: _____

PART 7—AUTO & SHOP INFORMATION

1. C	5. C	8. D	11. B	14. C	17. A	20. D	23. A
2. D	6. C	9. C	12. D	15. A	18. D	21. D	24. C
3. B	7. D	10. B	13. A	16. C	19. D	22. A	25. C
4. A							

Items
Answered
Incorrectly: ___; ___; ___; ___; ___; ___; ___; ___.

Items
Unsure
Of: ___; ___; ___; ___; ___; ___; ___; ___.

Total
Number
Answered
Correctly: _____

PART 8—MATHEMATICS KNOWLEDGE

1. C	5. D	8. D	11. B	14. D	17. D	20. A	23. A
2. D	6. D	9. D	12. D	15. D	18. A	21. B	24. A
3. C	7. D	10. C	13. C	16. A	19. C	22. B	25. C
4. B							

Items
Answered
Incorrectly: ___; ___; ___; ___; ___; ___; ___; ___.

Items
Unsure
Of: ___; ___; ___; ___; ___; ___; ___; ___.

Total
Number
Answered
Correctly: _____

PART 9—MECHANICAL COMPREHENSION

1. D	5. A	8. D	11. B	14. A	17. C	20. B	23. B
2. A	6. C	9. B	12. B	15. C	18. D	21. A	24. A
3. D	7. C	10. C	13. B	16. B	19. A	22. C	25. A
4. C							

Items
Answered
Incorrectly: ___; ___; ___; ___; ___; ___; ___; ___.

Items
Unsure
Of: ___; ___; ___; ___; ___; ___; ___; ___.

Total
Number
Answered
Correctly: _____

PART 10—ELECTRONICS INFORMATION

1. A	4. D	7. B	10. A	13. A	15. A	17. C	19. D
2. C	5. A	8. A	11. B	14. D	16. D	18. B	20. B
3. C	6. D	9. C	12. A				

Items
Answered
Incorrectly: ___; ___; ___; ___; ___; ___; ___; ___.

Items
Unsure
Of: ___; ___; ___; ___; ___; ___; ___; ___.

Total
Number
Answered
Correctly: _____

EXPLANATIONS—SECOND ASVAB SPECIMEN TEST

PART 1—GENERAL SCIENCE

1-C Citrus fruits include lemons, limes, oranges, and grapefruits.

2-D Water freezes at 0° on a centrigrade or Celsius thermometer. Water freezes at 32° Fahrenheit.

3-C The major chemical constituent of a cell by importance is protein, but by weight it is water.

4-A Of the metals listed, only mercury is a liquid at room temperature. The other three metals are solids at room temperature.

5-A The lack of apparent gravitational pull is termed weightlessness.

6-D Meteors or "shooting stars" come into the earth's atmosphere from outer space with high velocity. The resistance offered by the earth's atmosphere makes these meteors incandescent in flight.

7-C While the hereditary components of most diseases are still under study, the hereditary nature of sickle cell anemia is documented and well understood. Sickle cell anemia is most common among black people.

8-C Water boils at 212°F and freezes at 32°F. 212° − 32° = 180°.

9-B As viewed from space, one-half of the moon is always illuminated by the sun. However, as the moon changes its position in its orbit around the earth, different amounts of the illuminated side are visible from the earth.

10-A The salivary glands secrete the enzyme ptyalin which acts on carbohydrates.

11-D Vitamin K is useful in the coagulation of blood. Vitamin C prevents scurvy; vitamin E maintains muscle tone and aids in fertility; vitamin D prevents rickets.

12-B A bulkhead is a wall; the anchor keeps the ship from moving; and the prow is the front of the ship.

13-C The primary reason for lowering the center of gravity in automobiles is to increase stability. Stability is increased largely by lowering the center of gravity and by increasing the width of the automobile.

14-B A substance that changes the rate of a chemical reaction but is itself unchanged at the end of the reaction is called a catalyst.

15-C Ice changes into water when it melts or liquefies. This is an example of a physical change as the chemical composition remains the same.

16-D Ball-and-socket joints permit movement in almost all directions.

17-D Scurvy is a disease caused by a vitamin C deficiency. Limes are rich in vitamin C.

18-C The earth rotates 360° in 24 hours, therefore it rotates 45° in three hours.

19-B Vitamin C, contained in citrus fruits, tomatoes, and green vegetables, is also known as ascorbic acid.

20-A Radiation is the process by which energy is transferred in space.

21-C Barometric pressure is expressed in inches. The range is generally from 28 to 31 inches.

22-B A tumor is a growth. A malignant tumor or growth is a cancer.

23-A Steel is a compound of iron and carbon.

24-D The greatest danger during exercise under hot, dry conditions is that of dehydration. A person can survive for a relatively long period of time without food, but for only a short time without water. Hot, dry conditions make the need for water more urgent.

25-B The moon is a satellite of the earth.

PART 2—ARITHMETIC REASONING

1-B 3 for 20¢ × 4 = 12 for 80¢
80¢ − 70¢ = 10¢ profit per dozen
10¢ × 6 doz. = 60¢ total profit

2-B 60 ft. = 20 yd. The wall is
4 yd. × 20 yd. = 80 sq. yd.
$10.50 × 80 = $840.

3-D $6\frac{1}{2}$ pounds − 4 pounds = $2\frac{1}{2}$ pounds

There are 5 half-pounds in $2\frac{1}{2}$ pounds.

$9.26 + 5(1.06) = $9.26 + 5.30
= $14.56

4-D 20 peaches are 5 × 4 peaches; 4 peaches cost $.50; 5 × $.50 = $2.50

5-D
$$10 \times \$1.00 = \$10.00$$
$$9 \times .50 = 4.50$$
$$8 \times .25 = 2.00$$
$$16 \times .10 = 1.60$$
$$25 \times .05 = \underline{1.25}$$
$$\$19.35$$

6-B 60 minutes in one hour; 24 hours in one day; 60 × 24 = 1,440 minutes.

7-D There are 144 pencils in a gross; 144 × 6 = 864 pencils in all. 864 ÷ 24 = 36 weeks' worth of pencils.

8-C
$$\frac{3}{8} = \frac{9}{24}$$
$$\frac{1}{4} = \frac{6}{24}$$
$$\frac{1}{6} = \frac{4}{24}$$
$$\frac{19}{24}$$ of the pads were issued;

$\frac{5}{24}$ remained $\frac{5}{\cancel{24}} \times \frac{\cancel{600}^{25}}{1} = 125$ pads remained
                          ₁

9-B The regular cost of 4 records was
$6.98 × 4 = $27.92
The sale price of 4 records was
$12.50 × 2 = $25.00
$27.92 − $25.00 = $2.92

10-A 1 hour = 60 minutes. At 3 miles per hour, the student covers 1 mile every 20 minutes. Therefore she will need 40 minutes to walk 2 miles.

11-C 8 a.m. + 15 hours = 23 o'clock = 11 p.m.

12-B Express the relationship of games won to games played as a fraction: $\frac{8}{24}$.

Reduce to lowest terms: $\frac{8}{24} = \frac{1}{3}$.

Then convert to a percent:

$\frac{1}{3} = .33\frac{1}{3} = 33\frac{1}{3}\%$

13-B 80 cards × 7 hours = 560 cards filed; 800 − 560 = 240 cards remaining.

14-B To find percent of increase, subtract the original figure from the new figure. Then divide the amount of change by the original figure.
$380 − $350 = $30; $30 ÷ $350 = .0857
(which is approximately $8\frac{1}{2}\%$).

15-D 40 miles ÷ 20 mph = 2 hrs.

16-B $\frac{2}{\cancel{5}} \times \frac{\cancel{100}^{20}}{1} = 40$ gal.
        ₁

17-C If 20% is deducted, the net salary is 80%.
$20,000 × 80% = $20,000 × .80 = $16,000.

18-A $2,000 ÷ 100 = $20

19-B Add the three monthly totals, then divide by 3 to find the average monthly cost:

$42.30
 38.60 $123.90 ÷ 3 = $41.30
 43.00

$123.90

20-A 10 × ½ hour = 5 hours

21-B 1,400 miles ÷ 50 mph = 28 hours

22-C Let x = original price
x × .25 = .25x
x − .25x = $112.50
.75x = $112.50
$x = \dfrac{\$112.50}{.75} = \$150$

23-B $241.75 + $13.24 + $102.97 = $357.96
$627.04 − $357.96 = $269.08

24-B 250 × .08 = $20.00; 250 × .07 = $17.50; 500 erasers cost $37.50; $50.00 − $37.50 = $12.50. Let x = additional erasers purchased. x × .05 = 12.50; $x = \dfrac{12.50}{.05} =$ 250; 500 + 250 = 750 erasers.

25-B 1 : 200 = x : 375; 200x = 375; x = 375 ÷ 200 = 1.875 = $1\frac{7}{8}$ inches.

26-D $10\frac{1}{4}$ lbs. $\div \frac{1}{2} = \frac{41}{\cancel{4}_2} \times \frac{\cancel{2}^{1}}{1} = 20\frac{1}{2}$ boxes

27-C 4 feet = 48 inches;

$48 \div \frac{3}{4} = \frac{\cancel{48}^{16}}{1} \times \frac{4}{\cancel{3}_1} = 64$ magazines

28-D $\frac{1}{2}$ cup of spinach = 80 calories

$\frac{1}{2}$ cup of peas = 300 calories

1 cup of peas = 600 calories

$\frac{2}{3}$ cup of peas = 400 calories

400 ÷ 80 = 5 half cups of spinach

= $2\frac{1}{2}$ cups of spinach

29-B 30 min. for 6 pages; 1 hr. for 12 pages; 126 ÷ 12 = 10.5 hrs.

30-D 9 hrs. = 540 mins.; 540 ÷ 45 = 12 The night watchman stops at the storage area 12 times during his tour plus once at the beginning of his tour of duty for a total of 13 times.

PART 3—WORD KNOWLEDGE

1-D *Superiority* is *excellence.*

2-B *Absurd* means *irrational, unreasonable,* or *foolish.*

3-C *Inflammable* means *easily inflamed,* hence *explosive.*

4-D The word *intermittently* means recurring from time to time.

5-A The word *occurrence* is synonymous with *event* or *incident.*

6-B *Deception* means fraud or subterfuge.

7-D The *captive* is the one who was *captured* and made *prisoner,* regardless of the reason for his capture.

8-B The term *vegetation* includes all *plant life.*

9-A *Fictitious* means *imaginary.*

10-D To *suspend* is to *stop temporarily.*

11-A A *territory* is a *large expanse of land or water,* a *region.*

12-D *Huge* means *very large, enormous,* or *immense.*

13-D To *heed* is to *pay attention to* or to *take notice of.*

14-C *Vigorously* means *forcefully* and *energetically.*

15-A To *imitate* is to *copy.*

16-D *Alias* means an assumed or other name.

17-C *Impair* means to make worse or weaken.

18-A *Itinerant* means journeying or traveling.

19-C To *defend* is to *protect* from harm, verbal or bodily.

20-B An *aim* is an *intention* or *goal.* To aim is to direct towards the goal.

21-A To *assemble* is to *congregate,* to *convene,* or to *bring together.*

22-C To *instruct* is to *teach;* an *instructor* is a *teacher.*

23-B To *commend* is to *recommend* as *worthy of notice* or to *praise.*

24-D To *revolve* is to *turn around* or to *rotate.*

25-B The prefix *non* means *not.* That which is *not essential* is *unnecessary.*

26-A To *amplify* is to *enlarge* by adding illustrations or details, in short, to *expand.*

27-B *Intact* means *unimpaired, whole,* or *undamaged.*

28-A The word *tapestry* means a fabric woven to produce a design.

29-A *Terse* means concise or brief.

30-A The word *concoction* means a combination of ingredients.

31-D To *acquire* is to *get* or to *obtain* by any means.

32-C *Exhaustion* is the *using up of energy or resources, extreme tiredness* or *fatigue.*

33-D *Ajar* means *open.*

34-D *Steady* means *constant* and *regular.*

35-D To *emphasize* is to *stress.*

PART 4—PARAGRAPH COMPREHENSION

1-A The passage states that physical examinations are intended to increase efficiency and production, and that they do accomplish these ends.

2-C The first sentence states that a good or service has value only because people want it.

3-C When the activities of an individual come in conflict with the community interest, the individual's rights are no longer considered to be of greatest importance but actually become secondary.

4-B One chief justice plus eight associate justices equals nine justices.

5-C The last sentence in the passage states that the real danger is in a large leak which can cause an explosion.

6-A The business of publishing city directories is a private business operated for profit. As such, it is a commercial enterprise.

7-A The survey showed that of all the subjects, typing helped most in business. It was also considered valuable by college students in their schoolwork.

8-B The passage states that the X-ray machine "contributes to precision and accuracy in industry."

9-B See the first sentence in the reading passage.

10-D The second sentence states that crime is the result of opportunity plus desire. Accordingly, to prevent crime, it is each individual's responsibility to prevent the opportunity.

11-C The third sentence states that heating the drill will spoil its temper and cutting edges.

12-D The second sentence states that the drill point must be withdrawn frequently to cool it.

13-A The first sentence in the passage states that arsonists set fires deliberately or intentionally.

14-B The last sentence in the passage states that some arsonists just like the excitement of seeing the fire burn and watching the firefighters at work, and even helping fight the fire.

15-D The first three options are not supported by the passage. Different types of arsonists mentioned in the passage leads to the conclusion that arsonists are not all alike.

PART 5—NUMERICAL OPERATIONS

1-C $2 + 3 = 5$

2-B $8 - 5 = 3$

3-B $9 \div 3 = 3$

4-B $4 + 6 = 10$

5-D $6 \times 3 = 18$

6-A $9 + 5 = 14$

7-A $3 + 9 = 12$

8-B $7 + 8 = 15$

9-C $3 \times 8 = 24$

10-D $3 \times 2 = 6$

11-C $1 - 1 = 0$

12-C $2 \times 9 = 18$

13-D $9 + 3 = 12$

14-B $8 + 16 = 24$

15-B $9 - 4 = 5$

16-D $6 + 8 = 14$

17-C $4 \times 6 = 24$

18-B $3 \div 3 = 1$

19-C $5 + 8 = 13$

20-B $7 - 6 = 1$

21-A $8 - 3 = 5$

22-D $5 + 8 = 13$

23-C $20 \div 2 = 10$

24-B $15 - 7 = 8$

25-A $6 \div 2 = 3$

26-B $7 - 2 = 5$

27-C $10 \div 2 = 5$

28-A $15 \div 3 = 5$

29-B $2 \times 8 = 16$

30-C $1 + 6 = 7$

31-C $2 \times 9 = 18$

32-B $7 + 3 = 10$

33-D $30 \div 3 = 10$

34-C $7 + 9 = 16$

35-D $15 \times 5 = 75$

36-A $4 - 3 = 1$

37-D $7 + 5 = 12$

38-A $27 \div 9 = 3$

39-A $6 + 4 = 10$

40-C $6 \times 6 = 36$

41-B $8 + 9 = 17$

42-D $1 + 3 = 4$

43-A $16 \div 4 = 4$

44-D $9 \times 9 = 81$

45-C $5 + 7 = 12$

46-A $30 \div 15 = 2$

47-A $7 + 5 = 12$

48-D $3 \times 6 = 18$

49-A $9 - 6 = 3$

50-C $4 \times 6 = 24$

PART 6—CODING SPEED

There is no way to explain the answers to the Coding Speed questions; they are either right or wrong. If you still find yourself making many mistakes, try to develop a new strategy on the next specimen test.

PART 7—AUTO & SHOP INFORMATION

1-C Automobiles use internal combustion engines. Gasoline is exploded inside a cylinder to produce power.

2-D The four strokes of an internal combustion engine are the intake stroke, the compression stroke, the power stroke, and the exhaust stroke.

3-B Vapor-lock usually occurs when the gasoline in the gas line has turned to vapor and the carburetor does not get enough gasoline.

4-A The conditions stated indicate that the battery is not properly charged. The conditions are corrected generally by either recharging or replacing the battery.

5-C A dead battery, defective battery cables, or corrosion between the cables and the battery posts are common causes for failure of an automobile engine to "turn over." If the battery charge is normal, the next best thing to check is the connection between the battery cables and battery posts.

6-C The generator or alternator is usually mounted at the front of the engine and is linked by a fan belt to the engine's crankshaft pulley.

7-D If the spark plug gap was set closer than required, the spark plugs would fire sooner than necessary. This would cause a rougher idle speed and a longer power stroke.

8-D The device being described is a voltage regulator. When the battery becomes fully charged, a relay opens up so that the battery doesn't overcharge. A permanently closed voltage regulator will cause overcharging.

9-C The piston rings form a seal around the piston and the wall of the cylinder. Dirty oil in the crankcase will stop the rings from working properly.

10-B Water freezes at 32°F, or 0°C. Adding alcohol will cause the water to freeze at a lower temperature and will help prevent the engine block from cracking. *Note:* When water freezes it expands, and the pressure created can crack an engine block.

11-B The ignition coil in a gasoline engine builds up a low voltage current supplied by the battery to the high voltage needed by the spark plugs.

12-D A wooden mallet is used in woodworking. The other hammers are made of steel. They are too hard and might crack a wood chisel. Choice A is a ball peen hammer, choice B is a straight peen hammer, and choice C is a brick hammer.

13-A By placing a screwdriver at the end of a brace, you will have a much wider turning arc than by just using an ordinary screwdriver. The wider the turning arc, the more force that the screwdriver will exert. Screwdrivers with wide handles exert more force than those with narrow handles.

14-C This is a Philips-head screwdriver. It will turn Philips head screws with this shape:

15-A A jointer plane is used for planing wood when close tolerances are required.

16-C Tempering brings steel to the desired hardness and strength.

17-A Sheet metal is generally cleaned by using an industrial grade of sulphuric acid.

18-D The cut of a file refers to the kind of teeth it has. It may have single-cut or double-cut teeth. The teeth also have different degrees of fineness.

19-D One would not be able to see a defect in a painted ladder, such as a knot or a split in the wood. A ladder should *never* be painted.

20-D When a blade in the gauge matches the threads in the screw, the measure is the screw pitch.

21-D A lathe is a machine which rotates a piece of wood in order to create a uniform circular design when the wood is cut with a chisel. A baseball bat is the only round object.

22-A A rope is made from many separate strands of hemp or synthetic fiber, such as nylon. When a rope is cut, the strands can unravel if the ends are not whipped or wrapped with cord.

23-A The set is the angle at which the teeth are bent. It makes the teeth stand out from the rest of the saw and prevents the saw from getting stuck or binding to the stock.

24-C Lacquer thinner is a strong solvent and will dissolve hardened paint.

25-C The flattened part of tool C rests at the top of the hole and the ruler is then pushed down into the hole until it reaches the bottom. The depth of the hole is then read from the ruler.

PART 8—MATHEMATICS KNOWLEDGE

1-C An even number of negative signs when multiplying gives a positive product.
$(-4)(-3) = +12$

2-D $(2x - 1)(10) = 70$; divide both sides by 10
$2x - 1 = 7$; add 1 to both sides
$2x = 8$; divide both sides by 2
$x = 4$

3-C The formula to find the circumference of a circle is $2\pi r$. The formula to find the area of a circle is πr^2. The only number that has the same value when multiplied by 2 or squared is 2.

4-B $I = 500 + (500 \times .20 \times 2)$
$I = 500 + 200$
$I = 700$

5-D The lawn is $8' \times 12' = 96$ sq. ft.
$96 \times 5 = 480$ pints of water needed
8 pts. in 1 gal.; $480 \div 8 = 60$ gallons needed

6-D To place the decimal point in the product, add together the number of digits to the right of the decimal points in all of the multipliers.
$25.726 \times .04 = 1.02904$ (3 decimal places + 2 decimal places = 5 decimal places)

7-D The first step in finding a square root is grouping the digits into pairs, starting at the decimal point. If necessary, place a 0 to the left of the first digit to create a pair. Each pair represents one digit in the square root. The square root of 960 is a two digit number in the 30's because the square root of 09 is 3.

8-D Perform the operations within the parentheses first. Then remove the parentheses.

9-D $50\% = .50 = \dfrac{1}{2}$

$\dfrac{1}{2}x = 66$

$x = 66 \times 2$

$x = 132$

10-C $\dfrac{3}{8}x = 96$

$3x = 96 \times 8 = 768$

$x = 256$

11-B 6 words per line $\times$ 5 lines per inch $= 30$ words per inch
30 words per inch $\times$ 8 inches $= 240$ words
If the article has 270 words and there is space for only 240 words, then 30 words must be deleted.

12-D

```
        12345679
     9)111111111
        9
        ‾‾
        21
        18
        ‾‾
        31
        27
        ‾‾
        41
        36
        ‾‾
        51
        45
        ‾‾
        61
        54
        ‾‾
        71
        63
        ‾‾
        81
        81
        ‾‾
         0
```

13-C If ¾ are absent, ¼ are present. If ⅔ of the ¼ present leave, ⅓ of the ¼ remain.
⅓ × ¼ = 1/12 remain in the room

14-D $3^3 \times 3 = 27 \times 3 = 81$

15-D First convert to a 24-hour clock.

3:30 p.m. = 15:30 o'clock
$$15:30 \quad = 14:90$$
$$\underline{-8:50 \quad = \quad 8:50}$$
$$\qquad\qquad\quad 6:40 = 6 \text{ hours } 40 \text{ minutes}$$

To subtract a larger number of minutes from a smaller number of minutes, borrow 60 minutes from the hour to enlarge the smaller number.

16-A $\dfrac{2x}{7} = 2x^2; \quad 14x^2 = 2x; \quad \dfrac{\overset{7x}{\cancel{14x^2}}}{\underset{1}{\cancel{2x}}} = 1;$

$$7x = 1; \quad x = 1/7$$

17-D $A^2 = \dfrac{B^2}{C + D}; A^2(C + D) = B^2;$

$$C + D = \dfrac{B^2}{A^2}; C = \dfrac{B^2}{A^2} - D$$

18-A $-1(3-2) = -3 + 2$

19-C $\dfrac{5}{4}x = \dfrac{5}{4}$

$$x = \dfrac{5}{4} \div \dfrac{5}{4} = \dfrac{\overset{1}{\cancel{5}}}{\underset{1}{\cancel{4}}} \times \dfrac{\overset{1}{\cancel{4}}}{\underset{1}{\cancel{5}}} = 1; \quad 1 - 1 = 0$$

20-A For ease in division, convert the feet into inches. The piece of wood is 50 inches long.

$$50 \div 3 = 16\dfrac{2}{3} \text{ in.} = 1 \text{ ft. } 4\dfrac{2}{3} \text{ in. per part.}$$

21-B

$$0.017\overline{)5.100}^{\,300.}$$

To divide by a decimal, move the decimal point of the divisor to the right until the divisor becomes a whole number. Move the decimal point of the dividend to the right the same number of spaces. Place the decimal point of the quotient directly above the decimal point in the dividend.

22-B The formula for the area of a triangle is one half the base times the height.

23-A "Percent" means out of 100. If K percent are emotionally unstable, then K out of 100 are emotionally unstable. The remainder, 100 − K, are not unstable.

24-A The larger wheel is 3 times the size of the smaller wheel, so it makes one third the revolutions.
42 ÷ 3 = 14

25-C Angle ABC and angle ABD are supplementary angles. Since angle ABC = 90°, angle ABD must also equal 90° (180° − 90° = 90°). A right angle contains 90°.

PART 9—MECHANICAL COMPREHENSION

1-D Since the upper block is connected to an immovable hook, it must remain stationary.

2-A The distortion of the cam causes the valve to rise when contact is made. The amount of this distortion is the length Y.

3-D To move the pistons to the right, valves 1, 3, and 4 must be open. Valve 4 permits the air to enter the system; valve 3 allows the air to hit the left side of the piston; and valve 1 is an exhaust channel for the air.

4-C The circumference of the wheel is 20 in. One complete revolution will raise W2 20 in. and lower W1 20 in., a difference of 40 in.

5-A For every full rotation of the worm shaft, the gear will turn only 22°.

6-C The vertical component of the momentum of the ball is zero only at position C.

7-C The slowest points for lever AB are 3 and 7 where the direction reverses and the velocity momentarily becomes zero. The midpoint, 5, represents the maximum speed, as it is halfway between these minimum points.

8-D A yellow flame means too much fuel or too little oxygen is present during combustion. For complete combustion: fuel + oxygen → carbon dioxide + water. The best answer is to allow more air to enter and mix with the gas.

9-B Gear A turns in the opposite direction from gear B. A clockwise turn of A results in a counterclockwise revolution of B. Since the distance traversed by A (perimeter = $\pi \times$ diameter = $\pi \times 4$) is twice that of C (perimeter = $\pi \times 2$), the speed of C is doubled.

10-C The downward pull equals the 100-lb. weight being hoisted plus the 50-lb. effort. 100 lbs. + 50 lbs. = 150 lbs.

11-B Imagine the driven wheel as a record. For one rotation of the record, point y travels much further than point x. It takes more turns of the driver wheel to turn point y one complete revolution.

12-B The diameter of the handle is 3½ times ($^{28}/_8$) the diameter of the axle. When 50 lbs. of force is applied to the handle, it is multiplied by 3½ times, or, $^{28}/_8 \times 50$ = 175 lbs.

13-B There are only 4 different types of symbols shown in the pictures:

14-A To increase the efficiency of heating gas, baffles cause gases to mix more thoroughly and thereby to come in closer contact with the heating elements in a furnace.

15-C The problem here is that only part of a ruler is shown. Count 4 units on the 8th scale. This corresponds to $6\frac{1}{2}$ threads on the length to be threaded. Doubling the $6\frac{1}{2}$ threads (in $\frac{1}{2}$ inch) we get 13 threads in 1 inch.

16-B Boiling Point = 100°; Freezing Point = 0°; 100° − 0° = 100°.

17-C The air pressure on top of the liquid forces the liquid through the hose into the bucket.

18-D if pipe B is turned 4 revolutions and there are 8 threads per inch, the overall length would decrease by 4 threads, or $\frac{1}{2}$ inch.

19-A An inclined plane is a sloping, triangular shape, used here as a wedge to force open an axe cut made in the wood.

20-B The bolt thread makes one revolution per eighth of an inch, or has 8 threads in one inch.

21-A Once every second = 60 times a minute. With 10 projection rods on the wheel, the wheel must rotate at 6 rpm to make 60 rod contacts per minute.

22-C The film of water inside the loop would form a lens which would enlarge the printing on the page. if you look through a water-filled globe, objects will also appear larger.

23-B If the man moves to the back of the seesaw, his moment (weight × distance from center) will increase. The woman, who is lighter, will rise in the air.

24-A Insulating the pipes keeps warm moisture laden air from coming into contact with the cold pipes. This stops condensation.

25-A The measurements which can be made on the micrometer are: a) 2 major divisions and 1 minor division on the ruler-type scale, or: .2 + .025 = .225; b) 2 minor divisions above 0 on the rotating scale, or .002. Summing, we find the final measurement is: .225 + .002 = .227.

PART 10—ELECTRONICS INFORMATION

1-A Outdoor boxes and fittings must be weatherproof to withstand any problems caused by moisture.

2-C A rectifier is a device which converts AC current into DC current by allowing the current to flow in only one direction while blocking the flow of electricity in the reverse direction.

3-C The starting current of a motor is normally six times greater than its running current.

4-D A rectifier or diode is a device that changes AC to DC.

5-A When a kilowatt-hour meter is read, the number that comes just before the indicator is the number that is important. The answer would then be 9672 KwH.

6-D Converters change DC to AC. Rectifiers change AC to DC. Contactors are remote controlled switches frequently used as part of elevator controls. Transformers change voltages in AC circuits in accordance with the ratio of the number of turns in the secondary winding to the number of turns in the primary winding.

7-B A "2-line return-call" electric bell circuit would have 2 bells, 2 metallic lines, 2 return-call push buttons, and 2 sets of batteries. It might look like this:

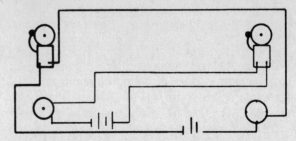

8-A Figure 1, a connector, is used to join two sections of aluminum pipe conduit.

9-C Grounding a fixture is a safety precaution used to lessen the chance of shock.

10-A A capacitor contains two conducting surfaces separated by an insulator and can, therefore, store static electrical charges. Caution should be exercised before touching capacitors. They should have their terminals "shorted" before being handled.

11-B All the other materials are very good insulators. Carbon has some resistance but still conducts more readily than the others. Resistors may contain some carbon.

12-A The windings in an AC motor are designed to offer a certain amount of impedance, which is a combination of inductive reactance and resistance, to the flow of AC. When DC is applied, only the pure resistance is available to limit the flow of current. Therefore, the direct current flow is larger than the alternating current would be at the same voltage. The increase in power consumption is dissipated as heat.

13-A Silver is a much better conductor than copper. It is not used in wires because it is very expensive.

14-D A household iron is the only device which depends on a thermostat to control its use. An

overheated iron will damage the clothing that it is supposed to press.

15-A An alternator is a device which is found in automobiles. It is used to produce AC In a car, the electronic circuitry changes AC to DC

16-D This is a mechanical or solderless connector. It does away with the need to solder wires and is found in house wiring.

17-C Two three-way switches will control a lamp from two different positions.

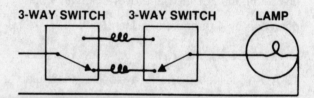

18-B A battery is an assembly of chemical cells. The common 9-volt battery found in transistor radios consists of six 1.5-volt cells connected in series to produce a total of six times 1.5 volts— or 9 volts.

19-D Rosin is used to remove copper-oxide from wires so that the solder can join the copper wires.

20-B In the letters RHW, R stands for rubber insulation, H stands for heat resistant, and W stands for waterproof.

TEST YOURSELF AGAIN AND NOTE FURTHER IMPROVEMENT

THIRD ASVAB SPECIMEN TEST

This section contains specimen answer sheets for use in answering the questions on each subtest, an actual specimen ASVAB test, answer keys for determining your scores on these subtests, and the rationale or explanation for each answer.

Remove (cut out) the specimen answer sheets on the following pages and use them to record your answers to the test questions. The ASVAB Specimen Test has the same format and content as the actual ASVAB test. Take this test under "real" test conditions. Time each subtest carefully.

Use the answer keys to obtain your subtest scores and to evaluate your performance on each subtest. Record the number of items you answered correctly, as well as the number of each item you answered incorrectly or wish to review, in the space provided below the answer keys for each subtest.

Review carefully and be certain to understand the explanations for the answers to all questions you answered incorrectly and for each of the questions which you answered correctly but are unsure of. This is absolutely essential in order to acquire the knowledge and expertise necessary to obtain the maximum scores possible on the actual ASVAB subtests.

Transfer your scores for each part of the third ASVAB Specimen Test to the Self-Appraisal Chart appearing on page 275. This will enable you to see the progress made as you continue to prepare for the actual test.

**Specimen Answer Sheet for
Answering Parts 1–5**

The answer sheet contains a CODE grid (17), a SOCIAL SECURITY NUMBER grid (16), and answer bubbles (A B C D) for:

- PART 1–GS: Practice (S1–S3) and items 1–25
- PART 2–AR: items 1–30
- PART 3–WK: items 1–35
- PART 4–PC: items 1–15
- PART 5–NO: items 1–50

**Specimen Answer Sheet for
Answering Parts 6–10**

**ANSWER SHEET
ARMED SERVICES VOCATIONAL
APTITUDE BATTERY**

MI / FIRST / LAST

PART 6—CS

1 A B C D E	15 A B C D E	29 A B C D E	43 A B C D E	57 A B C D E	71 A B C D E
2 A B C D E	16 A B C D E	30 A B C D E	44 A B C D E	58 A B C D E	72 A B C D E
3 A B C D E	17 A B C D E	31 A B C D E	45 A B C D E	59 A B C D E	73 A B C D E
4 A B C D E	18 A B C D E	32 A B C D E	46 A B C D E	60 A B C D E	74 A B C D E
5 A B C D E	19 A B C D E	33 A B C D E	47 A B C D E	61 A B C D E	75 A B C D E
6 A B C D E	20 A B C D E	34 A B C D E	48 A B C D E	62 A B C D E	76 A B C D E
7 A B C D E	21 A B C D E	35 A B C D E	49 A B C D E	63 A B C D E	77 A B C D E
8 A B C D E	22 A B C D E	36 A B C D E	50 A B C D E	64 A B C D E	78 A B C D E
9 A B C D E	23 A B C D E	37 A B C D E	51 A B C D E	65 A B C D E	79 A B C D E
10 A B C D E	24 A B C D E	38 A B C D E	52 A B C D E	66 A B C D E	80 A B C D E
11 A B C D E	25 A B C D E	39 A B C D E	53 A B C D E	67 A B C D E	81 A B C D E
12 A B C D E	26 A B C D E	40 A B C D E	54 A B C D E	68 A B C D E	82 A B C D E
13 A B C D E	27 A B C D E	41 A B C D E	55 A B C D E	69 A B C D E	83 A B C D E
14 A B C D E	28 A B C D E	42 A B C D E	56 A B C D E	70 A B C D E	84 A B C D E

PART 7—AS

1 A B C D	5 A B C D	9 A B C D	13 A B C D	17 A B C D	21 A B C D	25 A B C D
2 A B C D	6 A B C D	10 A B C D	14 A B C D	18 A B C D	22 A B C D	
3 A B C D	7 A B C D	11 A B C D	15 A B C D	19 A B C D	23 A B C D	
4 A B C D	8 A B C D	12 A B C D	16 A B C D	20 A B C D	24 A B C D	

PART 8—MK

1 A B C D	5 A B C D	9 A B C D	13 A B C D	17 A B C D	21 A B C D	25 A B C D
2 A B C D	6 A B C D	10 A B C D	14 A B C D	18 A B C D	22 A B C D	
3 A B C D	7 A B C D	11 A B C D	15 A B C D	19 A B C D	23 A B C D	
4 A B C D	8 A B C D	12 A B C D	16 A B C D	20 A B C D	24 A B C D	

PART 9—MC

1 A B C D	5 A B C D	9 A B C D	13 A B C D	17 A B C D	21 A B C D	25 A B C D
2 A B C D	6 A B C D	10 A B C D	14 A B C D	18 A B C D	22 A B C D	
3 A B C D	7 A B C D	11 A B C D	15 A B C D	19 A B C D	23 A B C D	
4 A B C D	8 A B C D	12 A B C D	16 A B C D	20 A B C D	24 A B C D	

PART 10—EI

1 A B C D	4 A B C D	7 A B C D	10 A B C D	13 A B C D	16 A B C D	19 A B C D
2 A B C D	5 A B C D	8 A B C D	11 A B C D	14 A B C D	17 A B C D	20 A B C D
3 A B C D	6 A B C D	9 A B C D	12 A B C D	15 A B C D	18 A B C D	

Third

ASVAB

Specimen Test

The introductory material for general orientation, as well as the general directions for taking the test, appears before the actual test questions in the ASVAB test booklet. However, as this material was covered previously in this book, it is not included in the specimen ASVAB test booklet.

Directions

This is a test of 25 questions to find out how much you know about general science as usually covered in high school courses. Pick the best answer for each question, then blacken the space on your answer form which has the same number and letter as your choice.

Here are three sample questions.

S1. Water is an example of a

S1-A solid
S1-B gas
S1-C liquid
S1-D crystal

Now look at the section of your answer sheet labeled Part 1, "Practice." Notice that answer space C has been marked for question 1. Now do practice questions 2 and 3 by yourself. Find the correct answer to the question, then mark the space on your answer form that has the same letter as the answer you picked. Do this now.

S2. Lack of iodine is often related to which of the following diseases?

S2-A beriberi
S2-B scurvey
S2-C rickets
S2-D goiter

S3. An eclipse of the sun throws the shadow of the

S3-A earth on the moon
S3-B moon on the earth
S3-C moon on the sun
S3-D earth on the sun

You should have marked D for quesion 2 and B for question 3. If you made any mistakes, erase your mark carefully and blacken the correct answer space. Do this now.

Your score on this test will be based on the number of questions you answer correctly. You should try to answer every question. Do not spend too much time on any one question.

When you begin, be sure to start with question number 1 of Part 1 of your test booklet, and number 1 in Part 1 on your answer form.

DO NOT TURN THIS PAGE UNTIL TOLD TO DO SO.

GENERAL SCIENCE

TIME: 11 Minutes—25 Questions

1. Which one of the following is *not* a fruit?

   1-A potato
   1-B tomato
   1-C cucumber
   1-D green pepper

2. The hammer, anvil, and stirrup bones lie in the

   2-A knee
   2-B hip
   2-C ear
   2-D elbow

3. Of the following, a condition *not* associated with heavy cigarette smoking is

   3-A shorter life span
   3-B slowing of the heartbeat
   3-C cancer of the lung
   3-D heart disease

4. The Wassermann test may indicate the presence of

   4-A syphilis
   4-B tuberculosis
   4-C measles
   4-D AIDS

5. Alcoholic beverages contain

   5-A wood alcohol
   5-B isopropyl alcohol
   5-C glyceryl alcohol
   5-D grain alcohol

6. The air around us is composed mostly of

   6-A carbon
   6-B nitrogen
   6-C hydrogen
   6-D oxygen

7. Spiders can be distinguished from insects by the fact that spiders have

   7-A hard outer coverings
   7-B large abdomens
   7-C four pairs of legs
   7-D biting mouth parts

8. An important ore of uranium is called

   8-A hematite
   8-B chalcopyrite
   8-C bauxite
   8-D pitchblende

9. Of the following, the lightest element known on earth is

   9-A hydrogen
   9-B oxygen
   9-C helium
   9-D air

10. Hearing an echo is most like seeing

    10-A around the corner through a periscope
    10-B fine print under strong illumination
    10-C stars at night that are invisible in the daytime
    10-D one's image in a mirror

11. A thermometer which indicates the freezing point of water at zero degrees and the boiling point of water at 100 degrees is called the

    11-A Centigrade thermometer
    11-B Fahrenheit thermometer
    11-C Reaumer thermometer
    11-D Kelvin thermometer

12. Refraction of light affects the aim one should take when

    12-A shooting at a fish that has jumped out of the water
    12-B spearing a fish in the water from the bank
    12-C spearing a fish under water when one is swimming under water
    12-D casting a fly on the surface of the water

GO ON TO THE NEXT PAGE.

13. A new drug for treatment of tuberculosis was being tested in a hospital. Patients in Group A actually received doses of the new drug; those in Group B were given only sugar pills. Group B represents

13-A a scientific experiment
13-B a scientific method
13-C an experimental error
13-D an experimental control

14. The statement that carrots help one to see in the dark is

14-A ridiculous
14-B reasonable because orange is a reflective color
14-C reasonable because carrots are high in vitamin A
14-D reasonable because rabbits see very well at night

15. Radium is stored in lead containers because

15-A the lead absorbs the harmful radiation
15-B radium is a heavy substance
15-C lead prevents the disintegration of the radium
15-D lead is cheap

16. The presence of coal deposits in Alaska shows that at one time Alaska

16-A had a tropical climate
16-B was covered with ice
16-C was connected to Asia
16-D was formed by volcanic action

17. If a person has been injured in an accident and damage to the back and neck is suspected, it is best to

17-A roll the person over so that he does not lie on his back
17-B rush the person to the nearest hospital
17-C force the person to drink water to replace body fluids
17-D wait for professional help

18. A 1,000-ton ship must displace a weight of water equal to

18-A 500 tons
18-B 1,500 tons
18-C 1,000 tons
18-D 2,000 tons

19. A lead sinker weighs 54 grams in air, 23.8 grams in liquid A, and 28.6 grams in liquid B. From this information, what conclusions can be drawn concerning the densities of the two liquids?

19-A Liquid A has a greater density than liquid B.
19-B Both liquids are more dense than water.
19-C Both liquids are less dense than water.
19-D No conclusions can be drawn concerning the densities of the two liquids.

20. After adding a solute to a liquid, the freezing point of the liquid is

20-A lowered
20-B the same
20-C raised
20-D inverted

21. Organisms that sustain their life cycles by feeding off other live organisms are known as

21-A parasites
21-B saprophytes
21-C bacteria
21-D viruses

22. The term *ft./sec.* is a unit of

22-A mass
22-B speed
22-C length
22-D density

23. A circuit breaker is used in many homes instead of a

23-A switch
23-B fire extinguisher
23-C fuse
23-D meter box

GO ON TO THE NEXT PAGE.

1

24. What is the name of the negative particle which circles the nucleus of the atom?

   24-A neutron
   24-B meson
   24-C proton
   24-D electron

25. Which of the following rocks can be dissolved with a weak acid?

   25-A sandstone
   25-B gneiss
   25-C granite
   25-D limestone

1

DO NOT GO ON UNTIL TOLD TO DO SO.
STOP! IF YOU FINISH BEFORE THE TIME IS UP, YOU
MAY CHECK OVER YOUR WORK ON THIS PART ONLY.

ARITHMETIC REASONING

Directions

This test has 30 questions about arithmetic. Each question is followed by four possible answers. Decide which answer is correct, then blacken the space on your answer form which has the same number and letter as your choice. Use your scratch paper for any figuring you wish to do.

Here are two sample questions.

> S1. A person buys a sandwich for 90¢, soda for 55¢, and pie for 70¢. What is the total cost?
>
> S1-A $2.00
> S1-B $2.05
> S1-C $2.15
> S1-D $2.25

The total cost is $2.15, therefore, C is the correct answer.

> S2. If 8 workers are needed to run 4 machines, how many workers are needed to run 20 machines?
>
> S2-A 16
> S2-B 32
> S2-C 36
> S2-D 40

The number needed is 40; therefore, D is the correct answer.

Your score on this test will be based on the number of questions you answer correctly. You should try to answer every question. Do not spend too much time on any one question.

Notice that Part 2 begins with question number 1. When you begin, be sure to start with question number 1 in Part 2 of your test booklet and number 1 in Part 2 on your answer form.

DO NOT TURN THIS PAGE UNTIL TOLD TO DO SO.

2

2

ARITHMETIC REASONING

TIME: 36 Minutes—30 Questions

1. A fruit picker gets $3.00 an hour plus 72¢ for every bushel over 40 that he picks in a day. If he works 8 hours and picks 50 bushels, how much will he get?

   1-A $29.76
   1-B $30.20
   1-C $31.20
   1-D $31.76

2. How many 36 passenger buses will it take to carry 144 people?

   2-A 4
   2-B 3
   2-C 5
   2-D 6

3. A gallon contains 4 quarts. A cartoning machine can fill 120 one-quart cartons a minute. How long will it take to put 600 gallons of orange juice into cartons?

   3-A 1 minute and 15 seconds
   3-B 5 minutes
   3-C 10 minutes
   3-D 20 minutes

4. A clerk spent his 35-hour work week as follows: $\frac{1}{5}$ of his time in sorting mail; $\frac{1}{2}$ of his time in filing letters; and $\frac{1}{7}$ of his time in reception work. The rest of his time was devoted to messenger work. The percentage of time spent on messenger work by the clerk during the week was most nearly

   4-A 6%
   4-B 14%
   4-C 10%
   4-D 16%

5. A dealer bought some bicycles for $4,000. He sold them for $6,200, making $50 on each bicycle. How many bicycles were there?

   5-A 40
   5-B 43
   5-C 38
   5-D 44

6. Many American cars feature speedometers which show kilometers per hour. If you are required to drive 500 miles, and you know that one kilometer is approximately $\frac{5}{8}$ of a mile, how many kilometers would you cover in that journey?

   6-A 625
   6-B 800
   6-C 850
   6-D 1,000

7. One year the postage rate for sending 1 ounce of mail first class was increased from 20 cents to 22 cents. The percent of increase in the 22 cent postage rate was most nearly

   7-A 2 percent
   7-B 10 percent
   7-C 11 percent
   7-D 15 percent

8. On a scale drawing, a line $\frac{1}{4}$ inch long represents a length of 1 foot. On the same drawing, what length represents 4 feet?

   8-A 1 inch
   8-B 2 inches
   8-C 3 inches
   8-D 4 inches

9. What is the greatest number of half-pint bottles that can be filled from a 10-gallon can of milk?

   9-A 160
   9-B 170
   9-C 16
   9-D 17

10. Soap, ordinarily priced at 2 bars for $0.66, may be purchased in lots of one dozen for $3.48. What is the saving per bar when it is purchased in this way?

    10-A 4 cents
    10-B 8 cents
    10-C 16 cents
    10-D 19 cents

GO ON TO THE NEXT PAGE

11. Twenty students contribute $25 each for a Christmas party. Forty percent of the money is spent for food and drinks. How much is left for other expenses?

11-A $125
11-B $200
11-C $300
11-D $375

12. A pole 24 feet high has a shadow 8 feet long. A nearby pole is 72 feet high. How long is its shadow?

12-A 16 feet
12-B 24 feet
12-C 32 feet
12-D 56 feet

2

13. A man deposited a check for $1,000 to open an account. Shortly after that, he withdrew $941.20. How much did he have left in his account?

13-A $56.72
13-B $58.80
13-C $59.09
13-D $60.60

14. A shopper bought 4 pillow cases that cost $4.98 apiece, 2 fitted sheets that cost $8.29 apiece, and 2 flat sheets that cost $8.09 apiece. What was her total bill?

14-A $52.58
14-B $51.68
14-C $52.68
14-D $21.36

15. The wage rate in a certain trade is $8.60 an hour for a 40-hour week and $1\frac{1}{2}$ times the base pay for overtime. An employee who works 48 hours in a week earns

15-A $447.20
15-B $498.20
15-C $582.20
15-D $619.20

16. A carton contains 9 dozen file folders. If a clerk removes 53 folders, how many folders are left in the carton?

16-A 37
16-B 44
16-C 55
16-D 62

17. A man had $25.00. He saw some ties that cost $4.95 apiece. How many of these ties could he buy?

17-A 6
17-B 7
17-C 5
17-D 3

18. A man earns $20.56 on Monday; $32.90 on Tuesday; $20.78 on Wednesday. He spends half of all that he earns during the three days. How much has he left?

18-A $29.19
18-B $31.23
18-C $34.27
18-D $37.12

19. It costs $1.00 per square yard to waterproof canvas. What will it cost to waterproof a canvas truck cover that is 15′ × 24′?

19-A $20.00
19-B $36.00
19-C $40.00
19-D $360.00

20. A part-time employee worked a total of 16½ hours during 5 days of the past week. What was this employee's average workday?

20-A 3 hours
20-B 3 hours, 15 minutes
20-C 3 hours, 18 minutes
20-D 3 hours, 25 minutes

21. A driver traveled 100 miles at the rate of 40 mph, then traveled 80 miles at 60 mph. The total number of hours for the entire trip was

21-A $1\frac{3}{20}$

21-B $1\frac{3}{4}$

21-C $2\frac{1}{4}$

21-D $3\frac{5}{6}$

GO ON TO THE NEXT PAGE

22. On her maiden voyage the *S.S. United States* made the trip from New York to England in 3 days, 10 hours, and 40 minutes, beating the record set by the *R.M.S. Queen Mary* in 1938 by 10 hours and 2 minutes. How long did it take the *Queen Mary* to make the trip?

22-A 3 days, 20 hours, 42 minutes
22-B 3 days, 15 hours, 38 minutes
22-C 3 days, 12 hours, 2 minutes
22-D 3 days, 8 hours, 12 minutes

23. Gary bought a shirt for $18.95. He gave the clerk $20.00. How much change should Gary get?

23-A $2.05
23-B $1.95
23-C $1.05
23-D $ .05

24. John bought 20 party favors for $66.00. What was the cost of each one?

24-A $3.35
24-B $3.30
24-C $2.45
24-D $3.50

25. In a 45-minute gym class, 30 boys want to play basketball. Only 10 can play at once. If each player is to play the same length of time, how many minutes should each play?

25-A 8
25-B 12
25-C 15
25-D 20

26. The library charges 5¢ for the first day and 2¢ for each additional day that a book is overdue. If a borrower paid 65¢ in late charges, for how many days was the book overdue?

26-A 15
26-B 21
26-C 25
26-D 31

27. How many slices of bread, each weighing 2 ounces, are needed to balance 2 pounds of apples?

27-A 8
27-B 12
27-C 16
27-D 24

28. A girl bought a sweater for $21.00, a blouse for $14.98, and a scarf for $4.97. What was the total cost of her purchases?

28-A $35.50
28-B $40.85
28-C $30.85
28-D $40.95

29. Don and Frank started from the same point and drove in opposite directions. Don's rate of travel was 50 miles per hour. Frank's rate of travel was 40 miles per hour. How many miles apart were they at the end of 2 hours?

29-A 90
29-B 160
29-C 140
29-D 180

30. A decorator went to a department store and ordered curtains for 5 windows. One pair of curtains cost $14.28; 2 pairs cost $33.26 apiece; and the remaining 2 pairs cost $65.38 apiece. What was the retail cost of the five pairs of curtains?

30-A $211.46
30-B $211.56
30-C $112.92
30-D $110.82

2

STOP! IF YOU FINISH BEFORE THE TIME IS UP, YOU MAY CHECK OVER YOUR WORK ON THIS PART ONLY. DO NOT RETURN TO PART ONE. DO NOT TURN THE PAGE UNTIL YOU ARE TOLD TO DO SO.

3

WORD KNOWLEDGE

3

Directions

This test has 35 questions about the meanings of words. Each question has an underlined word. You are to decide which one of the four words in the choices most nearly means the same as the underlined word, then mark the space on your answer form which has the same number and letter as your choice.

Now look at the two sample questions below.

S1. <u>Mended</u> most nearly means

    S1-A repaired
    S1-B torn
    S1-C clean
    S1-D tied

A REPAIRED is the correct answer. *Mended* means *fixed* or *repaired. Torn* (B) might be the state of an object before it is mended. The repair might be made by *tying* (D), but not necessarily. *Clean* (C) is wrong.

S2. It was a <u>small</u> table.

    S1-A sturdy
    S2-B round
    S2-C cheap
    S2-D little

Little means the same as small so the D answer is the best one.

Your score on this test will be based on the number of questions you answer correctly. You should try to answer every question. Do not spend too much time on any one question.

When you begin, be sure to start with question number 1 in Part 3 of your test booklet and number 1 in Part 3 on your answer form.

DO NOT TURN THIS PAGE UNTIL TOLD TO DO SO.

3

PART 3

WORD KNOWLEDGE

TIME: 11 Minutes—35 Questions

1. Double most nearly means

   1-A almost
   1-B half
   1-C twice
   1-D more than

2. Purchase most nearly means

   2-A charge
   2-B supply
   2-C order
   2-D buy

3. Hollow most nearly means

   3-A empty
   3-B brittle
   3-C rough
   3-D smooth

4. Deportment most nearly means

   4-A attendance
   4-B intelligence
   4-C neatness
   4-D behavior

5. Prior most nearly means

   5-A personal
   5-B more urgent
   5-C more attractive
   5-D earlier

6. Grimy most nearly means

   6-A ill-fitting
   6-B poorly made
   6-C dirty
   6-D ragged

7. Did the storm cease during the night?

   7-A start
   7-B change
   7-C continue
   7-D stop

8. The crowd received him with acclaim.

   8-A amazement
   8-B applause
   8-C booing
   8-D laughter

9. The town will erect the bridge.

   9-A paint
   9-B design
   9-C destroy
   9-D construct

10. The children pledged allegiance to the flag.

    10-A freedom
    10-B homeland
    10-C protection
    10-D loyalty

11. The cashier yearned for a vacation.

    11-A begged
    11-B longed
    11-C saved
    11-D applied

12. Summit most nearly means

    12-A face
    12-B top
    12-C base
    12-D side

13. Villainous most nearly means

    13-A untidy
    13-B dignified
    13-C homely
    13-D wicked

14. It is my conviction that you are wrong,

    14-A guilt
    14-B imagination
    14-C firm belief
    14-D fault

3

GO ON TO THE NEXT PAGE.

15. Punctual most nearly means

    15-A polite
    15-B thoughtful
    15-C proper
    15-D prompt

16. Irritating most nearly means

    16-A nervous
    16-B unsuitable
    16-C annoying
    16-D noisy

17. The cyclist pedaled at a uniform rate.

    17-A increasing
    17-B unchanging
    17-C unusual
    17-D very slow

18. Power most nearly means

    18-A size
    18-B ambition
    18-C force
    18-D success

19. We were told to abandon the ship.

    19-A relinquish
    19-B encompass
    19-C infiltrate
    19-D quarantine

20. Resolve most nearly means

    20-A understand
    20-B decide
    20-C recall
    20-D forget

21. Ample most nearly means

    21-A plentiful
    21-B enthusiastic
    21-C well shaped
    21-D fat

22. Bewildered most nearly means

    22-A worried
    22-B offended
    22-C puzzled
    22-D delighted

23. Conclusion most nearly means

    23-A theme
    23-B suspense
    23-C end
    23-D beginning

24. She likes the aroma of fresh-brewed coffee.

    24-A flavor
    24-B warmth
    24-C fragrance
    24-D steam

25. Startled most nearly means

    25-A surprised
    25-B chased
    25-C punished
    25-D arrested

26. Forthcoming events are published daily.

    26-A weekly
    26-B interesting
    26-C social
    26-D approaching

27. Verdict most nearly means

    27-A approval
    27-B decision
    27-C sentence
    27-D arrival

28. Blemish most nearly means

    28-A color
    28-B insect
    28-C flaw
    28-D design

29. The reply will be conveyed by messenger.

    29-A carried
    29-B guarded
    29-C refused
    29-D damaged

30. Pedestrian most nearly means

    30-A passenger
    30-B street-crosser
    30-C walker
    30-D traffic light

GO ON TO THE NEXT PAGE.

31. <u>Incessant</u> most nearly means

   31-A occasional
   31-B disagreeable
   31-C constant
   31-D noisy

32. <u>Solidity</u> most nearly means

   32-A unevenness
   32-B smoothness
   32-C firmness
   32-D color

33. <u>Increment</u> most nearly means

   33-A an improvisation
   33-B an account
   33-C an increase
   33-D a specification

34. <u>Vocation</u> most nearly means

   34-A school
   34-B examination
   34-C occupation
   34-D carpentry

35. One should eat only <u>mature</u> fruits.

   35-A edible
   35-B washed
   35-C ripe
   35-D sprayed

3

DO NOT TURN THIS PAGE UNTIL TOLD TO DO SO.
STOP! IF YOU FINISH BEFORE THE TIME IS UP, YOU
MAY CHECK OVER YOUR WORK ON THIS PART ONLY.

4

PARAGRAPH COMPREHENSION

4

Directions

This test contains 15 items measuring your ability to obtain information from written passages. You will find one or more paragraphs of reading material followed by incomplete statements or questions. You are to read the paragraph(s) and select one of the lettered choices which best completes the statement or answers the question.

Here are two sample questions.

> **S1.** From a building designer's standpoint, three things that make a home livable are the needs of the client, the building site, and the amount of money the client has to spend.
>
> According to the passage, to make a home livable
>
> S1-A the prospective piece of land makes little difference
>
> S1-B it can be built on any piece of land
>
> S1-C the design must fit the owner's income and site
>
> S1-D the design must fit the designer's income

The correct answer is that the designer must fit the owner's income and site, so C is the correct response.

> **S2.** In certain areas water is so scarce that every attempt is made to conserve it. For instance, on one oasis in the Sahara Desert the amount of water necessary for each date palm tree has been carefully determined.
>
> How much water is each tree given?
>
> S2-A no water at all
>
> S2-B exactly the amount required
>
> S2-C water only if it is healthy
>
> S2-D water on alternate days

The correct answer is exactly the amount required, so B is the correct response.

Your score on this test will be based on the number of questions you answer correctly. You should try to answer every question. Do not spend too much time on any one question.

When you begin be sure to start with question number 1 in Part 4 of your test booklet and number 1 in Part 4 on your answer form.

DO NOT TURN THIS PAGE UNTIL TOLD TO DO SO.

4

PARAGRAPH COMPREHENSION

TIME: 13 Minutes—15 Questions

1. Few drivers realize that steel is used to keep the road surface flat in spite of the weight of buses and trucks. Steel bars, deeply embedded in the concrete, are sinews to take the stresses so that the stresses cannot crack the slab or make it wavy.

   The passage best supports the statement that a concrete road

   1-A is expensive to build
   1-B usually cracks under heavy weights
   1-C looks like any other road
   1-D is reinforced with other material

2. Just as the procedure of a collection department must be clear-cut and definite, so the various paragraphs of a collection letter must show clear organization, giving evidence of a mind that has a specific end in view.

   The passage best supports the statement that a collection letter should always

   2-A be divided into several paragraphs
   2-B express confidence in the debtor
   2-C be brief but courteous
   2-D be carefully planned

3. You can tell a frog from a toad by its skin. In general, a frog's skin is moist, smooth, and shiny while a toad's skin is dry, dull, and rough or covered with warts. Frogs are also better at jumping than toads are.

   You can recognize a toad by its

   3-A great jumping ability
   3-B smooth, shiny skin
   3-C lack of warts
   3-D dry, rough skin

4. In a pole-vaulting competition, the judge decides on the minimum height to be jumped. The vaulter may attempt to jump any height above the minimum. Using flexible fiber-glass poles, vaulters have jumped as high as 18 feet 8¼ inches.

   According to the passage, pole vaulters

   4-A may attempt to jump any height in competition
   4-B must jump higher than 18′ 8¼″ to win
   4-C must jump higher than the height set by the judge
   4-D must use fiber-glass poles

5. With the exception of Earth, all of the planets in our solar system are named for gods and goddesses in Greek or Roman legends. This is because the other planets were thought to be in heaven like the gods and our planet lay beneath, like the earth.

   All the planets except Earth

   5-A were part of Greek and Roman legends
   5-B were thought to be in heaven
   5-C are part of the same solar system
   5-D were worshipped as gods

6. The location of a railway line is necessarily a compromise between the desire to build the line with as little expense as possible and the desire to construct it so that its route will cover that over which trade and commerce are likely to flow.

   The route selected for a railway line

   6-A should be the one over which the line can be built most cheaply
   6-B determines the location of commercial centers
   6-C should always cover the shortest possible distance between its terminals
   6-D cannot always be the one involving the lowest construction costs

7. Although rural crime reporting is spottier and less efficient than city and town reporting, sufficient data has been collected to support the statement that rural crime rates are lower than those in urban communities.

4

GO ON TO THE NEXT PAGE.

The paragraph best supports the statement that

7-A better reporting of crime occurs in rural areas than in cities

7-B there appears to be a lower proportion of crime in rural areas than in cities

7-C cities have more crime than towns

7-D no conclusions can be drawn regarding crime in rural areas because of inadequate reporting.

8. In the business districts of cities, collections from street letter boxes are made at stated hours, and collectors are required to observe these hours exactly. Anyone using these boxes can rely with certainty upon the time of the next collection.

The paragraph best supports the statement that

8-A mail collections in business districts are more frequent during the day than at night

8-B mail collectors are required to observe safety regulations exactly

8-C mail collections are made often in business districts

8-D mail is collected in business districts on a regular schedule

9. In large organizations some standardized, simple, inexpensive method of giving employees information about company policies

and rules, as well as specific instructions regarding their duties, is practically essential. This is the purpose of all office manuals of whatever type.

The paragraph best supports the statement that office manuals

9-A are all about the same

9-B should be simple enough for the average employee to understand

9-C are necessary to large organizations

9-D act as constant reminders to the employee of his or her duties

10. Unfortunately, specialization in industry creates workers who lack versatility. When a laborer is trained to perform only one task, he is almost entirely dependent for employment upon the demand for that particular skill. If anything happens to interrupt that demand, he is unemployed.

The paragraph best supports the statement that

10-A the demand for labor of a particular type is constantly changing

10-B the average laborer is not capable of learning more than one task at a time

10-C some cases of unemployment are due to laborers' lack of versatility

10-D too much specialization is as dangerous as too little

Questions 11 and 12 are based on the following passage.

When demand for new buildings rises sharply, prices of such buildings usually increase rapidly while construction invariably lags behind. The relation of supply to demand is one of the factors that may greatly influence prices. When demand for new buildings suddenly declines, their prices fall because the available supply cannot be immediately curtailed.

11. According to the above passage, a sharp increase in demand for new buildings usually results in

11-A fewer new buildings in proportion to buyers

11-B a proportionate increase in construction

11-C more builders of new buildings

11-D more sellers

12. When there is a sudden drop in the demand for new buildings, the immediately resulting effect on their prices is attributable mainly to the

12-A cessation in new construction

12-B curtailment in the supply of such buildings

12-C reduction in new construction

12-D static condition in the supply of such buildings

GO ON TO THE NEXT PAGE.

Questions 13–15 are based on the passage shown below.

The two systems of weights and measures are the English system and the metric system. The English system uses units such as foot, pound, and quart; the metric system uses meter, gram, and liter.

The metric system was first adopted in France in 1795 and is now used by most countries in the world. In the metric system, the unit of length is the meter, which is one ten-millionth of the distance from the Equator to the North Pole.

The British recently changed their system of weights and measures to the metric system; however, in the United States, there has been much opposition to this change. It would cost billions of dollars to change all our weights and measures to the metric system.

13. According to the passage above, the metric system is used

    13-A in all of Europe except Great Britain
    13-B in almost all countries of the world
    13-C in only a few countries
    13-D mostly in Europe

14. The United States has not changed to the metric system because

    14-A the system is too complicated
    14-B the change would be costly
    14-C the system is not accurate
    14-D it is difficult to learn

15. The meter is equal to

    15-A the distance from the Equator to the North Pole
    15-B 1/1,000,000 of the distance from the Equator to the North Pole
    15-C 1/10,000,000 of the distance from the Equator to the North Pole
    15-D 1/100,000,000 of the distance from the Equator to the North Pole

4

DO NOT TURN THIS PAGE UNTIL TOLD TO DO SO.
STOP! IF YOU FINISH BEFORE THE TIME IS UP, YOU
MAY CHECK OVER YOUR WORK ON THIS PART ONLY.

5

NUMERICAL OPERATIONS

5

Directions

This is a test to see how rapidly and accurately you can do 50 simple arithmetic computations. Each problem is followed by four answers, only one of which is correct. Decide which answer is correct, then blacken the space on your answer form which has the same number and letter as your choice.

Now look at the four sample problems below.

S1. $3 \times 3 =$

S1-A 6
S1-B 0
S1-C 9
S1-D 1

The answer is 9, so C is correct.

S2. $3 + 7 =$

S2-A 4
S2-B 6
S2-C 8
2S-D 10

The answer is 10, so D is correct.

S3. $5 - 2 =$

S3-A 2
S3-B 3
S3-C 4
S3-D 5

The answer is 3, so B is correct.

S4. $9 \div 3 =$

S4-A 3
S4-B 6
S4-C 9
S4-D 12

The answer is 3, so A is correct.

This is a speed test, so work as fast as you can without making mistakes. Do each problem as it comes. If you finish before time is up, go back and check your work. When the signal is given, you will turn the page and begin with question 1 in Part 5 of your test booklet and answer space 1 in Part 5 of your answer form.

DO NOT TURN THIS PAGE UNTIL TOLD TO DO SO.

NUMERICAL OPERATIONS

TIME: 3 Minutes—50 Questions

1. $5 - 3 =$

   1-A 2
   1-B 6
   1-C 8
   1-D 11

2. $8 - 6 =$

   2-A 7
   2-B 2
   2-C 12
   2-D 14

3. $12 \div 2 =$

   3-A 10
   3-B 3
   3-C 4
   3-D 6

4. $8 - 6 =$

   4-A 12
   4-B 5
   4-C 4
   4-D 2

5. $4 + 8 =$

   5-A 6
   5-B 10
   5-C 12
   5-D 14

6. $6 \times 8 =$

   6-A 24
   6-B 48
   6-C 42
   6-D 36

7. $18 - 14 =$

   7-A 4
   7-B 8
   7-C 10
   7-D 12

8. $2 \times 12 =$

   8-A 14
   8-B 22
   8-C 24
   8-D 34

9. $9 - 6 =$

   9-A 1
   9-B 2
   9-C 3
   9-D 4

10. $1 \times 6 =$

    10-A 5
    10-B 6
    10-C 7
    10-D 9

11. $7 - 2 =$

    11-A 5
    11-B 9
    11-C 14
    11-D 7

12. $5 - 0 =$

    12-A 0
    12-B 1
    12-C 5
    12-D 10

13. $10 - 6 =$

    13-A 4
    13-B 8
    13-C 14
    13-D 16

14. $1 + 5 =$

    14-A 0
    14-B 4
    14-C 5
    14-D 6

15. $4 \times 2 =$

    15-A 6
    15-B 16
    15-C 12
    15-D 8

16. $49 \div 7 =$

    16-A 6
    16-B 7
    16-C 8
    16-D 9

17. $3 \times 10 =$

    17-A 7
    17-B 13
    17-C 15
    17-D 30

18. $8 - 0 =$

    18-A 8
    18-B 0
    18-C 1
    18-D 80

19. $4 \times 3 =$

    19-A 1
    19-B 7
    19-C 12
    19-D 16

20. $8 - 3 =$

    20-A 3
    20-B 4
    20-C 5
    20-D 6

21. $7 \times 4 =$

    21-A 28
    21-B 30
    21-C 32
    21-D 34

22. $4 + 8 =$

    22-A 32
    22-B 24
    22-C 12
    22-D 4

23. $5 - 1 =$

    23-A 4
    23-B 5
    23-C 6
    23-D 15

24. $9 \div 3 =$

    24-A 3
    24-B 6
    24-C 9
    24-D 12

25. $4 + 5 =$

    25-A 25
    25-B 20
    25-C 11
    25-D 9

26. $7 \times 8 =$

    26-A 56
    26-B 48
    26-C 42
    26-D 72

27. $9 + 6 =$

    27-A 13
    27-B 14
    27-C 15
    27-D 16

28. $8 \div 2 =$

    28-A 4
    28-B 7
    28-C 1
    28-D 6

GO ON TO THE NEXT PAGE.

29. 7 − 1 =

    29-A 8
    29-B 0
    29-C 7
    29-D 6

30. 8 ÷ 8 =

    30-A 8
    30-B 0
    30-C 16
    30-D 1

31. 5 ÷ 5 =

    31-A 0
    31-B 1
    31-C 10
    31-D 25

32. 5 × 3 =

    32-A 8
    32-B 15
    32-C 18
    32-D 25

33. 16 ÷ 4

    33-A 2
    33-B 4
    33-C 6
    33-D 7

34. 6 × 2 =

    34-A 8
    34-B 4
    34-C 36
    34-D 12

35. 10 − 8 =

    35-A 80
    35-B 18
    35-C 12
    35-D 2

36. 7 ÷ 1 =

    36-A 1
    36-B 7
    36-C 0
    36-D 8

37. 9 ÷ 3 =

    37-A 3
    37-B 8
    37-C 9
    37-D 18

38. 4 × 8 =

    38-A 24
    38-B 28
    38-C 32
    38-D 42

39. 5 ÷ 5 =

    39-A 25
    39-B 10
    39-C 5
    39-D 1

40. 7 − 4 =

    40-A 11
    40-B 9
    40-C 6
    40-D 3

41. 4 − 0 =

    41-A 0
    41-B 4
    41-C 1
    41-D 5

42. 1 × 2 =

    42-A 1
    42-B 2
    42-C 3
    42-D 4

43. 12 + 2 =

    43-A 4
    43-B 6
    43-C 10
    43-D 14

44. 3 × 15 =

    44-A 12
    44-B 18
    44-C 35
    44-D 45

45. 25 ÷ 5 =

    45-A 4
    45-B 5
    45-C 6
    45-D 7

46. 3 × 4 =

    46-A 12
    46-B 7
    46-C 5
    46-D 1

47. 8 − 6 =

    47-A 2
    47-B 4
    47-C 12
    47-D 14

48. 8 ÷ 2 =

    48-A 6
    48-B 16
    48-C 10
    48-D 4

49. 20 ÷ 2 =

    49-A 40
    49-B 22
    49-C 18
    49-D 10

50. 8 − 7 =

    50-A 56
    50-B 15
    50-C 5
    50-D 1

5

DO NOT TURN THIS PAGE UNTIL TOLD TO DO SO.
STOP! IF YOU FINISH BEFORE THE TIME IS UP, YOU
MAY CHECK OVER YOUR WORK ON THIS PART ONLY.

6

CODING SPEED

6

Directions

This is a test of 84 items to see how quickly and accurately you can find a number in a table. At the top of each section, there is a number table or "key." The key is a group of words with a code number for each word.

Each question in the test is a word taken from the key at the top. From among the possible answers listed for each question, find the one that is the correct code number for that word.

Look at the sample key and answer the five sample questions below. Note that each of the questions is one of the words in the key. To the right of each question are possible answers listed under the options A, B, C, D, and E.

Sample Questions

Key

| green .... 2715 | man ..... 3451 | salt ...... 4586 |
| hat ...... 1413 | room..... 2864 | tree...... 5972 |

Sample Questions	Options				
	A	**B**	**C**	**D**	**E**
S-1. room	1413	2715	2864	3451	4586
S-2. green	2715	2864	3451	4586	5972
S-3. tree	2715	2864	3451	4596	5972
S-4. hat	1413	2715	2864	3451	4586
S-5. room	1413	2864	3451	4586	5972

By looking at the key you see that the code number for the first word, "room," is 2864. 2864 is listed under the letter C so C is the correct answer. The correct answers for the other four questions are A, E, A, and B.

This is a speed test, so work as fast as you can without making mistakes.

Notice that Part 6 begins at the top of the next answer form. When you begin, be sure to start with question number 1 in Part 6 of your test booklet and number 1 in Part 6 on your answer form.

DO NOT TURN THIS PAGE UNTIL TOLD TO DO SO.

CODING SPEED

TIME: 7 Minutes—84 Questions

Key

bird........ 7011	egg........ 1237	jury........ 2912	pump 3061	stump...... 8956
car 6300	ghost 9212	maroon 5873	rat......... 4643	window..... 6766

Questions			Options		
	A	**B**	**C**	**D**	**E**
1. maroon	4643	5873	6766	8956	9212
2. window	1237	2912	4643	6766	8956
3. jury	2912	3061	5873	6300	7011
4. rat	1237	3061	4643	6300	6766
5. ghost	2912	4643	5873	8956	9212
6. bird	3061	4643	6300	6766	7011
7. stump	5873	6300	6766	7011	8956
8. car	1237	3061	6300	6766	9212
9. egg	1237	2912	3061	5873	8956
10. pump	2912	3061	4643	6300	6766
11. window	3061	6300	6766	7011	9212
12. rat	3061	4643	5873	6766	8956

Key

axle........ 5614	club........ 1090	lamp....... 6686	muffin...... 3939	trip 8968
baby....... 9846	guitar 4379	mop 2545	noose...... 7867	waste 4886

Questions			Options		
	A	**B**	**C**	**D**	**E**
13. guitar	3939	4379	4886	6686	7867
14. waste	1090	2545	3939	4379	4886
15. axle	4379	4886	5614	6686	8968
16. mop	1090	2545	4379	7867	9846
17. trip	3939	4886	6686	8968	9846
18. lamp	2545	3939	4886	5614	6686
19. club	1090	4379	4886	5614	7867
20. muffin	2545	3939	4379	7867	8968
21. noose	4379	5614	7867	8968	9846
22. lamp	1090	3939	4886	6686	8968
23. baby	4379	4886	6686	7867	9846
24. noose	1090	6686	7867	8968	9846

GO ON TO THE NEXT PAGE.

Key

army....... 9234	disc........ 6957	line........ 1854	pain 2610	rug 5600
coast 4532	land 1620	man 3002	paint....... 7677	test........ 8406

Questions	Options				
	A	**B**	**C**	**D**	**E**
25. disc	1620	3002	5600	6957	8406
26. paint	1854	2610	4532	6957	7677
27. line	1620	1854	2610	3002	5600
28. test	1854	4532	6957	8406	9234
29. pain	2610	3002	5600	7677	8406
30. army	1620	2610	3002	6957	9234
31. rug	4532	5600	6957	8406	9234
32. man	3002	4532	6957	7677	8406
33. paint	1620	2610	7677	8406	9234
34. coast	2610	3002	4532	5600	6957
35. land	1620	1854	2610	3002	5600
36. rug	2610	4532	5600	6957	9234

6

Key

artist....... 3019	enemy 3417	hunter...... 4697	ruler 7419	umbrella.... 2499
current 6214	frost 9822	pirate 1347	ticket....... 5299	whale 8852

Questions	Options				
	A	**B**	**C**	**D**	**E**
37. frost	1347	4697	5299	7419	9822
38. whale	4697	5299	6214	8852	9822
39. enemy	2499	3417	4697	5299	6214
40. pirate	1347	2499	3019	8852	9822
41. ruler	3019	4697	5299	6214	7419
42. umbrella	1347	2499	3417	5299	6214
43. current	3417	5299	6214	7419	8852
44. hunter	2499	3019	3417	4697	5299
45. ticket	4697	5299	6214	8852	9822
46. artist	3019	4697	5299	7419	8852
47. whale	1347	2499	3417	4697	8852
48. pirate	1347	5299	6214	7419	9822

GO ON TO THE NEXT PAGE.

Key

book	3498	exam	2412	hotel	9804	navy	4404	sea	7602
boy	1518	guard	5249	motel	8940	pie	6765	thing	5521

Questions		Options				
		A	**B**	**C**	**D**	**E**
49.	guard	1518	4404	5249	5521	6765
50.	exam	1518	2412	5521	7602	9804
51.	thing	2412	5521	5249	6765	8940
52.	motel	3498	4404	6765	8940	9804
53.	sea	5249	6765	7602	8940	9804
54.	boy	1518	2412	4404	5521	7602
55.	navy	2412	3498	4404	5249	6765
56.	book	3498	5249	5521	7602	8940
57.	hotel	1518	2412	6765	8940	9804
58.	pie	5521	6765	7602	8940	9804
59.	navy	4404	5249	5521	6765	7602
60.	book	1518	2412	3498	4404	9804

Key

air	1230	cabin	5254	edge	6010	goose	4656	knee	3369
brush	8800	day	1010	fate	7946	island	9064	lever	2125

Questions		Options				
		A	**B**	**C**	**D**	**E**
61.	island	1010	3369	7946	8800	9064
62.	goose	1230	2125	4656	5254	6010
63.	knee	2125	3369	5254	7946	8800
64.	fate	1010	1230	3369	4656	7946
65.	brush	2125	4656	5254	8800	9064
66.	lever	1010	1230	2125	6010	8800
67.	cabin	3369	4656	5254	7946	9064
68.	edge	1230	2125	4656	6010	8800
69.	air	1230	3369	5254	7946	9064
70.	knee	1010	1230	2125	3369	4656
71.	cabin	1230	2125	3369	4656	5254
72.	day	1010	1230	6010	8800	9064

GO ON TO THE NEXT PAGE.

Key

arch 2641	coin........ 9559	fuzz........ 4769	hair........ 6931	puzzle 8724
battle 1686	dress 5959	green 3480	mud 7777	stew 4162

Questions			Options		
	A	**B**	**C**	**D**	**E**
73. puzzle	1686	4769	6931	8724	9559
74. fuzz	2641	3480	4162	4769	5959
75. stew	2641	4162	6931	7777	8724
76. battle	1686	2641	4162	6931	8724
77. mud	3480	4769	5959	7777	9559
78. green	1686	3480	4162	6931	8724
79. coin	2641	4162	5959	7777	9559
80. arch	2641	4162	4769	6931	8724
81. dress	1686	4769	5959	8724	9559
82. hair	4162	4769	5959	6931	7777
83. puzzle	1686	4162	6931	7777	8724
84. dress	2641	3480	4162	4769	5959

6

DO NOT TURN THIS PAGE UNTIL TOLD TO DO SO.
STOP!   IF YOU FINISH BEFORE THE TIME IS UP, YOU
MAY CHECK OVER YOUR WORK ON THIS PART ONLY.

7

Directions

This test has 25 questions about automobiles, shop practices, and the use of tools. Pick the best answer for each question, then blacken the space on your answer form which has the same number and letter as your choice.

Here are four sample questions.

S1. The most commonly used fuel for running automobile engines is

S1-A kerosene
S1-B benzine
S1-C crude oil
S1-D gasoline

Gasoline is the most commonly used fuel, so D is the correct answer.

S2. A car uses too much oil when which parts are worn?

S2-A pistons
S2-B piston rings
S2-C main bearings
S2-D connecting rods

Worn piston rings causes the use of too much oil, so B is the correct answer.

S3. The saw shown to the right is used mainly to cut

S3-A plywood
S3-B odd-shaped holes in wood
S3-C along the grain of the wood
S3-D across the grain of the wood

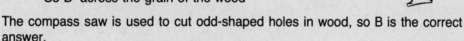

The compass saw is used to cut odd-shaped holes in wood, so B is the correct answer.

S4. Thin sheet metal should be cut with

S4-A ordinary scissors
S4-B a hack saw
S4-C tin shears
S4-D a jig saw

Tin shears are used to cut thin sheet metal, so C is the correct answer.

Your score on this test will be based on the number of questions you answer correctly. You should try to answer every question. Do not spend too much time on any one question.

When you are told to begin, be sure to start with question number 1 in Part 7 of your test booklet and number 1 in Part 7 on your answer form.

DO NOT TURN THIS PAGE UNTIL TOLD TO DO SO.

7

AUTO & SHOP INFORMATION

TIME: 11 Minutes—25 Questions

1. Most automobile engines run according to the

   1-A rotary cycle
   1-B intake-exhaust cycle
   1-C four-stroke cycle
   1-D two-stroke cycle

2. The most important rule for a driver to remember in the care of an automobile battery is to

   2-A make certain that the points are properly adjusted in the spark plugs
   2-B burn the headlights or play the radio occasionally while the ignition is turned on
   2-C have the battery discharged at regular intervals, weekly in the winter, biweekly in the summer
   2-D keep the level of the liquid above the plates

3. The function of the rotor is to

   3-A open and close the distributor points
   3-B rotate the distributor cam
   3-C distribute electricity to the spark plugs
   3-D rotate the distributor shaft

4. When the level of the liquid in a battery gets too low, it is necessary to put in some more

   4-A battery acid
   4-B hydroxide
   4-C water
   4-D antifreeze

5. After brakes have been severely overheated, what should be checked for?

   5-A water condensation in brake fluid
   5-B glazed brake shoes
   5-C wheels out of alignment
   5-D crystallized wheel bearings

6. A good lubricant for locks is

   6-A graphite
   6-B grease
   6-C mineral oil
   6-D motor oil

7. Of the following, which is the most likely cause if an engine is found to be missing on one cylinder?

   7-A a clogged exhaust
   7-B a defective spark plug
   7-C an overheated engine
   7-D vapor lock

8. If an automobile engine overheats while the radiator remains cold, the difficulty probably lies in

   8-A lack of engine oil
   8-B a stuck thermostat
   8-C improper ignition timing
   8-D an overloaded engine

9. It is best for an automobile's gas tank to be full or nearly-full to prevent

   9-A gasoline from vaporizing in the fuel lines
   9-B moisture from condensing in the gas tank
   9-C drying out of the fuel pump
   9-D loss of vacuum in the vacuum line

10. Upon the complete loss of oil pressure while a car is in operation, it is best that the car be

    10-A pulled over to the side of the road and the engine stopped immediately for inspection
    10-B pulled over to the side of the road and a repair truck called to install a new oil pump
    10-C driven a few miles to your favorite garage
    10-D driven as usual for the entire day and be dropped off at the garage in the evening

7

GO ON TO THE NEXT PAGE.

11. When painting, nail holes and cracks should be

   11-A filled with putty before starting
   11-B filled with putty after the priming coat is applied
   11-C filled with paint by careful working
   11-D ignored

12.

   The tool shown above is a

   12-A punch
   12-B drill holder
   12-C Phillips-type screwdriver
   12-D socket wrench

7

13. An expansion bolt is used to

   13-A enlarge a hole
   13-B fasten into hollow tile
   13-C allow for expansion and contraction
   13-D fasten into solid masonry

14. The length of a 10-penny nail, in inches, is

   14-A $2\frac{1}{2}$
   14-B 3
   14-C $3\frac{1}{2}$
   14-D 4

15. Glazier's points are used to

   15-A hold glass in a wooden window sash
   15-B scratch glass so that it can be broken to size
   15-C force putty into narrow spaces between glass and sash
   15-D remove broken glass from a pane

16. A number 10 wood screw is

   16-A thicker than a number 6
   16-B longer than a number 6
   16-C shorter than a number 6
   16-D thinner than a number 6

17. Paint is "thinned" with

   17-A linseed oil
   17-B varnish
   17-C turpentine
   17-D gasoline

18.

   The tool shown above is

   18-A an offset wrench
   18-B a box wrench
   18-C a spanner wrench
   18-D an open end wrench

19. In grinding a good point on a twist drill, it is necessary that

   19-A the point be extremely sharp
   19-B both cutting edges have the same lip
   19-C a file be used for the entire cutting process
   19-D the final grinding be done by hand

20. The tool used to locate a point directly below a ceiling hook is a

   20-A plumb bob
   20-B line level
   20-C transit
   20-D drop gauge

21. The sawing of a piece of wood at a particular angle, for example 45 degrees, is accomplished by using a

   21-A jointer
   21-B cant board
   21-C miter box
   21-D binder

22. The plane to use in shaping a curved edge on wood is known as

   22-A jack
   22-B spoke shave
   22-C smooth
   22-D rabbet

GO ON TO THE NEXT PAGE.

23. The wrench that is used principally for pipe work is

23-A
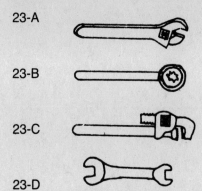

23-B

23-C

23-D

24. If an expander is used under an oil ring it must be

24-A of the diagonal joint type
24-B a rigid type
24-C of the step joint type
24-D of the vented type

25. A squeegee is a tool that is used in

25-A drying windows after washing
25-B cleaning inside boiler surfaces
25-C the central vacuum cleaning system
25-D clearing stoppages in waste lines

7

DO NOT TURN THIS PAGE UNTIL TOLD TO DO SO.
STOP! IF YOU FINISH BEFORE THE TIME IS UP, YOU
MAY CHECK OVER YOUR WORK ON THIS PART ONLY.

8

242

MATHEMATICS KNOWLEDGE

8

Directions

This is a test of your ability to solve 25 general mathematical problems. You are to select the correct response from the choices given. Then mark the space on your answer form which has the same number and letter as your choice. Use the scratch paper that has been given to you to do any figuring that you wish.

Now look at the two sample problems below.

S1. If $x + 6 = 7$, then x is equal to

S1-A 0
S1-B 1
S1-C -1
S1-D $\dfrac{7}{6}$

The correct answer is 1, so B is the correct response.

S2. What is the area of this square?

S2-A 1 square foot
S2-B 5 square feet
S2-C 10 square feet
S2-D 25 square feet

The correct answer is 25 square feet, so D is the correct response.

Your score on this test will be based on the number of questions you answer correctly. You should try to answer every question. Do not spend too much time on any one question.

When you are told to begin, be sure to start with question number 1 in Part 8 of your test booklet and number 1 in Part 8 on your answer form.

DO NOT TURN THIS PAGE UNTIL TOLD TO DO SO.

8

PART 8

MATHEMATICS KNOWLEDGE

TIME: 24 Minutes—25 Questions

1. If 30 is divided by .06, the result is

   1-A 5
   1-B 50
   1-C 500
   1-D 5,000

2. 36 yards and 12 feet divided by 3 =

   2-A 40 feet
   2-B 124 feet
   2-C $12\frac{1}{4}$ yards
   2-D 12 yards

3. 150 is what percent of 30?

   3-A 50
   3-B 150
   3-C 180
   3-D 500

4. R is what percent of 1,000?

   4-A .001R
   4-B 1R
   4-C .01R
   4-D .1R

5. A car owner finds he needs 12 gallons of gas for each 120 miles he drives. If he has his carburetor adjusted, he will need only 80% as much gas. How many miles will 12 gallons of gas then last him?

   5-A 90
   5-B 150
   5-C 96
   5-D 160

6. What fraction of 63 is $\frac{2}{7}$ of 21?

   6-A $\frac{1}{42}$
   6-B $\frac{7}{6}$
   6-C $\frac{2}{21}$
   6-D $\frac{1}{3}$

7. If the perimeter of an equilateral triangle is 6n − 12, what is the length of the base?

   7-A 3(2n − 4)
   7-B 2(3n − 6)
   7-C 3n − 6
   7-D 2n − 4

8. Which one of the following is a polygon?

   8-A circle
   8-B ellipse
   8-C star
   8-D parabola

9. A man walks once around a regular hexagonal (six-sided) field. If he starts in the middle of a side and follows the contour of the field, he will make 6

   9-A 30° turns
   9-B 45° turns
   9-C 60° turns
   9-D 120° turns

10. How many pints are equal to 2 gallons?

   10-A 8
   10-B 16
   10-C 4
   10-D 24

245 **GO ON TO THE NEXT PAGE.**

11. If x = y, find the value of 8 + 5(x − y).

    11-A 8 + 5x − 5y
    11-B 8 + 5xy
    11-C 13x − 13y
    11-D 8

12.

Triangle R is 3 times triangle S.
Triangle S is 3 times triangle T.
If triangle S = 1, what is the sum of the three triangles?

    12-A $2\frac{1}{3}$

    12-B $3\frac{1}{3}$

    12-C $4\frac{1}{3}$

    12-D 6

13. If ⅔ of a jar is filled with water in one minute, how many minutes longer will it take to fill the jar?

    13-A $\frac{1}{4}$

    13-B $\frac{1}{3}$

    13-C $\frac{1}{2}$

    13-D $\frac{2}{3}$

14. If 2 − x = x − 2, then x =

    14-A −2
    14-B 2
    14-C 0
    14-D $\frac{1}{2}$

15. What is the correct time if the hour hand is exactly ⅔ of the way between 5 and 6?

    15-A 5:25
    15-B 5:40
    15-C 5:30
    15-D 5:45

16. If .04y = 1, then y =

    16-A .025
    16-B 25
    16-C .25
    16-D 250

17. (3 + 2)(6 − 2)(7 + 1) = (4 + 4)(x). What is the value of x?

    17-A 13 + 2
    17-B 14 + 4
    17-C 4 + 15
    17-D 8 + 12

18. In the triangle below, angle B is 90 degrees. Which line in the triangle is longest?

    18-A AB
    18-B AC
    18-C neither
    18-D can't be determined from the information given

19. The reciprocal of 5 is

    19-A 1.0
    19-B 0.5
    19-C 0.2
    19-D 0.1

20. What is the area, in square inches, of a circle whose radius measures 7 inches? (Use ²²/₇ for pi)

    20-A 22
    20-B 44
    20-C 154
    20-D 616

GO ON TO THE NEXT PAGE.

8

21. Evaluate the expression 5a − 4x − 3y if a = −2, x = −10, and y = 5.

21-A +15
21-B +25
21-C −65
21-D −35

22. The area of circle O is 64π. The perimeter of square ABCD is

22-A 32
22-B 32π
22-C 64
22-D 16

23. The number of digits in the square root of 64,048,009 is

23-A 4
23-B 5
23-C 6
23-D 7

24. If 9 is 9% of x, then x =

24-A .01
24-B 100
24-C 1
24-D 9

25. 75% of 4 is the same as what percent of 9?

25-A 36
25-B 25
25-C 40
25-D 33⅓

8

DO NOT TURN THIS PAGE UNTIL TOLD TO DO SO.
STOP! IF YOU FINISH BEFORE THE TIME IS UP, YOU
MAY CHECK OVER YOUR WORK ON THIS PART ONLY.

9

MECHANICAL COMPREHENSION

9

Directions

This test has 25 questions about mechanical principles. Most of the questions use drawings to illustrate specific principles. Decide which answer is correct and mark the space on your separate answer form which has the same number and letter as your choice.

Here are two sample questions.

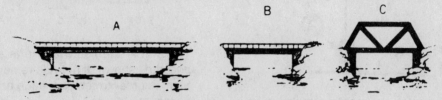

S1. Which bridge is the strongest?

    S1-A A
    S1-B B
    S1-C C
    S1-D All are equally strong

Answer C is correct.

   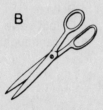    

S2. If all of these objects are the same temperature, which will feel coldest?

    S2-A A
    S2-B B
    S2-C C
    S2-D D

Answer B is correct.

Your score on this test will be based on the number of questions you answer correctly. You should try to answer every question. Do not spend too much time on any one question.

When you are told to begin, be sure to start with question number 1 in Part 9 of your test booklet and number 1 in Part 9 on your answer form.

DO NOT TURN THIS PAGE UNTIL TOLD TO DO SO.

MECHANICAL COMPREHENSION

TIME: 19 Minutes—25 Questions

9

1.

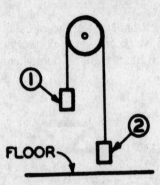

The figure above represents a pulley, with practically no friction, from which two ten-pound weights are suspended as indicated. If a downward force is applied to weight 1, it is most likely that weight 1 will

1-A come to rest at the present level of weight 2

1-B move downward until it is level with weight 2

1-C move downward until it reaches the floor

1-D pass weight 2 in its downward motion and then return to its present position

2.

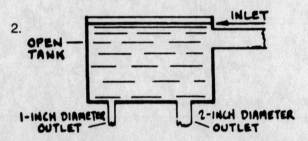

Eight gallons of water per minute are flowing at a given time from the one-inch outlet in the tank shown. What is the amount of water flowing at that time from the two-inch outlet?

2-A 64 gallons per minute

2-B 32 gallons per minute

2-C 16 gallons per minute

2-D 2 gallons per minute

3.

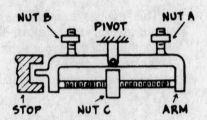

The arm in the figure above is exactly balanced as shown. If nut A is removed entirely then, in order to rebalance the arm, it will be necessary to turn

3-A nut C toward the right

3-B nut C toward the left

3-C nut B up

3-D nut B down

4. Automatic operation of a sump pump is controlled by the

4-A pneumatic switch

4-B float

4-C foot valve

4-D centrifugal driving unit

5.

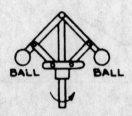

The figure above shows a governor on a rotating shaft. As the shaft speeds up, the governor balls will

5-A move down

5-B move upward and inward

5-C move upward

5-D move inward

GO ON TO THE NEXT PAGE.

6.

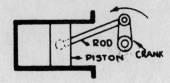

The figure above shows a crank and piston. The piston moves from mid-position to the extreme right if the crank

6-A makes $\frac{1}{2}$ turn

6-B makes a $\frac{3}{4}$ turn

6-C makes one turn

6-D makes $1\frac{1}{2}$ turns

7. If gear A makes 14 revolutions, gear B will make

7-A 9
7-B 14
7-C 17
7-D 21

8. If pulley A is the driver and turns in direction 1, which pulley turns fastest?

8-A A
8-B B
8-C C
8-D D

9. As cam A makes one complete turn, the setscrew will hit the contact point

9-A once
9-B twice
9-C three times
9-D not at all

10.

PRESSURE GAUGE

The reading shown on the above gauge is

10-A 10.35
10-B 13.5
10-C 10.7
10-D 17.0

11.

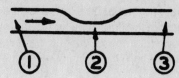

The figure above represents a pipe through which water is flowing in the direction of the arrow. There is a constriction in the pipe at the point indicated by the number 2. Water is being pumped into the pipe at a constant rate of 350 gallons per minute. Of the following, the most accurate statement is that

11-A the velocity of the water at point 2 is the same as the velocity of the water at point 3

11-B a greater volume of water is flowing past point 1 in a minute than is flowing past point 2

11-C the velocity of the water at point 1 is greater than the velocity at point 2

11-D the volume of water flowing past point 2 in a minute is the same as the volume of water flowing past point 1 in a minute

9

12.

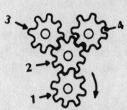

Four gears are shown in the figure above. If gear 1 turns as shown, then the gears turning in the same direction are

12-A 2 and 3
12-B 2 and 4
12-C 3 and 4
12-D 2, 3, and 4

13. The main purpose of expansion joints in steam lines is to

13-A provide for changes in length of heated pipe

13-B allow for connection of additional radiators

13-C provide locations for valves

13-D reduce breakage of pipe due to minor movement of the building frame

GO ON TO THE NEXT PAGE.

14. What effort must be exerted to lift a 60-pound weight in the figure of a first-class lever shown below (disregard weight of lever in your computation)?

14-A 30 pounds
14-B 36 pounds
14-C 45 pounds
14-D 60 pounds

15.

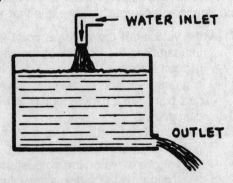

If water is flowing into the tank at the rate of 120 gallons per hour and flowing out of the tank at a constant rate of one gallon per minute, the water level in the tank will

15-A rise 1 gallon per minute
15-B rise 2 gallons per minute
15-C fall 2 gallons per minute
15-D fall 1 gallon per minute

16. A characteristic of a rotary pump is

16-A a rapidly rotating impeller moves the liquid through the discharge piping
16-B two gears, meshed together and revolving in opposite directions, move the liquid to the discharge pipe
16-C valves are required on the discharge side of the pump
16-D it is usually operated at high speeds up to 3,600 RPM

17.

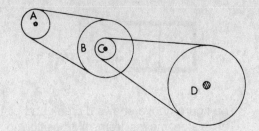

In the diagram above, pulley A drives a system of pulleys. Pulleys B and C are keyed to the same shaft. Use the following diameters in your computations: A = 1 inch; B = 2 inches; C = $\frac{1}{2}$ inch; and D = 4 inches. When pulley A runs at an rpm of 2,000, pulley D will make

17-A 125 rpm
17-B 500 rpm
17-C 250 rpm
17-D 8,000 rpm

18. The weight is being carried entirely on the shoulders of the two persons shown below. Which person bears the most weight?

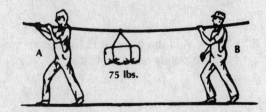

18-A A
18-B B
18-C Both are carrying the same weight.
18-D It cannot be determined.

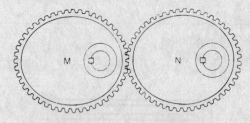

19. If gear N turns at a constant rpm, gear M turns at

19-A the same constant rpm as N
19-B a faster constant rpm than N
19-C a slower constant rpm than N
19-D a variable rpm

GO ON TO THE NEXT PAGE.

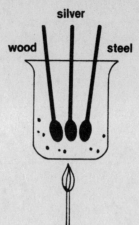

24.

Which spoon is hottest?

24-A wood
24-B silver
24-C steel
24-D silver and steel are equally hot

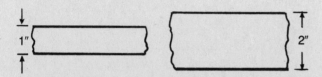

20. The figure above shows a lever-type safety valve. It will blow off at a lower pressure if weight W is

20-A increased
20-B moved to the right
20-C increased and moved to the right
20-D moved to the left

21. With the same water pressure, the amount of water that can be carried by a 2-inch pipe as compared with a 1-inch pipe is

21-A the same
21-B twice as much
21-C 3 times as much
21-D 4 times as much

22. In order to stop a faucet from dripping, your first act should be to replace the

22-A cap nut
22-B seat
22-C washer
22-D spindle

23. In the figure given below, assume that all valves are closed. For air flow from R through G and then through S to M, open

There are twenty teeth on the front sprocket and ten teeth on the rear sprocket on the bicycle above. Each time the pedals go around, the rear wheel will

25-A go half way around
25-B go around once
25-C go around twice
25-D go around four times

9

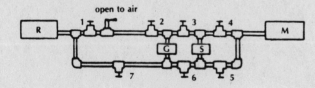

23-A valves 7, 6, and 5
23-B valves 7, 3, and 4
23-C valves 7, 6, and 4
23-D valves 7, 3, and 5

DO NOT TURN THIS PAGE UNTIL TOLD TO DO SO.
STOP! IF YOU FINISH BEFORE THE TIME IS UP, YOU
MAY CHECK OVER YOUR WORK ON THIS PART ONLY.

10

ELECTRONICS INFORMATION

10

Directions

This is a test of your knowledge of electrical, radio, and electronics information. There are 20 questions. You are to select the correct response from the choices given. Then mark the space on your answer form which has the same number and letter as your choice.

Now look at the two sample questions below.

1S. What does the abbreviation AC stand for?

    1S-A additional charge
    1S-B alternating coil
    1S-C alternating current
    1S-D ampere current

The correct answer is alternating current, so C is the correct response.

2S. Which of the following has the least resist-ance?

    2S-A wood
    2S-B silver
    2S-C rubber
    2S-D iron

The correct answer is silver, so B is the correct response.

Your score on this test will be based on the number of questions you answer correctly. You should try to answer every question. Do not spend too much time on any one question.

When you are told to begin, be sure to start with question number 1 in Part 10 of your test booklet and number 1 in Part 10 on your answer form.

DO NOT TURN THIS PAGE UNTIL TOLD TO DO SO.

ELECTRONICS INFORMATION

TIME: 9 Minutes—20 Questions

1. The core of an electromagnet is usually

   1-A aluminum
   1-B brass
   1-C lead
   1-D iron

2. An electrician should consider all electrical equipment "alive" unless he definitely knows otherwise. The main reason for this practice is to avoid

   2-A doing unnecessary work
   2-B energizing the wrong circuit
   2-C personal injury
   2-D de-energizing a live circuit

3. If *voltage* is represented by V, *current* by I and *resistance* by R, then the one of the following that correctly states Ohm's Law is

   3-A $R = V \times I$
   3-B $R = \dfrac{I}{V}$
   3-C $V = I \times R$
   3-D $V = \dfrac{I}{R}$

4. When working near lead acid storage batteries extreme care should be taken to guard against sparks, essentially to avoid

   4-A overheating the electrolyte
   4-B an electric shock
   4-C a short circuit
   4-D an explosion

5. The voltage that will cause a current of 5 amperes to flow through a 20 Ohm resistance is

   5-A $\dfrac{1}{4}$ volt
   5-B 4 volts
   5-C 20 volts
   5-D 100 volts

6. Receptacles in a house-lighting system are regularly connected in

   6-A parallel
   6-B series
   6-C diagonal
   6-D perpendicular

7. The oscilloscope image shown above represents

   7-A steady DC
   7-B resistance in a resistor
   7-C AC
   7-D pulsating DC

8. Voltage drop in a circuit is usually due to

   8-A inductance
   8-B capacitance
   8-C resistance
   8-D conductance

9. Which of the following sizes of electric heaters is the largest one that can be used in a 120-volt circuit protected by a 15-ampere circuit breaker?

   9-A 1000 watts
   9-B 1300 watts
   9-C 2000 watts
   9-D 2600 watts

10. Low Potential is a trade term which refers to

   10-A 700 volts
   10-B 600 volts or less
   10-C 1,200 volts
   10-D 900 volts

GO ON TO THE NEXT PAGE.

11. The purpose of having a rheostat in the field circuit of a DC shunt motor is to

    11-A control the speed of the motor
    11-B minimize the starting current
    11-C limit the field current to a safe value
    11-D reduce sparking at the brushes

12. A polarized plug generally has

    12-A two parallel prongs of the same size
    12-B prongs at an angle with one another
    12-C magnetized prongs
    12-D prongs marked plus and minus

13. In comparing Nos. 00, 8, 12, and 6 A.W.G. wires, the smallest of the group is

    13-A No. 00
    13-B No. 8
    13-C No. 12
    13-D No. 6

14.

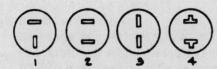

The convenience outlet that is known as a *polarized* outlet is number

    14-A 1
    14-B 2
    14-C 3
    14-D 4

15. In a house bell circuit, the push button for ringing the bell is generally connected in the secondary of the transformer feeding the bell. One reason for doing this is to

    15-A save power
    15-B keep line voltage out of the push button circuit
    15-C prevent the bell from burning out
    15-D prevent arcing of the vibrator contact points in the bell

16. Operating an incandescent electric light bulb at less than its rated voltage will result in

    16-A shorter life and brighter light
    16-B brighter light and longer life
    16-C longer life and dimmer light
    16-D dimmer light and shorter life

17.

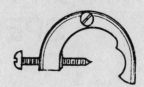

The device shown above is a

    17-A C-clamp
    17-B test clip
    17-C battery connector
    17-D ground clamp

10

18. When the electric refrigerator in a certain household kitchen starts up, the kitchen light at first dims considerably and then it increases somewhat in brightness while the refrigerator motor is running; the light finally returns to full brightness when the refrigerator shuts off. This behavior of the light shows that most likely the

    18-A circuit wires are too small
    18-B refrigerator motor is defective
    18-C circuit fuse is too small
    18-D kitchen lamp is too large

19. In electronic circuits, the symbol shown below usually represents a

    19-A transformer
    19-B capacitor
    19-C transistor
    19-D diode

20. In electronic circuits, the symbol shown below usually represents a

    20-A diode
    20-B magnetron
    20-C transistor
    20-D triode

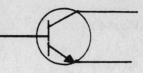

END OF EXAMINATION

IF YOU FINISH BEFORE THE TIME IS UP, YOU MAY CHECK OVER YOUR WORK ON THIS PART ONLY.
DO NOT GO BACK TO ANY PREVIOUS PART.

ANSWER KEY—THIRD ASVAB SPECIMEN TEST

Use these answer keys to determine the number of correct answers you received on each part and to list those items which you answered incorrectly or which you are unsure of how to arrive at the correct answer.

Be certain to review carefully and understand the rationale for arriving at the correct answer for all questions you answered incorrectly, as well as those you answered correctly but are unsure of. This is absolutely essential in order to acquire the knowledge and expertise necessary to obtain the maximum scores possible on the actual ASVAB subtests.

Transfer the scores you obtained on each part of the Third ASVAB Specimen Test to the Self-Appraisal Chart appearing on page 275. This will enable you to see the progress made as you continue to prepare for the actual test.

PART 1—GENERAL SCIENCE

1. A	5. D	8. D	11. A	14. C	17. D	20. A	23. C
2. C	6. B	9. A	12. B	15. A	18. C	21. A	24. D
3. B	7. C	10. D	13. D	16. A	19. A	22. B	25. D
4. A							

Items
Answered
Incorrectly: ___; ___; ___; ___; ___; ___; ___; ___.

Items
Unsure
Of: ___; ___; ___; ___; ___; ___; ___; ___.

Total
Number
Answered
Correctly: _____

258

PART 2—ARITHMETIC REASONING

1. C	5. D	9. A	13. B	17. C	21. D	25. C	28. D
2. A	6. B	10. A	14. C	18. D	22. A	26. D	29. D
3. D	7. B	11. C	15. A	19. C	23. C	27. C	30. B
4. D	8. A	12. B	16. C	20. C	24. B		

Items
Answered
Incorrectly: ___; ___; ___; ___; ___; ___; ___; ___.

Items
Unsure
Of: ___; ___; ___; ___; ___; ___; ___; ___.

Total
Number
Answered
Correctly: _____

PART 3—WORD KNOWLEDGE

1. C	6. C	11. B	16. C	20. B	24. C	28. C	32. C
2. D	7. D	12. B	17. B	21. A	25. A	29. A	33. C
3. A	8. B	13. D	18. C	22. C	26. D	30. C	34. C
4. D	9. D	14. C	19. A	23. C	27. B	31. C	35. C
5. D	10. D	15. D					

Items
Answered
Incorrectly: ___; ___; ___; ___; ___; ___; ___; ___.

Items
Unsure
Of: ___; ___; ___; ___; ___; ___; ___.

Total
Number
Answered
Correctly: _____

PART 4—PARAGRAPH COMPREHENSION

1. D	3. D	5. B	7. B	9. C	11. A	13. B	15. C
2. D	4. C	6. D	8. D	10. C	12. D	14. B

Items
Answered
Incorrectly: ___; ___; ___; ___; ___; ___; ___; ___.

Items
Unsure
Of: ___; ___; ___; ___; ___; ___; ___; ___.

Total
Number
Answered
Correctly: _____

PART 5—NUMERICAL OPERATIONS

1. A	8. C	15. D	21. A	27. C	33. B	39. D	45. B
2. B	9. C	16. B	22. C	28. A	34. D	40. D	46. A
3. D	10. B	17. D	23. A	29. D	35. D	41. B	47. A
4. D	11. A	18. A	24. A	30. D	36. B	42. B	48. D
5. C	12. C	19. C	25. D	31. B	37. A	43. D	49. D
6. B	13. A	20. C	26. A	32. B	38. C	44. D	50. D
7. A	14. D						

Items Answered Incorrectly: ___; ___; ___; ___; ___; ___; ___; ___.

Items Unsure Of: ___; ___; ___; ___; ___; ___; ___; ___.

Total Number Answered Correctly: _____

PART 6—CODING SPEED

1. B	12. B	23. E	34. C	45. B	55. C	65. D	75. B
2. D	13. B	24. C	35. A	46. A	56. A	66. C	76. A
3. A	14. E	25. D	36. C	47. E	57. E	67. C	77. D
4. C	15. C	26. E	37. E	48. A	58. B	68. D	78. B
5. E	16. B	27. B	38. D	49. C	59. A	69. A	79. E
6. E	17. D	28. D	39. B	50. B	60. C	70. D	80. A
7. E	18. E	29. A	40. A	51. B	61. E	71. E	81. C
8. C	19. A	30. E	41. E	52. D	62. C	72. A	82. D
9. A	20. B	31. B	42. B	53. C	63. B	73. D	83. E
10. B	21. C	32. A	43. C	54. A	64. E	74. D	84. E
11. C	22. D	33. C	44. D				

Items Answered Incorrectly: ___; ___; ___; ___; ___; ___; ___; ___.

Items Unsure Of: ___; ___; ___; ___; ___; ___; ___; ___.

Total Number Answered Correctly: _____

PART 7—AUTO & SHOP INFORMATION

1. C	5. B	8. B	11. B	14. B	17. C	20. A	23. C
2. D	6. A	9. B	12. D	15. A	18. D	21. C	24. D
3. C	7. B	10. A	13. D	16. A	19. B	22. B	25. A
4. C							

Items
Answered
Incorrectly: ___; ___; ___; ___; ___; ___; ___; ___.

Items
Unsure
Of: ___; ___; ___; ___; ___; ___; ___; ___.

Total
Number
Answered
Correctly: _____

PART 8—MATHEMATICS KNOWLEDGE

1. C	5. B	8. C	11. D	14. B	17. D	20. C	23. A
2. A	6. C	9. D	12. C	15. B	18. B	21. A	24. B
3. D	7. D	10. B	13. C	16. D	19. C	22. C	25. D
4. D							

Items
Answered
Incorrectly: ___; ___; ___; ___; ___; ___; ___; ___.

Items
Unsure
Of: ___; ___; ___; ___; ___; ___; ___; ___.

Total
Number
Answered
Correctly: _____

PART 9—MECHANICAL COMPREHENSION

1. C	5. C	8. A	11. D	14. B	17. A	20. D	23. D
2. B	6. B	9. A	12. C	15. A	18. A	21. D	24. B
3. A	7. D	10. D	13. A	16. B	19. A	22. C	25. C
4. B							

Items
Answered
Incorrectly: ___; ___; ___; ___; ___; ___; ___; ___.

Items
Unsure
Of: ___; ___; ___; ___; ___; ___; ___; ___.

Total
Number
Answered
Correctly: _____

PART 10—ELECTRONICS INFORMATION

1. D	4. D	7. D	10. B	13. C	15. B	17. D	19. D
2. C	5. D	8. C	11. A	14. A	16. C	18. A	20. C
3. C	6. A	9. B	12. B				

Items
Answered
Incorrectly: ____; ____; ____; ____; ____; ____; ____; ____.

Items
Unsure
Of: ____; ____; ____; ____; ____; ____; ____; ____.

Total
Number
Answered
Correctly: _____

EXPLANATIONS—THIRD ASVAB SPECIMEN TEST

PART 1—GENERAL SCIENCE

1-A Fruits have seeds. Tomatoes, cucumbers, and green peppers have seeds. A potato is a tuber.

2-C The hammer, anvil, and stirrup are the three tiny bones that connect the eardrum with the inner ear.

3-B Cigarette smoking can speed up the heartbeat.

4-A The Wassermann test, developed by a German bacteriologist in 1906, is a blood test for syphilis.

5-D Wood alcohol is methyl alcohol, which is extremely toxic; drinking it may cause blindness. Isopropyl alcohol is rubbing alcohol. Glyceryl alcohol is an industrial solvent.

6-B Nitrogen constitutes about four-fifths of the earth's atmosphere, by volume.

7-C All spiders have four pairs of legs. True insects have three pairs of legs.

8-D Uranium is found in pitchblende and other rare metals. Hematite is a source of iron; chalcopyrite is an ore of copper; bauxite is a source of aluminum.

9-A The atomic weight of hydrogen is 1.0080, that of helium 4.003, and of oxygen 16.00. Air is not an element, but a mixture of gases.

10-D An echo is the repetition of a sound caused by the reflection of sound waves. An image is an optical appearance of an object produced by reflection from a mirror.

11-A With the centigrade scale, the fixed points are the freezing and boiling points of water. The interval is divided into 100 parts so that the freezing point of water is 0°C and the boiling point is 100°C.

12-B When a beam of light passes obliquely from a medium of one optical density to a medium of another optical density, it is refracted or bent. From the bank, a person viewing a fish under water will find that the fish is not where it appears to be because of the refraction of light traveling from air into water.

13-D Group B served as the control group. If the condition of patients in Group A were to improve significantly more than that of patients in Group B, scientists might have reason to believe in the effectiveness of the drug.

14-C Vitamin A deficiency leads to poor night vision. Since carrots are high in vitamin A, they should have a positive effect upon night vision, although eating large quantities of carrots will not in itself insure perfect night vision.

15-A Radiation cannot pass through lead.

16-A Coal is formed by the partial decomposition of vegetable matter under the influence of moisture, pressure, and temperature and in the absence of air. If there is coal in Alaska, there must once have been abundant vegetation in Alaska.

17-D Damage to the neck and back is especially dangerous because the spinal cord is so vulnerable. Once the spinal cord is severed, paralysis is inevitable and irreversible, so if there is any question of back or neck injury the person should be moved only by a skilled professional.

18-C Like displaces like.

19-A The denser the liquid, the less the weight of the lead sinker. Accordingly, liquid B has less density than liquid A.

20-A The lowering of the freezing point of a solution is generally proportional to the solute particles in the solution. A practical application of this principle is the throwing of salt on a snow or ice covered sidewalk to help melt the snow or ice.

21-A Organisms that live on or in the body of other live organisms from which food is obtained are called parasites.

22-B $\dfrac{\text{Distance}}{\text{Time}} = \text{Speed}$

23-C Circuit breakers serve exactly the same function as fuses. Should wires become overheated for any reason, the circuit breaker will "trip," thus breaking the circuit and interrupting the flow of electricity. Fuse burnout creates the same protective interruption of current.

24-D An electron is a negative particle. A proton is positively charged; a neutron is neutral and without charge; a meson has both positive and negative charges.

25-D Limestone, a sedimentary rock composed of calcium carbonate, can be dissolved with a weak acid.

PART 2—ARITHMETIC REASONING

1-C $3.00 per hour for 8 hours = $24.00
50 − 40 = 10 bushels
10 bushels @ $.72/bushel = $7.20
$24.00 + $7.20 = $31.20

2-A $\dfrac{144}{36} = 4$ buses

3-D 600 gallons = 2400 quarts

$\dfrac{2400}{120} = 20$ minutes

4-D The number of hours in the clerk's work week is irrelevant. Figure the percent of his time that he spent at the enumerated tasks. The difference between that percent and his full week (100%) is the percent of his time spent on messenger work.

$$\frac{1}{5} = \frac{14}{70}$$
$$\frac{1}{2} = \frac{35}{70}$$
$$\frac{1}{7} = \frac{10}{70}$$
$$\frac{59}{70} = .84 = 84\%; \; 100\% - 84\%$$
$$= 16\% \text{ on messenger work}$$

5-D $6,200 − $4,000 = $2,200 is the amount he made.
$2,200 ÷ $50 (profit on each bicycle) = 44 bicycles sold.

6-B Convert the miles to kilometers by dividing them by $\frac{5}{8}$.

$$500 \text{ miles} \div \frac{5}{8} = \frac{\overset{100}{\cancel{500}}}{1} \times \frac{8}{\underset{1}{\cancel{5}}} = 800 \text{ kilometers}$$

7-B To find the percent of increase, subtract the original figure from the new figure. Then divide the amount of change by the original figure.
22¢ − 20¢ = 2¢; 2 ÷ 20 = .10 = 10%

8-A $4 \times \frac{1}{4}$ inch = 1 inch

9-A 8 pts. in 1 gal.; 80 pts. in 10 gal.; 160 $\frac{1}{2}$ pts. in 10 gal.

10-A Cost per bar when purchased in small amounts = $0.33;
$\frac{\$3.48}{12}$ = $0.29, cost per bar when purchased in lots of one dozen
$0.33 − $0.29 = $0.04, savings per bar

11-C $25 × 20 = $500 in contributions
$500 × .40 = $200 spent for food and drinks
$500 − $200 = $300 remaining for other expenses

12-B Let x = length of nearby pole's shadow.
24 : 8 = 72 : x; 24x = 8 × 72;
$$x = \frac{8 \times \overset{3}{\cancel{72}}}{\underset{1}{\cancel{24}}} = 24 \text{ feet}$$

13-B $1,000.00 − $941.20 = $58.80

14-C
$$\begin{aligned}\$4.98 \times 4 &= \$19.92 \\ +8.29 \times 2 &= 16.58 \\ +8.09 \times 2 &= \underline{16.18} \\ &\quad\ \$52.68\end{aligned}$$

15-A 48 − 40 = 8 hours overtime
Salary for 8 hours overtime:

$$1\frac{1}{2} \times \$8.60 \times 8 = \frac{3}{\underset{1}{\cancel{2}}} \times \$8.60 \times \overset{4}{\cancel{8}}$$
$$= \$103.20$$

Salary for 40 hours regular time:

$8.60 × 40 = $344.00

Total salary = $344.00 + $103.20
= $447.20

16-C The carton contains 9 × 12 = 108 folders.
108 − 53 = 55 remain in carton.

17-C $25 ÷ $4.95 = 5.05—He could buy 5 ties.
$4.95 × 5 = $24.75. After buying 5 ties the man would still have 25¢ left.

18-D
$$\begin{aligned}\$20.56 \\ 32.90 \\ +\underline{20.78} \\ \$74.24 \div 2 = \$37.12 \text{ left}\end{aligned}$$

19-C 15′ × 24′ = 5 yards × 8 yards = 40 square yards
40 square yards × $1.00 = $40.00

20-C 16½ hours = 15 hours + 90 minutes; ¹⁵⁄₅ = 3 hours; ⁹⁰⁄₅ = 18 minutes; 3 hours + 18 minutes = 3 hours, 18 minutes

21-D 100 miles @ 40 mph = 2½ hours = 2³⁄₆ hours
80 miles @ 60 mph = 1⅓ hours = 1²⁄₆ hours
2³⁄₆ hours + 1²⁄₆ hours = 3⁵⁄₆ hours

22-A
$$\begin{aligned}3 \text{ days } 10 \text{ hrs. } 40 \text{ min.} \\ +\underline{10 \text{ hrs. } 2 \text{ min.}} \\ 3 \text{ days } 20 \text{ hrs. } 42 \text{ min.}\end{aligned}$$

23-C $20.00 − $18.95 = $1.05

24-B $66.00 ÷ 20 = $3.30

25-C Only 10 boys can play at one time. Therefore, the 30 boys must be divided into 3 groups. Each group can then play 45 min. ÷ 3 = 15 min.

26-D 65¢ − 5¢ for the first day = 60¢ for the other days. 60¢ ÷ 2¢ = 30 other days. The book was 31 days overdue.

27-C 1 lb. = 16 oz.; 2 lb. = 32 oz.; 32 oz. ÷ 2 oz. = 16 slices

28-D $21.00 + $14.98 + $4.97 = $40.95

29-D Don drove 50 miles × 2 hours = 100 miles. Frank drove 40 miles × 2 hours = 80 miles. Since they drove in opposite directions, add the two distances to learn that they were 180 miles apart.

30-B

$$\begin{array}{rr} \$14.28 \times 1 = & \$14.28 \\ +33.26 \times 2 = & 66.52 \\ \underline{65.38 \times 2 =} & \underline{130.76} \\ & \$211.56 \end{array}$$

PART 3—WORD KNOWLEDGE

1-C *Double* means *twofold* or *twice* as much.

2-D To *purchase* is to *buy* for a price.

3-A *Hollow* means *empty.*

4-D *Deportment* means *behavior* or *conduct.*

5-D *Prior* means *previous* or *earlier.*

6-C Grimy and ragged often go together, but *grimy* means *dirty.*

7-D The word *cease* means to stop or come to an end.

8-B The word *acclaim* is synonymous with applause or approval.

9-D The word *erect* means to build or construct.

10-D *Allegiance* means *devotion* or *loyalty.*

11-B To *yearn* is to *have a great desire for* or to *be filled with longing.*

12-B The *summit* is the *top.*

13-D *Villainous* means *wicked* or *evil.*

14-C One who has a *conviction* is *fully convinced,* so holds a *firm belief.*

15-D *Punctual* means *prompt* or *on time.*

16-C To *irritate* is to *incite impatience or displeasure,* to *exasperate,* or to *annoy.*

17-B *Uniform* means *all the same, consistent,* or *unchanging.*

18-C *Power* is *strength* or *force.* All the other choices are attributes which might help one to attain power.

19-A The word *abandon* means to give up or relinquish.

20-B *Resolve* means to determine or decide.

21-A *Ample* means abundant or plentiful.

22-C To be *bewildered* is to be *confused* or *puzzled*.

23-C The *conclusion* is the *end*.

24-C An *aroma* is a *pleasing smell* or *fragrance*.

25-A *Startled* means *frightened suddenly,* though not seriously, hence *surprised.*

26-D *Forthcoming* means *coming up* or *approaching.*

27-B A *verdict* is a *decision* or *judgment.*

28-C A *blemish* is a *mark of deformity,* a *defect* or a *flaw.*

29-A To *convey* is to *transmit,* to *transport,* or to *carry.*

30-C A *pedestrian* is a *foot traveler,* a *walker.* Pedestrians walk across the street.

31-C *Incessant* means unceasing or constant.

32-C *Solidity* means firmness or the quality of being solid.

33-C *Increment* means an addition or increase.

34-C One's *vocation* is one's *occupation* or *calling.*

35-C That which is *mature* is *fully aged* or *ripe.*

PART 4—PARAGRAPH COMPREHENSION

1-D The first three options are not supported by the passage. The second sentence in the passage states that steel bars, deeply embedded in the concrete, are sinews (a source of strength) to take the stresses.

2-D If the collection letter must show clear organization and show evidence of a mind that has a specific end in view, it should be carefully planned.

3-D The second sentence states that a toad's skin is both dry and rough.

4-C The vaulter may attempt to jump any height above the minimum which is set by the judge.

5-B The second sentence states that the other planets were thought to be in heaven.

6-D The key word is "compromise." A railroad line must be built along logical trade and commerce routes even if construction is more expensive.

7-B The passage says that enough data has been collected to draw the conclusion that the rural crime rates are lower than those in urban communities.

8-D See the first sentence in the reading passage.

9-C The passage states that office manuals are a necessity in large organizations.

10-C A laborer who has only one skill may find himself unemployed if that skill is not in demand. A more versatile worker can find a job requiring another skill.

11-A The first sentence states that when there is a sharp rise in demand for new buildings, construction invariably lags behind; that is, there are fewer new buildings in proportion to buyers.

12-D The last sentence states that when there is a sudden drop in the demand for new buildings, their prices fall because the available supply cannot be curtailed.

13-B See the second paragraph in the reading passage.

14-B See the last paragraph in the reading passage.

15-C A meter is one ten-millionth of the distance from the Equator to the North Pole. One ten-millionth = 1/10,000,000.

PART 5—NUMERICAL OPERATIONS

1-A $5 - 3 = 2$

2-B $8 - 6 = 2$

3-D $12 \div 2 = 6$

4-D $8 - 6 = 2$

5-C $4 + 8 = 12$

6-B $6 \times 8 = 48$

7-A $18 - 14 = 4$

8-C $2 \times 12 = 24$

9-C $9 - 6 = 3$

10-B $1 \times 6 = 6$

11-A $7 - 2 = 5$

12-C $5 - 0 = 5$

13-A $10 - 6 = 4$

14-D $1 + 5 = 6$

15-D $4 \times 2 = 8$

16-B $49 \div 7 = 7$

17-D $3 \times 10 = 30$

18-A $8 - 0 = 8$

19-C $4 \times 3 = 12$

20-C $8 - 3 = 5$

21-A $7 \times 4 = 28$

22-C $4 + 8 = 12$

23-A $5 - 1 = 4$

24-A $9 \div 3 = 3$

25-D $4 + 5 = 9$

26-A $7 \times 8 = 56$

27-C $9 + 6 = 15$

28-A $8 \div 2 = 4$

29-D $7 - 1 = 6$

30-D $8 \div 8 = 1$

31-B $5 \div 5 = 1$

32-B $5 \times 3 = 15$

33-B $16 \div 4 = 4$

34-D $6 \times 2 = 12$

35-D $10 - 8 = 2$

36-B $7 \div 1 = 7$

37-A $9 \div 3 = 3$

38-C $4 \times 8 = 32$

39-D $5 \div 5 = 1$

40-D $7 - 4 = 3$

41-B $4 - 0 = 4$

42-B $1 \times 2 = 2$

43-D $12 + 2 = 14$

44-D $3 \times 15 = 45$

45-B $25 \div 5 = 5$

46-A $3 \times 4 = 12$

47-A $8 - 6 = 2$

48-D $8 \div 2 = 4$

49-D $20 \div 2 = 10$

50-D $8 - 7 = 1$

PART 6—CODING SPEED

There is no way to explain the answers to the Coding Speed questions. A few mistakes are inevitable. If you made many mistakes, look to see if they fall into any pattern. Slow down a bit on the next specimen test.

PART 7—AUTO & SHOP INFORMATION

1-C The most popular engine has a four-stroke cycle. The four cycles are intake, compression, power, and exhaust.

2-D The most important rule is to maintain the level of the liquid. This liquid—usually water—acts as an electrolyte, a necessary component when electricity is discharged from a battery. Without it, no electricity will be produced.

3-C The rotor determines which spark plug is to ignite. It is found under the distributor cap. The rotor is connected by a shaft to the engine and is timed to ignite the spark plug at the top of the power stroke.

4-C Batteries in a car are refilled with distilled water. The other chemicals either will not work or will damage the battery.

5-B Overheating the brake shoe will cause the brake material to glaze and become slippery. Slippery brakes are dangerous because they take longer to stop a car.

6-A Graphite, which is powdered carbon, is very slippery and will not bind the small springs and metal parts of a lock.

7-B Although all of the options may cause an engine to miss, a defective spark plug is the likely cause if the engine misses only on one cylinder.

8-B If an automobile engine overheats while the radiator remains cold, it is probably a faulty thermostat. The thermostat cuts off the flow of the coolant to the radiator when the engine is cold and allows the coolant to flow to the radiator as the coolant temperature rises. A stuck thermostat prevents this flow to the radiator, resulting in an overheated engine and a cool radiator.

9-B Moisture enters with the air, especially on damp days. Condensation forms inside the gas tank and collects in the bottom of the tank to form a rust or create a thick sludge. Keeping the gas tank as nearly full as possible allows less room for formation of condensation.

10-A If an engine loses oil pressure, the car must be stopped immediately. Otherwise, it will overheat and become damaged.

11-B Nail holes are filled with putty after applying the priming coat, before you apply the finishing coat of paint.

12-D Although this tool looks like a screwdriver, the head will fit into a hex nut and works like a socket wrench.

13-D An expansion bolt is put into a hole that has been drilled into solid masonry. The bolt is then tightened, forcing apart the sides of the expansion bolt. This anchors into the concrete.

14-B A 10-penny nail is 3 inches long. For each 2-penny increase, the length increases by ½ inch. So, a 4-penny nail is 1½ inches long and a 12-penny nail is 3½ inches long.

15-A Glazier's points are triangular-shaped pieces of metal which are inserted into a window frame to prevent the glass from being pushed out.

16-A The number on the box of wood screws tells the thickness. The higher the number, the thicker the screw. A number 10 wood screw will be thicker than a number 6 wood screw.

17-C Paint is made thinner or easier to apply by diluting it with turpentine. Linseed oil and varnish are not used as paint thinners.

18-D The opened face on this tool shows that it is an open end wrench.

19-B In twist drill grinding, it is important to have equal and correctly sized drill-point angles, equal length cutting tips, correct clearance behind the cutting lips, and correct chisel-edge angle. Option B is the only correct option.

20-A A plumb bob is a weight, often of lead, used in a line to determine vertical direction.

21-C A miter box is a device for guiding a handsaw at the proper angle when making a miter joint in wood.

22-B A spoke shave is used to plane a dowel-shaped surface. The other planes are used to smooth flat surfaces.

23-C Figure C is a pipe wrench; A is a crescent or expandable wrench; B is a ratchet wrench; and D is an open-end wrench.

24-D An oil ring expander must be of the vented type. As piston rings heat up, they expand. The vent is necessary to allow for expansion.

25-A A squeegee is a rubber wiper that removes water from a wet window.

PART 8—MATHEMATICS KNOWLEDGE

1-C When dividing by a decimal, move the decimal place in the divisor to the right to create a whole number. Move the decimal point in the dividend to the right the same number of places. Place the decimal point of the quotient directly above the decimal point of the dividend.

$$.06\overline{)30.00} = 500.$$

2-A 36 yards = 108 feet; 108 feet + 12 feet = 120 feet; 120 feet ÷ 3 = 40 feet

3-D To find what percent one number is of another number, create a fraction by putting the part over the whole. Reduce the fraction, if possible, then convert it to a decimal (*remember:* the line means *divided by,* so divide the numerator by the denominator), and change to a percent by multiplying by 100, moving the decimal point two places to the right.

$$\frac{\overset{5}{\cancel{150}}}{\underset{1}{\cancel{30}}} = 5 \times 100 = 500\%$$

4-D To find what percent one number is of another number, create a fraction by putting the part over the whole. Then convert to a decimal by dividing the numerator by the denominator and change to a percent by multiplying by 100.

$$\frac{R}{1,000} = .001R = .1R\%$$

5-B Right now he gets 120 mi. ÷ 12 gal. = 10 mpg. After carburetor adjustment, he will need 80% of 12 or 9.6 gal. to go 120 miles. He will then get 120 mi. ÷ 9.6 gal. = 12.5 mpg. 12 gal × 12.5 mpg = 150 miles on 12 gal.

6-C $\dfrac{2}{7} \times \dfrac{\overset{3}{\cancel{21}}}{1} = 6; \dfrac{6}{63} = \dfrac{2}{21}$

7-D An equilateral triangle has 3 equal sides. Therefore if its perimeter is 6n − 12, each side is $\dfrac{6n - 12}{3} = 2n - 4$.

8-C Only the star is a closed plane figure bounded by straight lines.

9-D The sum of angles of a hexagon = 180° (6 − 2) = 180° × 4 = 720°. As a hexagon contains 6 angles, 720°/6 = 120° = measure of each angle.

10-B There are 8 pints in 1 gallon so there are 16 pints in 2 gallons.

11-D 8 + 5(x − y) = 8 + 5x − 5y
Since x = y, 5x = 5y and 5x − 5y = 0
Substituting: 8 + 0 = 8

12-C
$S = 1$
$+R = 3 \times 1$
$+T = \dfrac{1}{3}$
_____
$4\dfrac{1}{3}$

13-C If ⅔ of the jar is filled in 1 minute, then ⅓ of the jar is filled in ½ minute. Since the jar is ⅔ full, ⅓ remains to be filled. The jar will be full in another ½ minute.

14-B The quickest way to answer this question is to try substituting the given values. If x = 2, then 2 − 2 = 2 − 2 is a true statement.
To solve algebraically: 2 − x = x − 2 (add 2)
4 = 2x (divide by 2)
2 = x

15-B $\dfrac{2}{3}$ of 60 min. = 40 min.
5:00 + 40 min. = 5:40

16-D .04y = 1
y = 1 ÷ .04 = 250

17-D (3 + 2)(6 − 2)(7 + 1) = (4 + 4)(x)
(5)(4)(8) = 8x
8x = 160
x = 20 = 8 + 12

18-B The hypotenuse, the side opposite the right angle, is the longest side.

19-C Reciprocal of 5 = 1/5 = .20 = 0.2

20-C Area $= \pi r^2 = \dfrac{22}{7} \times 7^2 = 22 \times 7 = 154$ sq. in.

21-A 5a − 4x − 3y = 5(−2) − 4(−0) − 3(5) = −10 + 40 − 15 = +15

22-C The formula for the area of a circle is πr^2. In this problem, $r^2 = 64$ so r = 8. The circle is tangent with the square on all four sides; the radius is exactly $\dfrac{1}{2}$ the length of a side of the square. Each side, then, is 16 units long. The formula for the perimeter of a square is P = 4s, so 4 × 16 = 64.

23-A The first step to finding the square root of a number is to pair the digits to each side of the decimal point. Each pair represents one digit in the square root. 64 04 80 09.

24-B 9% of x = 9
.09x = 9
x = 100

25-D 75% of 4 = 3
$3 = 33\dfrac{1}{3}\%$ of 9

PART 9—MECHANICAL COMPREHENSION

1-C Newton's Law of Motion states that a body at rest will stay at rest unless acted on by an outside force. Conversely, a body in motion stays in motion unless acted on by an outside force. In this picture, both objects are at rest (equilibrium). When an outside force is added to weight 1, the equilibrium changes, moving this weight downward. Since the pulley has practically no friction, the weight strikes the floor.

2-B The volume is dependent on the area of the outlet. Since $A = \pi r^2$ and $r = d/2$, then $A = \pi(d^2/4)$ where A is the area and d is the diameter. The volume is proportional to the diameter squared (d^2). When the volumes of the 1-inch and 2-inch outlets are compared, we see that the latter will produce 4 times as great a volume. If the 1-inch outlet has an 8-gallon flow, then the 2-inch outlet will have a 32-gallon flow.

3-A If nut A were removed, it would be necessary to move nut C to the right to counterbalance the loss of the weight of nut A.

4-B When the water level rises past the safe area, the float turns on the sump pump. When the level of water in the sump pump goes down, the float also goes down and will shut off the sump pump.

5-C The centrifugal force acts to pull the balls outward. Since the two balls are connected to a yolk around the center bar, this outward motion pulls the balls upward.

6-B The piston is now in part of the compression stroke; $\frac{1}{4}$ turn will move it to full compression; $\frac{1}{2}$ more turn will move it to the end of the power stroke. Adding $\frac{1}{4} + \frac{1}{2} = \frac{3}{4}$ turn.

7-D Gear A has 15 teeth; gear B has 10 teeth. Let x = number of revolutions gear B will make. $15 \times 14 = x \times 10$; $10x = 15 \times 14$; $x = \frac{15 \times 14}{10}$; $x = 21$.

8-A Pulley A has the smallest circumference and therefore turns the fastest.

9-A Study the diagram on page 513 and note that with each complete turn of the cam, the setscrew will hit the contact point once.

10-D Each division marks 2 units: 20 units/10 divisions = 2 units/division. The pointer is 3½ divisions above 10 or 2 units/division × 3½ divisions = 7;7 + 10 = 17.

11-D The volume of water flowing at points 1, 2, and 3 must be the same because of the conservation of mass: mass in = mass out. Also, since no water is added or removed after point 1, there cannot be any change of volume.

12-C Gear 1 turns clockwise; gear 2 turns counterclockwise; gears 3 and 4 turn clockwise.

13-A When steam flows through pipes, it expands. The pipes would burst if extra space were not provided for expansion and contraction.

14-B Let x = effort that must be exerted. $60 \times 3 = x \times 5$; $180 = 5x$; $x = {}^{180}\!/_5 = 36$

15-A The water is filling up in the tank at a rate of 120 gallons per hour, or 2 gallons per minute ($^{120}\!/_{60} = 2$). The tank is also emptying at a rate of 1 gallon per minute. The net flow is increasing by 1 gallon per minute, since 2 gal./min. input − 1 gal./min. output = 1 gal./min. increase. *Note:* The easiest way to find the answer is to change all measurements to gallons per minute.

16-B Two gears, moving together, turn in opposite directions. Liquid is thus forced through the pipe.

17-A The larger the pulley, the more distance it must cover, and therefore, the smaller the RPM. If A turns at 2,000 RPM, B (twice as large) turns at 1,000 RPM; C is attached to B and turns at the same rate. Finally, D (8 times larger than C), turns at 1,000/8 or 125 RPM.

18-A The weight is not centered but is closer to A. The distance from the center of the load to A is less than the distance from the center of the load to B. Therefore, A would support the greater part of the load.

19-A Gears M and N are eccentric oval gears that are identical in size, shape, and number of teeth. The point of contact of the gears shifts from the right to the left with each revolution. However, if gear N turns at a constant rpm, gear M will turn at the same constant rpm as N.

20-D By reducing the length of the lever arm, you are reducing the effort and will permit the valve to blow off at a lower pressure.

21-D The amount of water which can leave an outlet depends upon the size or area of the opening. The area of a circular opening is proportional to the radius squared (area = πr^2). Therefore, the 2-inch pipe outlet will carry 4 times the amount of water as will the 1-inch opening. Mathematically,

$$\frac{\text{Area of 2-inch}}{\text{Area of 1-inch}} = \frac{\pi(2)^2}{\pi(1)^2} = \frac{\pi 4}{\pi 1} = 4.$$

22-C The simplest and least expensive thing to do is to change the washer, which may have deteriorated due to excessive wear.

23-D Option A does not permit air flow through G and S; option B does not permit air flow through S; option C does not permit air flow through G; option D is correct.

24-B Wood is an insulator. Silver is a better conductor than steel.

25-C One revolution of the rear wheel causes 10 teeth to rotate completely. But one revolution of the front sprocket causes 20 teeth to rotate completely, making the 10-teeth rear sprocket revolve twice.

PART 10—ELECTRONICS INFORMATION

1-D Soft iron has the property of being easily magnetized or demagnetized. When the current is turned on in an electromagnet, it becomes magnetized. When the current is turned off, the iron loses its magnetism.

2-C This is a general safety question. Never assume that there is no current in a piece of electrical equipment; the results could be shocking.

3-C Using algebraic rules, Ohm's Law can be written in three equivalent ways:

$$R = \frac{V}{I}; \quad I = \frac{V}{R}; \quad V = IR.$$

4-D Lead acid batteries give off highly explosive hydrogen gas. This is a normal product of the acid reacting with the lead plates when electricity is made. A single spark can explode the gas.

5-D According to Ohm's law:
$V = IR; V = 5 \times 20; V = 100$ volts.

6-A receptacles in a house are connected in parallel. In parallel circuits, the current increases as more appliances are added but the voltage remains the same. $E_t = E_1 = E_2 = \ldots E_n I_t = I_1 + I_2 + \ldots I_n$

7-D The image shows the current rising and falling from some minimum value indicated by the straight line portions of the image. The current, therefore, pulses without changing direction. AC involves a reversal of direction.

8-C Ohm's law; $V = IR$ gives the voltage drop across a resistor. Inductance and capacitance do not produce a voltage drop. Conductance is the reciprocal of resistance. A high resistance has a low conductance.

9-B Maximum wattage that will cause a 15-ampere breaker to trip is (15 amps) (120 volts) = 1800 watts. Accordingly, 1300 watts is the largest heater that will operate without causing the circuit breaker to trip.

10-B In electrical terms, potential or E.M.F. is the voltage. Electricians consider any voltage of 600 volts or less to be Low Potential.

11-A A rheostat regulates the amount of voltage to the motor. The more voltage to a motor, the faster it will turn.

12-B A polarized plug is used so that the plug can only go into the receptacle in one way. The prongs are at an angle to one another.

13-C The number on the wires is in reverse order to the amount of current that they can carry. No. 12 is the smallest of the wires.

14-A The plug can go into the outlet in only one way in a polarized outlet. In the other outlets, the plug can be reversed.

15-B Connecting the bell to a 6- or 12-volt source on the secondary of a transformer is done as a safety precaution. The other way would be dangerous.

16-C An incandescent electric light bulb is a typical light bulb found in the home. When the incandescent bulb, which is rated for 110 volts, is run at 90 volts, it will not burn as brightly. Since the 110-volt capacity is not being used, it will last longer.

17-D This object is a ground clamp. It will be tightened around a cold water pipe. A grounding wire will be attached to the screw and thus stray electricity will be grounded.

18-A When a refrigerator motor starts up, it draws considerable current. This takes current away from the bulb. Thicker wires would allow more electricity to pass through, but they would be too expensive and impractical.

19-D The symbol shows a semiconductor diode. These usually contain silicon and sometimes germanium. They conduct only in the direction shown by the arrow. Currents flowing in the opposite direction meet with high resistance and are effectively blocked. For these reasons, silicon diodes are often used to rectify AC to DC.

20-C The transistor contains semiconductor material. Two varieties, NPN and PNP, are manufactured. The one shown in the diagram is of the NPN type.

SELF-APPRAISAL CHART

After you score your answers on the First ASVAB Specimen Test, record the subtest results on this Self-Appraisal Chart. For those subtests on which you scored low, further study is strongly recommended. As you take and record your results on the Second and Third ASVAB Specimen Tests, you will see the progress made through study and practice in preparing for the actual test.

SUBTEST	NUMBER OF QUESTIONS	NUMBER ANSWERED CORRECTLY		
		FIRST SPECIMEN TEST	SECOND SPECIMEN TEST	THIRD SPECIMEN TEST
1. General Science	25			
2. Arithmetic Reasoning	30			
3. Word Knowledge	35			
4. Paragraph Comprehension	15			
5. Numerical Operations	50			
6. Coding Speed	84			
7. Auto & Shop Information	25			
8. Mathematics Knowledge	25			
9. Mechanical Comprehension	25			
10. Electronics Information	20			

YOUR ASVAB RESULTS

The ASVAB Results Sheet, consisting of three parts, is provided for each student taking ASVAB-14. One part is for the student, one for the school counselor, and the third is a detachable postcard that can be used to notify parents that the scores are available. Only the parts for the student and the school counselor contain the test scores. ASVAB results are mailed by the military to the schools within 30 days after testing.

The information printed on the front of the student section of the results sheet, shown in Part A of Figure 8, contains

- Student identification information (name, grade, social security number, sex, and school)
- Percentile scores for *academic* and *occupational composites* by grade and sex
- Percentile scores for *academic* and *occupational composites* by youth population
- Graphic representation of student grade/sex percentile scores in a profile format using brackets to indicate probable range of true composite scores
- An interpretive guide to help students understand their results

The *Counselor Summary,* shown in Part B of Figure 8, is a record of the test results for each student tested.

The *Parent Postcard,* shown in Part C of Figure 8, is a postcard that can be mailed to parents and guardians by the school. It is important that parents are informed that their daughter or son has received ASVAB results so that these results may be discussed by them.

The Grade/Sex Percentile Scores compare the student to a nationally representative sample of the same grade and sex.

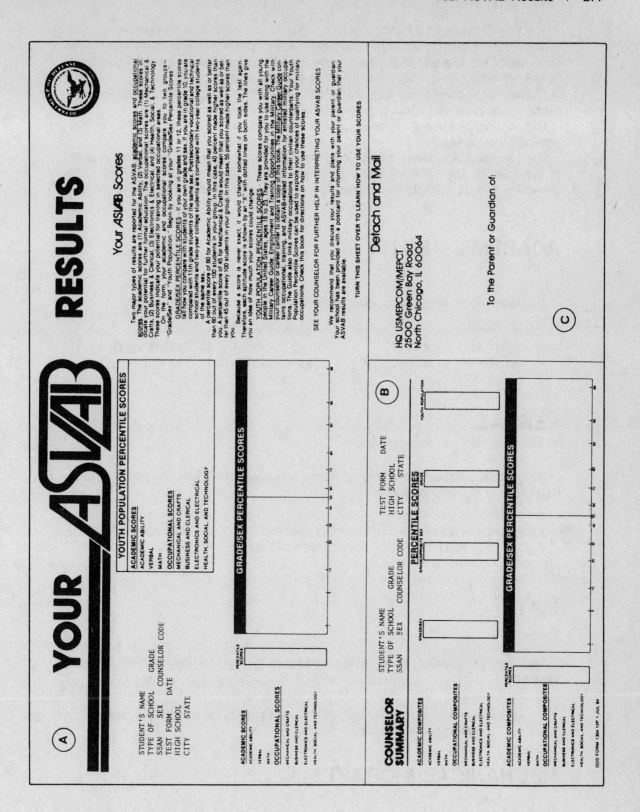

Figure 8. *ASVAB Results Sheet* (Front). (Part A is *Your ASVAB Results*, Part B is the *Counselor Summary*, and Part C is the *Parent Postcard*.)

The Youth Population Percentile Scores compare the student to the population of all youths ages 18 through 23. It has the advantage of putting all scores on a common scale regardless of grade or sex and can be used to explore the likelihood of qualifying for military service and assignment for training in a specialty.

The *academic scores* estimate your potential for further formal education and predict performance in general areas requiring verbal and mathematical skills.

The *occupational scores* estimate your potential for successful performance in four general career areas.

The composite scores you receive are combinations of results of two or more parts of the ASVAB. The following indicates what each composite score measures and shows the various subtests that contribute to each composite score.

ACADEMIC ABILITY

Academic Ability is a general indicator of verbal and mathematical abilities.

$$\text{ACADEMIC ABILITY} = \left[\text{WORD KNOWLEDGE} + \text{PARAGRAPH COMPREHENSION} \right]^* + \text{ARITHMETIC REASONING}$$

VERBAL

Verbal measures performance on questions requiring vocabulary, reading skills, and knowledge of high school science.

$$\text{VERBAL} = \text{WORD KNOWLEDGE} + \text{PARAGRAPH COMPREHENSION} + \text{GENERAL SCIENCE}$$

MATH

Math measures ability to use mathematical principles and arithmetic skills to solve problems.

$$\text{MATH} = \text{ARITHMETIC REASONING} + \text{MATHEMATICS KNOWLEDGE}$$

MECHANICAL & CRAFTS

Mechanical & Crafts measures arithmetic skills; understanding of mechanical principles; information concerning automobiles, shop terminology, and practices; and

---

* *Scores of subtests in brackets are combined and weighted as one unit.*

electricity and electronics. The score is an estimate of potential for successful performance in the mechanical and crafts career area.

$$\begin{array}{c}\text{MECHANICAL} \\ \text{\& CRAFTS}\end{array} = \begin{array}{c}\text{ARITHMETIC} \\ \text{REASONING}\end{array} + \begin{array}{c}\text{MECHANICAL} \\ \text{COMPREHENSION}\end{array} + \begin{array}{c}\text{AUTO \& SHOP} \\ \text{INFORMATION}\end{array} + \begin{array}{c}\text{ELECTRONICS} \\ \text{INFORMATION}\end{array}$$

BUSINESS & CLERICAL

Business & Clerical measures vocabulary, reading, coding, and mathematical skills. This score is an estimate of potential for successful performance in the business and clerical career area.

$$\begin{array}{c}\text{BUSINESS \&} \\ \text{CLERICAL}\end{array} = \left[\begin{array}{c}\text{WORD} \\ \text{KNOWLEDGE}\end{array} + \begin{array}{c}\text{PARAGRAPH} \\ \text{COMPREHENSION}\end{array}\right]^* + \begin{array}{c}\text{CODING} \\ \text{SPEED}\end{array} + \begin{array}{c}\text{MATHEMATICS} \\ \text{KNOWLEDGE}\end{array}$$

ELECTRONICS & ELECTRICAL

Electronics & Electrical measures ability to solve problems requiring knowledge of mathematics, electricity and electronics, and science. This score is an estimate of potential for successful performance in the electronics and electrical career area.

$$\begin{array}{c}\text{ELECTRONICS \&} \\ \text{ELECTRICAL}\end{array} = \begin{array}{c}\text{ARITHMETIC} \\ \text{REASONING}\end{array} + \begin{array}{c}\text{MATHEMATICS} \\ \text{KNOWLEDGE}\end{array} + \begin{array}{c}\text{ELECTRONICS} \\ \text{INFORMATION}\end{array} + \begin{array}{c}\text{GENERAL} \\ \text{SCIENCE}\end{array}$$

HEALTH, SOCIAL & TECHNOLOGY

Health, Social & Technology measures the ability to answer questions requiring vocabulary, reading, arithmetic reasoning, and mechanical reasoning skills. This score is an estimate of potential for successful performance in the health, social, and technology career area. This career area includes occupations such as air traffic controller, medical technician, and police officer.

$$\begin{array}{c}\text{HEALTH,} \\ \text{SOCIAL \&} \\ \text{TECHNOLOGY}\end{array} = \left[\begin{array}{c}\text{WORD} \\ \text{KNOWLEDGE}\end{array} + \begin{array}{c}\text{PARAGRAPH} \\ \text{COMPREHENSION}\end{array}\right]^* + \begin{array}{c}\text{ARITHMETIC} \\ \text{REASONING}\end{array} + \begin{array}{c}\text{MECHANICAL} \\ \text{COMPREHENSION}\end{array}$$

If your percentile score in an area is 60, you scored as well as or better than 60 out of 100 students. If you scored in the 30th percentile, this means that 70% of the group did better than you in the area.

* *Scores of subtests in brackets are combined and weighted as one unit.*

In general, the higher your score, the greater your chances of doing well in either formal education programs or the types of occupations shown in the groupings below.

OCCUPATIONAL GROUPINGS

MECHANICAL & CRAFTS

SAMPLE OCCUPATIONS

Machinist
Auto Mechanic
Jet Engine Mechanic
Diesel Mechanic
Sheet Metal Worker

Refrigeration Mechanic
Plumbing Systems Tester
Shipfitter
Cement Mason
Carpenter

BUSINESS & CLERICAL

SAMPLE OCCUPATIONS

Clerk Typist
Personnel Clerk
Transportation Agent
Data Entry Operator
Post Office Clerk

Paralegal Assistant
Payroll Clerk
Stock Control Clerk
Radio Telegraph Operator
Stenographer

ELECTRONICS & ELECTRICAL

SAMPLE OCCUPATIONS

TV & Radio Repairer
Automatic Equipment Technician
Electric Motor Repairer
Instrument Mechanic
Audio Video Repairer

Line Installer/Repairer
Electrician
Auto Electrician
Electronics Mechanic
Missile Electronics Technician

HEALTH, SOCIAL & TECHNOLOGY

SAMPLE OCCUPATIONS

Weather Observer
Medical Service Technician
Reporter
Exterminator
Air Traffic Controller

Dental Assistant
Police Officer
Intelligence Specialist
Cook
Flight Operations Specialist

To use the test results in career exploration, you should consider them in connection with other important things you know about yourself, such as your interests, skills, school grades, motivation, and your goals. An aptitude test score is only one very general indicator, along with all these other factors, to be used in exploring those careers you are considering.

Talking to a counselor, teacher, parent, or people employed in occupations you are considering can be very helpful.

For those interested in entering the military, enlistment processing occurs at 68 Military Entrance Processing Stations located around the country. At these stations, applicants typically take the ASVAB.

ASVAB results are used to determine if the applicant qualifies for entry into a service and if the applicant has the specific aptitude level required for job specialty training programs.

If you have taken the ASVAB in high school or postsecondary school, you can use your scores to determine whether you qualify for entry into the military services, provided the scores are not more than two years old.

The Armed Forces Qualification Test (AFQT) raw score is derived from the raw scores obtained on the ASVAB, as follows:

AFQT Raw Score = Word Knowledge Raw Score
+
Paragraph Comprehension Raw Score
+
Arithmetic Reasoning Raw Score
+
Mathematics Knowledge Raw Score

This AFQT Raw Score is then converted into a Percentile Score which is used to determine eligibility for entrance into the military.

Applicants without prior military service who receive an AFQT percentile score of 10 or higher are eligible for continued processing at the Military Entrance Processing Station. However, the services usually reject those who fail to score in the top three categories. Typically, the services prefer applicants who score in Category I (Percentile score: 93 and over), Category II (Percentile score: 65 to 92), and Category III (Percentile score: 31 to 64). However, under certain circumstances and depending upon the needs of the service, they may accept a very limited number of Category IV (Percentile score: 10 to 30). Final determination of acceptability remains with the services.

Applicants with prior military service who wish to return to the military are processed for enlistment at the discretion of the service, regardless of AFQT score.